GREAT SHIP DISASTERS

Other Books by A. A. HOEHLING

GREAT
SHIP
DISASTERS

A. A. HOEHLING

COWLES BOOK COMPANY, INC.

NEW YORK

"O, hear us when we cry to Thee
For those in peril on the sea!"
                    —William Whiting

Contents

1.

The ANDREA DORIA– STOCKHOLM Collision

OFF SABLE ISLAND, ONE JULY NIGHT IN 1898, THE FRENCH liner *La Bourgogne*, of nearly seventy-five hundred tons, collided in a deep fog with the iron-hulled, three-masted schooner *Cromartyshire*. The steamer sank in fifteen minutes. All but 164 persons of the 725 aboard went down with her in the cold Nova Scotian waters. Most of the survivors were crewmen.

The July 4 disaster, accompanied by the French sailors' animal-like struggle in the dark seas, was abruptly sobering to a nation still exulting over Admiral Sampson's victory at Santiago Harbor, just one day earlier, virtually climaxing the Spanish-American War. Admiral Cervera's fleet had been totally obliterated.

On a reflective note, *The New York Times* mused that the vessel had "succumbed to the one peril of the sea which it seems that the progress of science can do nothing to avert. That is, the peril of collision in a fog."

Little more than a decade later, science remained wanting. The White Star liner *Republic,* with twice the displacement of the *La Bourgogne,* was rammed in fog off Nantucket shoals by the smaller Italian steamship *Florida.* However, the use of wire-

1

less for the first time in a major sea accident that night of January 23, 1909, kept the loss of life to a minimum. Only two of the 440 passengers aboard the *Republic* were lost, and the name of Jack Binns, the radio operator who flashed the distress call "CQD!", became a household phrase.

By 1956, it was estimated that more than eleven hundred ships of all types had been wrecked off Nantucket Island, as storms linked in villainy with a shifting green wilderness of shoals and sandbars. No one could be quite sure how many more vessels, especially fishing craft, had plunged below in the austere seas between Nantucket and Cape Sable, Nova Scotia.

Yet, the "progress of science" in all fields, afforded unusual impetus by World War II, had made giant strides since *The New York Times* had lamented its shortcomings in 1898. There was, in particular, radar with its electronic optic nerve that could pierce night, fog, smoke, and other shrouds hitherto opaque to the human eye.

If radar were unable to "avert . . . the peril of collision in a fog," then, seemingly, nothing could or ever would.

One captain, at least, had come to depend upon it much as the very air he breathed. That warm July night of 1956, Captain Piero Calamai, fifty-nine-year-old master of the 29,000-ton, $29 million queen of the Italian Line, *Andrea Doria,* was guiding his ornate command inbound through thick fog at almost top speed.

When the fog rolled over her bows in midafternoon, Wednesday, July 25, off Nantucket, Calamai cut back from 23.2 to 22 knots. As he would explain, "We were not in crowded waters; there were no ships around to cross my path." However, "without radar"—and the sleek *Andrea Doria* was equipped with two sets —he figured he'd have dropped to "twelve-fourteen knots."

An hour late because of a storm in the crossing from Genoa, the liner was due at 9 A.M. Thursday, at her West Forty-fourth Street pier. Scheduled port time, with its shambling hordes of longshoreman, had to be paid for whether utilized or not.

The passengers, totaling 1,134 this trip (about double the crew of 572), probably didn't care if they *were* late. The *Andrea*

2

Doria was one of the most comfortable, beautiful vessels afloat. Her long, black hull contrasted smartly with her predominantly white superstructure and tapered funnel green-painted in company colors. Her interior decor was subdued modern, accenting murals and indirect light from low ceilings ("overheads," to the nautical-minded).

Best of all, with tasteful elegance, the Italian steamship was "safe," as a headline in *The New York Times* proclaimed in January, 1953, prior to her maiden voyage. "The hull of the 697-foot vessel," the article went on to say, "is subdivided into 11 watertight compartments . . . assuring that the ship will stay afloat if two compartments, even adjacent ones, should become flooded."

Compartmentation, as a matter of fact, was far from a new idea in marine engineering. Returning from China in the thirteenth century, Marco Polo described how junks were divided by bulkheads to keep them from foundering and, at least, to afford the crew time to abandon.

All the remaining Wednesday afternoon and into the evening the *Andrea Doria* pounded toward the Nantucket lightship through fog which the mates on watch estimated had reduced visibility to a minimum of half a mile at times, and never better than three miles. About 10:20 P.M. the small, red-hulled light vessel was passed—according to the radar—about one mile to the north.

Approximately twenty minutes later, another "pip" appeared on the *Andrea Doria's* radars. This time, its changing positions spoke of an approaching vessel about seventeen miles distant, when the signal was first apparent.

Calamai did not "deem it necessary" to change course "because the radar indicated we were going to pass safely green to green," that is, the *Andrea Doria* would steam by to the south of the other ship.

However, by the rules of the road, ships on converging course should ideally pass "red to red," *i.e.,* the port running lights rather than starboard green should be facing each other.

3

At 11:05 P.M., when the two ships were approximately three miles apart, the captain, still believing the stranger was "on a parallel course always on our right," saw no necessity either to alter the *Andrea Doria*'s heading or to chart the successive bearings and distances of the rapidly approaching "target."

At the same time, the third officer, Eugenio Giannini, apparently less confident than the master, wondered aloud:

"Why don't we hear him? Why doesn't he whistle?"

The *Andrea Doria* herself had been sounding her horn "continuously" for the last eight hours, Calamai would attest. It was audible for nearly four miles. The liner's speed was now 21.8 knots, only .2 knots less than her average since 3 P.M.

Seconds later, Giannini's suspense was over. He noticed a "glow" ahead, perhaps as little as 1.1 miles distant.

"There she is!" he shouted. "Do you see?"

"Yes," Calamai replied. He was standing on the wing of the bridge, eighty feet above waterline.

Not, however, until "two white lights" on the approaching ship's mast were suddenly sighted did Calamai call the order:

"All left!"

There would be disagreement whether any more than the "two white lights" had been observed—that is, if anyone on the bridge of the *Andrea Doria* had, at the same time, spotted a green starboard light or red port light looming through the swirling mists. One light or the other would have given clear indication on which side the stranger would pass, right or left in landsman's or highway terminology.

Like most liners of her tremendous bulk, *Andrea Doria* did not at once answer to the command to "turn!" The response was somewhat analogous to that of a sailing ship in a near-calm, with tiller hard over.

While the *Andrea Doria* had been plunging through a gray, opaque, and clammy world that afternoon, another liner—the 12,600-ton *Stockholm*, carrying the crown of the Swedish-American Line—was outbound for Göteborg, Sweden, under

4

bright summer skies at eighteen knots. This was a spanking average for the medium-sized motorship.

Even as the Italian vessel presented at least the illusion of massiveness (yet only one-third the gross tonnage for example, of the *Queen Elizabeth*), the all-white *Stockholm* resembled nothing so much as an oversized yacht. On this crossing she was home to 535 passengers, somewhat more than her designed capacity, and crew of 215.

Captain H. Gunnar Nordenson, at sixty-three, was, like Calamai, a veteran, able master. And he, too, placed his faith in radar. That night, however, with caressing breezes and a moon, he had no cause to reflect upon blind navigation. Actually, in that part of the ocean there was no fog.

During the evening, such matters were left to the discretion of Third Officer Ernst Carstens-Johannsen, who had the eight-thirty–midnight trick. The Nantucket lightship was still some sixty miles north when the twenty-six-year-old watch officer picked up the radar pip of an approaching ship. It appeared to be twelve miles distant and slightly to port.

He did not notify Captain Nordenson. In fact, when the pip had finally materialized into a visual object, the master still was below in his cabin, tending to his papers. At that time, the helmsman, Ingemar G. Bjorkman sang out:

"Light to port!"

The radar told Carstens-Johannsen that the oncoming vessel was some 1.8 miles away. He ordered a turn to starboard which, in conjunction with the *Andrea Doria*'s move to port, put the ship virtually on a collision course. The next four minutes seemingly passed in a blank on the *Stockholm*'s bridge for, suddenly, the third officer looked in horror to see the green running lights of a towering vessel sweeping across his bow.

"Hard a-starboard," he cried to his helmsman while ringing "full speed astern" on the engine room mechanical telegraph.

Down in the tourist lounge, a youthful resident of Pittsburgh, Dr. Leonard Laufe, bound for Stockholm's Karolinska Institute to study radium, found his chair suddenly sliding over the deck-

5

ing. It did not stop until it had careened completely across the room. At the same time, he saw the base fiddle fly out of the hands of one of the members of the string quartet.

All in all, it looked like a performance out of Mack Sennett.

"There was a horrible screeching noise and a terrible crash," the physician, who was a Korean War veteran, would recall. "But the lights stayed on."

On the *Andrea Doria,* the lights flickered, but did not wink out. Mrs. Henrietta Freeman, of San Francisco, was awakened by "a terrific bump." The elderly widow, who had survived the great earthquake and fire of 1906, was phlegmatically contemplating a second attempt at sleep when she heard "men's loud voices in the corridor."

She decided that the "bump" might have been serious.

Her watch, she noticed as she hurriedly dressed, told her it was 11:10 P.M.

To another first-class passenger, Stewart Coleman, vice president and a director of the Standard Oil Company of New Jersey, standing on the promenade deck, the collision sounded like a "muffled crumpling." He was returning from a vacation with his wife and two teen-age daughters.

But to Aurelio Monasterio, of Mexico City, the experience was not "muffled" or cushioned in any fashion. Reading in bed, he was thrown to the deck "by some brutal force . . . a red haze blinds me for a moment. My hands fly to my face and when I take them down they are red from blood. . . . I can't imagine what has occurred."

Neither had the officers on the bridge of either liner "imagined" for a few dazed, unbelievable minutes. The *Stockholm'*s tough bow, designed to butt through icy Scandinavian waters, had penetrated the starboard side of the *Andrea Doria* to a depth of nearly thirty feet (one-third the beam) just below the bridge and the promenade deck down to the double bottom. Like an inverted triangle, or giant wedge, the slash was estimated to be about forty feet across on top, tapering down to a point.

It was a fearful gash.

Since the *Stockholm*'s engines were in reverse at the time, the liner quickly pulled away. There was little left of her bow.

The *Andrea Doria,* light and not ballasted, immediately assumed a list of 17, 18, then 19 degrees, and in moments hung giddily on her starboard side at 20 degrees—an angle that defeated the purpose of all the watertight compartments and watertight doors. Water would slosh over and flow from compartment into compartment, enabling more and more water to come in all the while, like a long row of tilted buckets.

Calamai ordered the engines stopped, the watertight doors shut. The starboard turbines were ruptured and ruined, anyhow. It was necessary only to close off the port turbines.

It required perhaps ten minutes for distress messages to be framed and rushed to the radio shacks to be sparked out into the night. Both liners transmitted their "SOS's" at approximately 11:22 P.M. Positions were given that indicated both were nineteen miles west of Nantucket lightship, or forty-five miles south of Nantucket Island itself.

The Coast Guard picked the calls up at once and immediately relayed the intelligence:

"Andrea Doria and *Stockholm* collided!"

This was the first that either of the stricken ships knew the identity of the other.

The *Stockholm* was temporarily moored, not by her anchors (smashed into wreckage of the bow), but by the two anchor chains, which had unwound their seven-hundred-foot lengths, then caught onto some obstacle—an old wreck perhaps—on the ocean floor. While Captain Nordenson sought to determine if his damaged vessel could stay afloat, Dr. Laufe and two other doctors aboard went to work in the ship's hospital and in a special dispensary hurriedly set up in the dining saloon.

Broken bones of crewmen and a few skull fractures were the principal casualties. Three young seamen, in fo'c'sles up forward, had completely disappeared as the bow disintegrated.

Through an opened porthole, Dr. Laufe began to hear a peculiar wailing chorus. A ship's nurse explained that old Swedes

7

were singing hymns on deck, certain that the *Stockholm* had struck an iceberg and they would surely perish.

While the situation aboard the *Stockholm* was rapidly stabilizing, the list—now 25 degrees—of the *Andrea Doria* was enough to inspire panic in all but the most phlegmatic.

An apparent delay in sounding a general alarm or making announcements—at least in English—over the loudspeakers kept passengers in a state of bewilderment. The baggage-stacked passageways (preparatory to the next morning's scheduled debarkation) compounded the physical problem of keeping one's balance against the wild list.

Aurelio Monasterio finally struggled to a higher deck seeking his *punto di riunione* (muster station), to be informed by a sailor:

"Nothing! I know nothing. We are sinking. We are going down. . . !"

The resident of Mexico City, seeing that the Italian seaman's face was "livid with panic," added: "I realize that there are a great many people on deck. The heavy oil that covers the deck floor makes stability impossible. Men in tails, bare-necked women. And anguish, despair, loneliness staring out of the stark eyes of the passengers.

" 'Lord God in heaven,' cries a voice, 'help us!' "

Ordinary people, rich people, a few well-known names, all were pushing upward, over broken glass and splintered marble table tops and furniture.

The mayor of Philadelphia, Richardson Dilworth, and Mrs. Dilworth were among the mass surging toward the *uscitas,* or exits.

Another was Ruth Roman, the actress, who had been dancing in the Belvedere Room, the Salone delle Feste, to the popular "Arrivederci Roma" ("Till we meet again in Rome"). She rushed to her cabin and grabbed up her three-year-old son, reassuring him: "We are going on a picnic, Dickie!"

Most of those on board did not think they were en route to a picnic or anything remotely festive. Nicola Difiore, for example, of Scotch Plains, New Jersey, resignedly gathered a raincoat and a few toiletries, then started from his cabin.

It seemed like old times. He had survived two transport torpedoings in the war.

Mrs. Barbara Boggs, of New York, traveling with her husband Robert and two of her four children—Barbara and Bob—found it best to lie "flat on the tilting promenade deck, trying not to kick the heads of people stacked up at our feet." She was "waiting to hear something over the loudspeaker system," but all she could make out was "the crew talking to each other in Italian."

Barbara thought of her children at home, "who were at camp and the fact that they would be orphaned. . . . I thought of so many things I had meant to do, and cursed myself for not having done more for them . . . life had suddenly become infinitely precious and desirable. . . ."

She also was smitten by the illusion that the liner was listing "more and more every minute," although the *Andrea Doria* hung at 30 degrees to starboard. This prolonged state of personal imbalance had the attendant effect of intensifying her doubts as to whether any ships at all were steaming to the liner's aid.

Actually, quite a fleet was hammering at flank speed toward the scene in answer to the distress calls. The largest ship was the thirty-year-old but still handsome *Ile de France*. At 44,500 tons, she remained among the world's largest liners.

Her master, Baron Raoul de Beaudean, had wirelessed he should be at the Italian ship's side by one-thirty.

The first on the scene was the small United Fruit freighter, *Cape Ann*, returning empty from Bremerhaven. As soon as she hove to, at twelve thirty-six, with the lights of the two stricken ships visible in the lifting fog, the *Cape Ann* launched eight lifeboats.

It was a thrilling exhibition of rapid coordination and seamanship to those peering from the tilting starboard decks of the *Andrea Doria*.

Even so, they were beaten by three *lancia,* or lifeboats, from

9

the *Andrea Doria* which arrived at the side of the *Stockholm*. As their occupants filed aboard and some hurried into the evacuation hospital, Dr. Laufe's sense of expectation was considerably dampened. He noted in disbelief the identity of the survivors: all Italian crewmen, most of them from the third-class stewards' department.

The 146-person–capacity boats were each less than half filled. There was not one woman, child, or any other passenger in this lot, adding up, conceivably, to something less than the proudest moment in Italian maritime history. It was evocative of the *La Bourgogne*.

Meanwhile, on the *Andrea Doria*, Aurelio Monasterio found it impossible to remain erect. "The oil and water makes us slip. Our bare feet fasten on to bits of glass, broken pieces of wood, anything that offers foothold. Nobody knows anything about anything. Not a single alarm . . . the bell remains silent."

Stewart Coleman took an exceptionally bad spill, sliding across slimy, tilting passageways, and "ending up on the starboard side of the ship." A sailor who made the perilous misadventure with him came to the aid of Coleman, who had been "knocked out."

His benefactor revived him with a splash of salt water in the face.

Priests were much in evidence. Mrs. Freeman, sitting in a chair of an upper lounge, saw one of them, a young fellow, praying in the center of a group of three nuns.

As the ship abruptly lurched, Mrs. Freeman's chair "started sliding downhill." The priest stopped his prayers, fell onto hands and knees and crawled over to the San Francisco lady.

"Are you all right?" he asked.

Almost before she was able to reassure him, one of the nuns lost her balance and went sliding about the deck. The priest now crawled toward her.

Yet another man of the cloth, carrying a cup and apparently offering communion, paused to advise Barbara Boggs in the art of "holding one's nose, on account of the oil in the water, and

10

the other hand pulling down one's lifejacket so at impact it would not break one's neck."

He explained he had served as a wartime chaplain in the navy.

Religion and eternity had assumed a forefront this early morning off Nantucket Island. A Spanish woman wailed to Monasterio:

"It's no use. Everything is over! Let us commit ourselves to God and resign ourselves!"

Her despair was premature. In addition to the *Cape Ann,* the U.S. Navy transport *Thomas* and the *Stockholm* were all sending lifeboats and motor launches toward the *Andrea Doria* by 1:30 A.M., or some two and a third hours after the collision. The *Ile de France* and the tanker *Robert E. Hopkins* were very close.

Abandoning ship commenced in an often wild and disorganized fashion. People leaped fifty feet into the water. Were it not for the list, the drop from the promenade deck would have been seventy-five feet. Those who dove or jumped paid no attention as to whether sufficient boats were yet within swimming distance. At least the water was fairly warm and the passengers wore their life preservers.

A few mothers hysterically tossed small children from the decks, hoping someone would catch them. Most, but not all were fished safely out of the black waters.

One, a four-year-old girl who had landed in a lifeboat on her head, arrived at Dr. Laufe's emergency ward. Pinned to her nightgown was a note: "This is a little Italian girl."

The "little Italian girl"—whose name turned out to be Norma—had suffered a fatal concussion. It was too late, the physician found, to "depress" the swelling or otherwise relieve pressure. He also set the fractures of a small boy, thrown from the *Andrea Doria.* His internal hurts, however, would prove mortal.

Linda Morgan, fourteen-year-old daughter of Edward P. Morgan, a radio news commentator, and stepdaughter of Camille

11

Cianfarra, foreign correspondent for *The New York Times,* had been asleep in Cabin 52, of the upper deck, which bore the concentrated fury of the impact. Linda was hurled back into what was left of the *Stockholm*'s bow. She was discovered there, crying and bewildered, by Swedish sailors. Her several broken bones were nonetheless not mortal.

Linda's eight-year-old sister, Joan Cianfarra, died in the same crumpled cabin. Down the corridor, her stepfather lay dead. Mrs. Cianfarra, projected into a nearby cabin by the collapse of a bulkhead, was pinioned under broken furniture and entwining bedsprings.

The cabin's actual occupant, a husky Upper Montclair, New Jersey, chiropractor, Thure Peterson, had freed her by the use of a pair of pliers, assisted by a crewman with a huge carving knife. Dr. Peterson's wife, Martha, succumbed, however, before she, too, could be rescued.

People like Barbara Boggs found the abandonment process, haphazard as it was, "nothing compared to that horrible period of waiting." In spite of the earnest advice from the priest, Barbara "couldn't conceive of jumping from where we were—it was about three stories high." She continued:

"We decided that my husband would hang on to Bobby, and Barbara and I would hang on to each other if we had to go in the ocean. . . .

"Finally a steward came and said that women and children were to follow him, but he didn't say where we were going. There ensued a scene in which my son refused to leave his father, until the steward who knew us said to him, 'Bobby, you must take care of your mother and your sister,' and changed his mind for him. . . .

"I slid up against a rail somewhere, looked up and saw enormous bright lights, the *Ile de France.* God, what a sight that was.

"When our turn came we slid down ropes into a lifeboat."

Plucky Mrs. Freeman was making good progress down a rope ladder though it was "wet and slippery" when she thought she had come to its end and was abruptly "dangling in mid-air."

12

She was, however, much relieved when the swaying ladder straightened out to its full length and hands reached upward from the boat to help her through the remaining descent.

The male passengers, even as their predecessors on the *Titanic* forty-four years earlier, conducted themselves, with few exceptions, in the best traditions of gallantry and stoicism. Injured as he was from his severe fall, Stewart Coleman waited until the list was so severe that he could "jump into the lifeboat."

When his wife and daughters had left, it had been nearly a forty-foot climb down to the growing numbers of craft from the rescue fleet. Not a lifeboat could be launched from the port side, due to the steep angle. They remained well lashed down, uselessly in neat array along this now towering *ponte lance,* or boat deck.

Abandoning had come almost as anticlimax to Monasterio who had hoped until the very last that there would be time "to save the luggage and that we will receive our clothes, goods and other effects on arrival in New York."

Wearily, he had observed the passengers' "grimness" toward the *"Doria*'s sailors," an attitude the traveler from Mexico believed had finally become "openly aggressive." It occurred to him, however, that the seamen were "poor creatures . . . merely the instruments, the contacts between the officers and the ship."

And then it was Monasterio's turn to leave:

"I am among the last to let myself down the rope ladder that leads to the lifeboat assigned to my position on the gunwale. Carefully and steadily I creep down the endless seventeen meters that lead me away from the theater of the tragedy I lived during the last three hours—those last blinded and deaf hours assailed by sorrow, impotence, loneliness and a tremendous bitterness."

Perhaps none that morning was so consumed with "sorrow" and "loneliness" as Piero Calamai. By five-thirty, satisfied that no living person remained aboard, the captain shuffled off a deck and into a lifeboat. He had lost his ship and forty-five of those who had been aboard—all of whom happened to be passengers.

The *Ile de France,* carrying 753 survivors, had already departed for New York. The *Stockholm,* with 572, the *Cape Ann,*

13

with 168, and the *Thomas,* with 158, would soon follow. The remainder from the Italian liner were distributed among a sprinkling of other rescue vessels, including Coast Guard patrols and even helicopters.

The *Stockholm*'s fettering anchor chains had been cut free by acetylene torches. Aboard her it was almost time to relax. A grateful Captain Nordenson asked Dr. Laufe what he could do for him. The Pittsburgh physician, whose night's work had included the preparation and labeling of some fourteen plaster casts or splints, did not long ponder the offer.

"I'd like a sauna bath, please," he replied.

At nine-thirty, the Italian liner lay on her side at an angle of 50 degrees. She hung there for half an hour in an attitude as "impossible" as the accident itself. This was a paradox of her buoyancy. Then, she absorbed so many more thousand tons of additional seawater that she became hopelessly bow-heavy.

Her long struggle was over. She could float no longer.

Some of her lifeboats bobbed free in a circle of mixed flotsam. The magnificent liner showed her portside propeller and name—"*Andrea Doria,* Genoa."

Edward McCarthy, pool correspondent for the United Press, wrote from a Coast Guard plane, circling low, that after "several huge geysers" apparently coming from ruptured portholes, "the ship turned turtle. Her nose was forward in the water with her stern completely out of the water. She hung there for three or four minutes and then [at ten-ten, by McCarthy's watch] disappeared."

She went so quietly as to court anticlimax.

It was Thursday, an hour after the *Andrea Doria* should be docking at West Forty-fourth Street. In moments, the mortally wounded vessel rested in 225 feet of shoaly water, about one-third of the great ship's length. She had drifted only some two miles southeast of her point of collision.

The survivors, at that, were most fortunate.

"Only very favorable weather conditions," noted the Merchant Marine Council of the United States Coast Guard, "and

14

splendid rescue efforts by other vessels at the scene prevented a very much larger loss of life (a total of fifty-one killed on both ships). The possible extent of such loss is realized when one considers that the *Andrea Doria* carried some seventeen hundred persons and that because of the excessive list it was possible for her to launch only lifeboats on the starboard side, with normal capacity for about half this number.

"To many persons, this catastrophe, shocking as it was, certainly raised the question, how could it happen? How did it happen?"

The collision had occurred outside of territorial waters. The Coast Guard, therefore, had no authority to attempt to answer the query it had posed.

The passengers themselves remained bitter.

"The collision was due," asserted (to this writer) Stewart Coleman, hospitalized for his vertebra injury, "to notably bad seamanship on the part of the *Stockholm*. The east and westbound steamship lanes were arbitrarily set and not mandatory. The *Stockholm* was steaming eastward in the westbound lane in a heavy fog. I could only compare this with going in the wrong direction on a one-way street in the dark."

Captain Calamai, along generally similar lines, had also disputed the *Stockholm*'s side of the nautical road. Captain Nordenson quickly denied these allegations, stating that there was no track agreement in the Atlantic Ocean between the steamship companies.

Mrs. Barbara Boggs, now Mrs. Peter Benziger, had a hunch "both captains" were probably to blame. (So she wrote this author).

Still furious some days after his rescue, Monasterio sought counsel.

"I accuse the Italian Line of oversight, irresponsibility, inefficiency, neglect," he charged, along with many other allegations. Neither these nor further charges from other passengers could be proved and they became, necessarily, personal opinions.

Travelers on the *Stockholm* who did not have to abandon

their ship in the early hours of the morning tended to be rather neutral, although Dr. Laufe believed that the *Andrea Doria* had, in effect, "zigged when she should have zagged."

And those in the *Ile de France*'s luxurious suites were even more neutral. They did not know what had transpired until they arrived at their breakfast tables.

The crux of fault obviously lay in the interpretation, or noninterpretation of radar. There was no dispute that the sets themselves on both vessels were operating normally, This relegated speculation to the province of human error.

"Radar," editorialized the magazine *Marine Engineering Log,* "does not advise the deck officer to maintain full rpm's [revolutions per minute of the propellers] in fog, nor can it order necessary course changes for prompt evasive action. [It] never was meant to be a substitute for good seamanship."

Further than that, by the accepted rules of the road, a vessel in fog is supposed to be steaming at such speed as will permit her to stop in half the distance of existing visibility. With full speed astern, the *Andrea Dorea* required an oceanway of more than three miles to halt.

In other words, when the visibility, as Calamai reported, was down to half a mile, he should have been navigating—according to the letter of this standard of maritime practice, if not wholly a law—so slowly as to be able to come "dead in the water" in a quarter of a mile. Again, applying the same desideratum, the Italian steamship, at twenty-two knots, was plowing ahead twelve times faster than it theoretically should have.

The *Stockholm,* on the other hand, had no reason to reduce speed as long as she was running in clear weather.

The imponderable which was never clarified either by informal statements by the passengers or formal testimony by the officers in courts: Was there or was there not fog at the moment of impact?

Third officer Ernst Carstens-Johannsen, of the *Stockholm,* swore the sky was clear, the moon shining. It was dark and foggy, according to Third Officer Giannini, on the Italian liner.

16

Certain only is the fact that it was night time, and somewhere off treacherous Nantucket Island were familiar patches of fog.

The public remained consumed with curiosity. *Whose* fault was "that" collision off Nantucket? It mattered not for the overwhelming part it was none of the public's business. Few American lives had been claimed. Neither ship was of United States registry.

Yet, the tragedy had become a sort of Perry Mason mystery, of watery motif.

The owners themselves wanted to know, and the Italian Line arrived at court first, suing the Swedish-American Line for $30 million. The latter retorted with a counter suit for $2 million, largely to cover repairs to the *Stockholm*.

There was testimony in court which, however, proved inconclusive. Then, it was announced that the two important steamship companies had agreed to settle out of court.

The man on the street would never have an official or legal answer to the question. In fact, open or printed assessment of guilt remains gratuitous and in the province of libel.

In World War II, numbers of aviation cadets perished because of a fatal fascination with the up-rushing ground when practicing diving and dive-bombing. This transfixion, augmented by an acquired confidence in the invulnerability of their aircraft, could prove a combination as fatal as a bullet in the temple.

The glittering, though shielded dial of a radar on a navigation bridge at night time can itself act as a Lorelei, a crutch to those haunted by uncertainty, even as a massive steamship herself assumes an aspect of permanence comparable to the earth itself.

Quoting from further Proceedings of the Merchant Marine Council: ". . . in the hands of an incompetent operator, radar sometimes produces a false sense of security which will lead him to continue at a high rate of speed in areas of limited visibility, so that if a collision does occur, the resulting damage will be extremely severe."

The semiofficial writer was necessarily generalizing. But who can discount the considerations and fixations that might have exerted their influence on reasoning and decision-making one tragic night aboard two ocean liners speeding toward one another on a collision course?

2.

The ESSEX

THE LOSS OF THE *Andrea Doria* BECAME A "CLASSIC" OF THE seas. It captured the imagination of people and baffled them. Such a perplexing disaster should not have occurred in the first place. It mocked scientific acumen and the orderliness of things just past midpoint of the wonderful twentieth century.

It overshadowed even a far costlier transportation tragedy, measured in human souls, just four weeks earlier when two airliners collided over the Grand Canyon. All 128 aboard perished.

Historically, the *Andrea Doria–Stockholm* disaster presented no unique occurrence, no superlatives in magnitude, other than the bulk of the vessels themselves. Nor, against the backdrop of human behavior and capacity to err, was it especially surprising.

Great and lesser waters have claimed the unwary since recorded time and, quite certainly, long before. Who will ever know how many lives it cost the Phoenicians nearly twelve centuries before Christ to maintain stature as traders and masters of the sea?

Nor did it require a Salamis or a Trafalgar to inspire the frequent and familiar obituary: "lost at sea."

Who can ever count the numbers of fishermen who readied nets and headed their canoes or schooners toward open water— and oblivion?

19

The total losses at sea would manifestly be staggering. Lloyd's of London, beginning in 1866, has tallied in the "missing" category alone the great total of 4,022 vessels. "Accidents" are larger still.

Even now, every week of the year, approximately twenty-one ships on some ocean or waterway of the world violently collide, usually with some loss of life.

Yet they who have gone "down to the sea in ships" to "do business in great waters," as the psalmist phrased it, did not do so with trepidation, or with a conviction that their "business" was especially hazardous. When, for example, Captain George Pollard, Jr., sailed his square-rigged *Essex* out of Nantucket that August day, 1819, he could have nurtured premonitions of nothing more serious than storms.

With a crew of twenty, Pollard was following the profession of his Quaker ancestors of the New England island—whaling. He was taking his three-masted, 238-ton vessel in search of the giant sperm whale. Headed around Cape Horn for the Pacific, Pollard did not expect to see home or family for at least two years.

When he did once more raise the familiar green headlands, he might have aboard close to one thousand barrels of whale oil, bones for corset hoops and other strengthening purposes, as well as waxy fluid from the mammal's head known as spermaceti. This was used as tallow and for salves. In other words, there could be a fortune in the *Essex*'s holds.

The sperm whale, sixty feet long and no less than one-third the weight of the *Essex,* was—and remains—one of the largest mammals in existence. A harpooner had to do his work with the utmost strength and skill or face a wounded monster more formidable than the largest of grizzly bears.

Pollard brought along a friend as first mate—Owen Chase who, at twenty-three, was only six years the captain's junior. Thomas Nickerson, fifteen, was the youngest crew member. Six Negroes were among the crew, all of whom were free, salaried men. There were no slaves on Nantucket.

In spite of the usual "heavy westerly gales and a most

20

tremendous sea" off Cape Horn, the sturdy *Essex* safely gained the coast of Chile and calmer Pacific waters in mid-January. At the Galápagos Islands, three hundred live turtles were stowed below, providing "a most delicious food," in the opinion of Owen Chase, the chronicler of the voyage. Weighing at least as much as a man, the Galápagos turtle was a seafarer's delight, requiring neither food nor water, and it could be eaten as needed by the crew.

More than a year after the whalers had put out from home waters, on November 20, 1820, the ship sailed into a large school of their quarry, twenty-four hundred miles due west of the coast of Ecuador, a few miles above the Equator.

"Thar she blows!" called the lookout from his giddy perch atop the masthead.

All boats were lowered, as customary, when the ship was about half a mile away from the telltale air and steam spouts. Owen Chase himself threw the first harpoon. As had happened earlier, in October, in another hunting ground, the wounded sperm whale swung around "in agony" and smashed his powerful tail against the boat.

Although his boat had been completely wrecked in the previous encounter, Chase this time cut the line loose and stuffed the sailors' jackets into the hole which had been knocked in the keel. Thus, he was able to guide the damaged craft back to the *Essex*. There, he quickly effected semipermanent repairs with canvas and was ready to put over again. However, as he wrote:

> I observed a very large spermaceti whale . . . about 85 feet in length . . . he spouted two or three times and then disappeared. In less than two or three seconds he came up again, about the length of the ship off and made directly for us at the rate of about three knots.

The angered mammal, in spite of desperate last-moment efforts to turn the helm away, smashed the ship bow-on with its huge, armored-like head. The effect was as if the *Essex* had been staggered by a battering ram.

21

Stunned, knocked off their feet, "deprived almost of the power of speech," the crewmen were aware of the huge sea creature "grazing" the keel beneath the water, then watched it surface alongside seemingly to observe the havoc it had wrought.

The "rogue" whale made off "to leeward" as the pumps were started and the first mate surveyed the extent of damage. He was not far along in his assessment when again Chase sighted the monster:

> . . . apparently in convulsions on the top of the water, enveloped in the foam of the sea that his continual and violent thrashing about had created. I could distinctly see him smite his jaws together as if distracted with rage and fury.

The *Essex,* meanwhile, had been settling and Owen held scant hope of saving her. Then, came the cry from one of the crew:

"Here he is. He is making for us again!"

Maddened, obviously, by the concussion to its head, the huge mammal plowed in so fast that:

> . . . surf flew in all directions about him . . . his course toward us was marked by white foam a rod [sixteen and half feet] in width which he made with the continual violent thrashing of his tail. His head was about half out of water, and in that way he came upon and again struck the ship.

The whale "completely stove in the bow," before he swam off, this time not to return.

Within ten minutes after the first attack, the *Essex* had turned on her beam ends and floated half-awash. Those on board salvaged two quadrants and other navigational aids and leaped into "the spare boat."

When shortly the whale hunters in the other ship's boats, including the captain, returned, Pollard, at first not seeing any sign of the *Essex,* asked in mounting wonderment and consternation:

"My God, Mr. Chase, what is the matter?"

"We have been stove by a whale," the first mate unhesitatingly responded.

The entire crew now went to work on the derelict, chopping through decking to the storerooms. When the difficult and perilous task was completed, six hundred pounds of "hard bread," two hundred gallons of water, sails, a musket, carpenter's tools, and "a few turtles" were distributed evenly among the three boats, containing seven persons each.

In late afternoon, November 22, two days after the disaster, the survivors of the *Essex* abandoned their nearly sunken wreck containing 750 barrels of whale oil, and set sail for the Marquesas Islands, fifteen hundred miles southwest of their last estimated position. There seemed no unusual sense of urgency since the provisions were calculated as sufficient to sustain the whalers for two months.

However, within the first week, heavy winds, bringing rain and rough seas started the boats leaking and slowed the islandward progress. One of the three was violently attacked during the night by what looked like a huge shark. The creature was driven off but only after causing the craft to leak.

By the middle of December, the weather was warmer and generally improved. But the last turtle had been devoured along with most of the bread and water. There was no sign of land, anywhere. Some of the sailors began to sip of the ocean, which only served to further inflame "the raging fever of the throat. Sufferings, especially in periods of calm, when not a foot of progress was registered almost exceeded human belief."

On December 20, after nearly a month at sea, the castaways sighted land. It proved to be an uninhabited island about six miles long, some three hundred miles east of of Pitcairn Island where mutineers from HMS *Bounty* had landed three decades earlier.

The semimountainous and rocky island did not abound in animal life or vegetation; there was a little water, a few birds, some edible fish to be caught in the shallows. Nonetheless three of the crew, led by Thomas Chapelle, as the senior member, elected to remain behind as the remaining survivors of the *Essex* set sail two days after Christmas for Easter Island, eight hundred miles to the east.

On January 10, Matthew Joy, the second mate, died. He was the first to succumb. Ten days later, Richard Peterson, one of the Negroes, also perished and was buried at sea.

On the ninth of February, Isaac Cole, a crewman, breathed his last after convulsions and fits which finally culminated in paralysis. Before Cole, too, was dropped overboard, Owen Chase had an idea, revolving inescapably about "the painful subject of keeping the body for food." The first mate would write:

> We separated the limbs from the body and cut all the flesh from the bones, after which we opened the body—took out the heart, closed it again, sewing it up as decently as we could—and then committed it to the sea.
>
> We now first commenced to satisfy the immediate cravings of nature from the heart, which we eagerly devoured. We then ate sparingly of a few pieces of the flesh, after which we hung up the remainder, cut in thin strips, about the boat to dry in the sun. We made a fire and roasted some of it to serve us during the next day.

Five days later, all the flesh of the cannibalized crewman and remaining bread was consumed.

Meanwhile, on Captain Pollard's boat, which had separated from the mate's, the privation had become even more acute. Cannibalism had been resorted to three times. Still, the appetites of the dwindling survivors were unsatisfied.

On February 1, the captain and the remaining three in his boat agreed to leave it to chance who would be shot, for food purposes, and who would pull the trigger. Pollard's recollection of the event is as follows:

> We looked at each other with horrid thoughts in our minds, but we held our tongues. I am sure that we loved one another as brothers all the time; and yet our looks told plainly what must be done.

We cast lots and the fatal one fell on my poor cabin boy [seventeen-year-old Owen Coffin]. I started forward instantly and cried out, "My lad, my lad, if you don't like your lot I'll shoot the first man that touches you!"

The poor emaciated boy hesitated a moment or two; then quietly laying his head down on the gunnel [gunwale] of the boat, he said, "I like it as well as any other!"

Charles Ramsdell, who had drawn the lot of executioner, remonstrated until the unlucky Coffin, a relative of the captain, as so many on Nantucket Island were kinfolk, urged his shipmate to get on with the grizzly task. Pollard's tale concluded:

He was soon dispatched, and nothing left of him. . . . After some more days of horror and despair, when some were lying down in the bottom of the boat not able to rise and scarcely one of us could move a limb, a vessel hove in sight.

This was three weeks after Coffin had been shot. Pollard and Ramsdell were the only two remaining in the boat which was hauled aboard the Nantucket whaler *Dauphin*, ten miles off the coast of Chile.

When the gaunt, sun-parched, and heavily bearded captain attempted to tell his essentially nauseating tale, his "head" seemed to come "on fire at the recollection." He believed it must have been some nightmare.

Four days previously, Chase and the two survivors in his boat had been rescued by the brig *Indian*, of London.

The five were soon reunited in Valparaiso, Chile, after their remarkable if ghastly voyage of some thirty-five hundred miles in open boats, lasting more than three months. The accomplishment had been exceeded only by that of Captain William Bligh, of the *Bounty*, who, after being set adrift by the mutineers, had navigated four thousand miles across the South Pacific to the island of Timor in forty-seven days.

In April, Thomas Chapelle and his two shipmates were picked up from their island, later named Henderson, by the British vessel *Surrey*. They had subsisted on small black birds and berries. Skeletons found in caves mutely spoke of earlier castaways.

The third boat from the *Essex* was never seen again.

The whaling folk of Nantucket harbored no malice of record against the five survivors for their collective cannibalism and one murder. The sea was austere and cruel. Those who cast their fortunes upon it must guide their destinies as circumstances demanded—such was the philosophy upon the small, windblown island.

Pollard returned to sea to lose his next command, the *Two Brothers*. That was enough. He retired in 1825 and worked as a watchman. He died in 1870 at the age of eighty-one.

The first mate of the *Essex,* who continued a whaler's life as captain, was married four times. He succumbed also as an old man, the year before his onetime captain's passing. A son, William Henry Chase, met the New York-born author, Herman Melville, at sea in 1841, when the younger Chase was sixteen years old. From the son's accounts and Melville's perusing of the chronicles of his father's, those of Pollard's and also of Chapelle (who fabricated his erstwhile berth as that of second mate), the allegorical novel *Moby Dick* was born.

Thus, the *Essex,* if not the first or last vessel attacked and possibly destroyed by a whale, would, for various reasons, become the most famous, and also notorious.

3.

The Gold Rush Days:
the Unsinkable Mrs. Bates

THE WHALERS WERE PROFESSIONAL SALTS. THEY KNEW WHAT
they were doing. But this much could not be said for the "forty-
niners."

Responding to a gold strike at Sutter's Mill, the future site
of Sacramento, California, in January, 1848, students, farmers,
merchants, men, and women swarmed westward by ship from the
eastern ports as ignorant of the sea as they were of mining or
the hardships of pioneers. Crops were left untended as harvesters
abandoned the fields. Even the Nantucket and New Bedford
whaling fleets sailed forth as transports, unsuited as they were to
such accommodations.

The women would have to make do for dress hoops and oil
to fuel their lamps.

A group of divinity students tossed away their theology texts
and chartered a six-hundred-ton bark. When they could not round
up a crew quickly enough, they themselves set the sails and
guessed at the direction of the wind.

Foreshadowing "group fares" of a century hence, 124 similar emigrant companies were formed to buy or hire other ships.

Experienced mates and even captains, in their frenzy to mine and pan the yellow stuff, shipped out as ordinary seamen on the next barks casting off for the gold coast. One man smuggled himself aboard in a sugar box at sailing time.

From relatively modest attention to marine matters in preceding years, newspaper columns suddenly bulged and, in effect, swam with shipping notices.

"Ho for California!" read one such advertisement in the New York *Herald*. ". . . to sail on the 25th Instant, the splendid ocean steamer *Senator* of 754 tons burthen, 240 feet long by 30 feet beam. . . ."

Frequently, the notice extolled the abilities and even the sobriety of captain, mates, and chief engineer. Fares ranged from $130 for a shared fo'c'sle to $600 for something described as a private cabin.

The *Boston Transcript* of December 7, 1849, contained an increasingly familiar item:

> Collision at Sea—The ship *Galena*, from New Orleans, 22d ult., for New York, came in collision with the British brig *Charles* from Cardiff, bound to Wilmington, instantly reducing the latter to a wreck, so that she sunk in about three minutes. Seven of the crew were drowned.

In the same column, farther down, the *Transcript* also reported:

> In the *Galena*, at New York, from New Orleans, Mr. Chauncey P. Parker.
> In the *Crescent* from Salem for San Francisco, Messrs. Henry W. Haskell and Henry R. Neal, of Boston, and 59 others.

Adams and Co. Express offered monthly special messengers to San Francisco on the first and fifteenth, for letters and "small parcels."

The *Marcia Cleaves* sailed the same date for San Francisco. Three hours after an advertisement for the brig *Two Friends*

28

appeared in the New York papers, her one hundred cabins were overbooked, at $150 to $400 apiece. The charter price of $30,000, which happened to represent three times the value of the partially seaworthy hulk, was paid back, not even including the freight (at $60 a ton).

Even the voyage out, apparently, was good business.

Crowding and overcrowding became inescapably the rule rather than the exception. There were few groups arriving in San Francisco among which virtually every voyager did not hate his or her shipmate. Captain Samuel Plumer, of the *Washington Irving*, after a more or less average six-months' sail, delivered his fifty-three passengers with the adieu:

"I'd rather ship a cargo of wild animals than you folks!"

Sometimes, the seafarers did more than grumble. On the brig *Cachelot* a delegation of sturdy males earnestly promised the captain they would toss him into the South Atlantic if food wasn't improved. The fare, as described by one aboard, appeared to consist mainly of:

"Isthmus-made molasses with dirt, gravel and sticks in it besides some curious looking things which I did not exactly understand."

The menus improved after the passengers, including a few women, commandeered the galley. The master did not have to swim. However, even the best intentioned of skippers, without the bonus of refrigeration, were hard put to keep food from spoiling.

"In point of fact," wrote historian Oscar Lewis, "the gold rush got underway in an atmosphere not much different from that of wartime."

And those men who did not entertain illusions about California's social climate or even safety aboard ship, set forth as though they were, in reality going off to battle. Elliott W. Cook, of Lockport, New York, for one, listed among his inventory of personal luggage: "One rifle, two holster pistols, one half-cocking same [pistol] and three knives." (These were revolvers, by today's nomenclature, since there were no automatic pistols in 1849.)

The lonesomeness and the tedium of the experience was also noted by Cook who would write, "dreampt of Her last night, of my wife in her girlish days." Later, he observed, "am getting very dirty from using salt water to wash with."

Those rugged emigrants not poisoned by the food, stricken with some fatal fever, or beaten if not killed by brigand shipmates were faced with unending boredom. One passenger offered $10 for a completely new joke or any personal recollection not recounted many times already. Still later, he repeated the reward for anyone on the vessel who consistently did not talk to him at all.

Newspapers were read again and again until they disintegrated. Books and periodicals held up a little longer. Some ships published their own papers—*The Barometer,* for one, on the schooner *Edward Everett.* Card playing and fishing, when becalmed, and even palmistry added to the random diversions.

It was 14,500 land miles around the Horn from New York to the Golden Gate, 5,789 miles if the traveler wished to transfer ships at the Isthmus of Panama. Many did so to save two months' traveling time.

However, the ten-mile or longer trek across the Isthmus was beset by heat, quicksands, snakes, insects, and diseases such as cholera in the jungles, as well as savage Indians and highwaymen. Discarded baggage and clothing marked the trails of the exhausted, sweating travelers.

Those to whom such prospects or the equally distressing ones of the transcontinental route were too formidable had to endure the merciless storms and icebergs rounding the Horn. And, even at journey's end, the treacherous Farallone Islands threatened inbound ships off the Golden Gate.

The beautiful, towering California clippers in the 1850s could sail the whole voyage in a remarkable ninety days. The paddlewheelers of the Pacific Mail Steamship Co., such as the *California,* could make the run around the Horn in as little as two months, often with 350 on board, but not altogether in comfort.

It wasn't easy for any travelers to reach California. It was unlikely, however, that any of the nineteenth-century argonauts surmounted such continuing challenges as did Mrs. D. B. Bates, of Kingston, Massachusetts.

Mrs. Bates sailed from Baltimore on July 27, 1850, aboard her husband's *Nonantum*. The small vessel carried only six other passengers, some fifty tons of "light freight," and coal.

Off the Falkland Islands, the *Nonantum* caught fire. Although she was a total loss, passengers and crew made it safely to those rocky outcroppings in the Atlantic just above Cape Horn.

Now Captain Bates had no command. But the gold fields still beckoned, as brilliantly as the *Nonantum* had blazed.

After a month of watching seabirds on the lonely little British colony, Mrs. Bates and her husband spotted the *Humayoon,* newly arrived from Dundee. This bark was down to her gunwales under a cargo of tar, rum, and—coal.

The Bates's obtained, after much entreaty, accommodations on the crowded *Humayoon*. Tagging along this time was a shaggy goat, acquired on the Falklands.

The Scotch ship did not last as long even as the *Nonantum*. The *Humayoon's* inflammable freight burst into multicolored red, blue, and yellow flames off Tierra del Fuego. Mrs. Bates later wrote:

> Nothing could exceed the almost profoundness of the solitude by which we were surrounded, a silence broken only by the roaring and crackling of the flames as they wreathed and shot upward, illuminating the midnight darkness, and casting the reflection of their fiery glare far out over the lonely deep . . . it is quite improbable to convey by language an adequate conception of the solemn magnificence of this midnight scene.

With husband, goat, and carpetbag, Mrs. Bates was transferred to the first vessel that happened by, the coaler *Fanchon,* from Newburyport. The *Humayoon's* captain and mates, continuing their fight against the flames, waved farewell as the dinghy pulled off, bearing its human cargo toward shore—and further adventure.

Captain Lunt, the *Fanchon's* master, appeared to be "a judicious disciplinarian," and maintained his command in "the greatest neatness and order imaginable," affording an atmosphere of confidence to those who might need it. At last, thought Mrs. Bates, she could hope for "a speedy termination of our voyage."

The trouble with the other ships' incinerating themselves, the captain confided to Mrs. Bates, was their "want of proper ventilation."

However, on the evening of December 25, as she sat below with her husband and her newest shipmates, she began to smell a disturbingly familiar gaseous odor. When she asked Mr. Bates if he thought the coal was on fire, he replied: "Pshaw!"

And that was that. They went back to their modest Yuletide repast and conviviality. Her account continues:

> The third day, as Captain Lunt was watching one of the large ventilators on deck, he saw something having the appearance of smoke escaping therefrom. He sprang down between decks—there was no appearance of smoke or fire whatever—and raised the lower hatch. All appeared us usual. He then ordered the second mate to dig down into the coal, and soon proofs beyond a doubt were too apparent.
>
> The coal was so hot, it could not be taken in the hand. The whole body of coal, two or three feet below the surface, was red hot. The same preparations for a life on board a burning ship were again repeated that it had been my fortune twice previously to witness. In this instance, we had not to contend with the elements of wind and water as well as fire; for the ocean, at times, was as smooth and transparent as a glass.
>
> For a time, Captain Lunt shaped his course for the Galápagos Islands, what wind there was being favorable to waft us in that direction; and, our distance from the islands and the mainland being nearly equal, he was undecided for some time which port would be our destination. Being within the tropics, the weather was exceedingly pleasant—almost too much so for our benefit.

For several days in succession, it would remain perfectly calm. The nights were beautifully serene; not a cloud, or the slightest film of vapor, appeared on the face of the deep blue canopy of the heavens. . . .

Signal lights were kept burning in the hope of attracting the attention of some vessel which might be passing. For days lookouts were stationed aloft, and more than once our ears gladdened with the joyful cry of "Sail, ho!" which as often proved a vain illusion. The strained vision and anxious solicitude of those on the lookout caused them to imagine they saw that which they vainly desired to behold.

I was induced, by the entreaties and advice of my husband, seconded by those of Captain Lunt, to adopt gentlemen's apparel. Considering the danger and exposure we might be subjected to, should we be compelled to remain any length of time, it was not therefore considered a bad idea. . . . Accordingly, from the captain's wardrobe was selected a pair of black pants, a green hunting-coat, black satin vest, bosom and collar worn a la Byron and a purple velvet smoking cap. . . . I was scarcely recognizable by my friends on board.

Finally, the *Fanchon* dropped anchor in a small bay, two miles off the coast of Peru, with the towering Andes as a rugged backdrop. There was, however, no time to lose. Mrs. Bates's account goes on:

We threw overboard all the spare spars upon deck, and everything that would float. We had no provisions or water to take on shore, and had been refreshed with none through the day. There was one pig on board that had left Baltimore in the ship, and one hen. These, together with my pet goat, the sailors took under their own immediate protection, and succeeded in landing them on the beach.

The pig, in the height of his terror, beat an instantaneous retreat into one of the numerous caves, or recesses, situated at the base of perpendicular cliffs, which rose nearly two hundred feet, and presented an effectual barrier to any attempt that might be made to scale them. How intently I watched the foaming surf we were fast approaching, and which had already engulfed the boat in advance; the roaring and splashing of water, voices heard above the din of all, giving directions, dragged, minus bonnet

33

and shawl, through the surf upon the sandy beach. After removing everything off the ship's deck, they ran her still nearer in, and scuttled her; but the fire had made such progress, it was impossible to save her.

In two hours after we left her deck, she burst out into a sheet of flame. The fire caught to the sails, which were spread to the breeze, and she was a sheet of fire to the mastheads. Here, in this lonely bay, lay the fine ship *Fanchon*, and burnt to the water's edge. Nothing could exceed the almost awful profoundness of the solitude by which we were surrounded—a silence broken only by the roaring and crackling of the flames, as they wreathed and shot far upward, illuminating the midnight darkness, and casting the reflection of their fiery glare far out over the lonely deep—and the deep roar of the eternally restless waves, as they dashed in rapid succession upon the beach at our feet.

It is quite impossible to convey by language an adequate conception of the solemn magnificence of this midnight scene.

Mr. and Mrs. Bates and their goat languished for two long months in Valparaiso awaiting yet another vessel. Finally, the steamer *Republic* dropped anchor, needing food and fuel. The captain would take the Massachusetts couple, jinx that he had learned they were, but passage would cost them $1,200.

They could bring along the goat, but only on the condition it be presented to the cook. It was.

Ten months after they had left Kingston, Massachusetts, the Bateses arrived in the gold fields.

At least half of the broadly estimated 100,000 adventurers who answered the lure of "Eldorado" traveled by sea. Even less reliable was any total of how many lives were lost on that long, dangerous route.

The masts and ribs of many rotting, abandoned ships from Panama to San Francisco harbor and up along the brackish shores of the Sacramento River attested to the vast numbers of men who risked everything in their wild, feverish rush to get to the goldfields by sea. Many died en route in fire, and sinkings; others arrived safely but were too late to cash in on the "Rush," or found the competition too keen and the pickings too thin.

On Sunday, July 27, 1862, the large and popular side-wheeler *Golden Gate* caught fire fifteen miles north of Manzanillo, Mexico. At least 223 of the 338 aboard died and $1.5 million in gold specie slid to the bottom of these coastal sands of the Pacific. The disaster was like a flaming "amen" to the gold rush.

With the fever spent, people could pause belatedly, to ask, "Was it *really* worth it?" The three million ounces of gold teased out of the earth was, at least, disproportionate to the incredible effort to claim it.

Besides, the Civil War had been aflame for three months. There were other things to occupy one's attention.

4.

The ARCTIC and the AUSTRIA

MRS. BATES WAS ONE OF THE MANY WHO HAD EXPERIENCED tribulations in reaching the gold fields. Yet, travelers upon other oceans also learned that it was far from routine to journey to any destination via the water route, and invariably impossible to attempt to do so and survive as well.

The 1840s and 1850s proved especially perilous for the immigrants. "Lost at sea" became all too familiar an obituary in family Bibles from Boston, Massachusetts, to Birmingham, England. Some ships vanished without trace, as did many on the "gold run" around the Horn. It could only be surmised whether they had collided with another vessel, an iceberg, burned or gone aground upon some rocky coast.

Perhaps the most baffling disappearance was that of the Liverpool and Philadelphia Steamship Company's *City of Glasgow,* which sailed from Liverpool in March, 1854, and carried 399 persons into total oblivion. Even the specter of piracy had been offered as one of numerous explanations.

Those who lived through a shipwreck to tell their children and grandchildren of that supreme experience were among the fortunate few. Such, for example, was the case of the passengers aboard the *City of Philadelphia,* bound from Liverpool for her namesake city on her maiden voyage, when she smashed onto the banks off Cape Race, Newfoundland, on September 17, 1854.

Six hundred passengers and crew—all who had put westward from England—survived.

Exactly three days after this "lucky" wreck, another sidewheeler paddled out of the Mersey River in Liverpool, bound for New York. She was the handsome Collins liner *Arctic,* of 3,500-tons register, 284 feet over-all, built in 1850 to give transatlantic travelers a bit of extra comfort. The latter was an extravagance little known or even expected in the first half of the century.

Her blandishments included carpeting in the main saloons and first-class cabins (booking at $125), sofas, arm chairs, and exceptionally bright lamps using clockwork to force-feed the oil. French *spécialités de maison* were featured at dinner.

Second-class passage, at $70, was considered the most pleasant on the North Atlantic run.

In February, 1852, the *Arctic*'s superheated boilers helped her to set a record eastbound crossing of nine days, seventeen hours.

On her passage this September, 1854, the liner carried 282 passengers and a crew of 153. Her holds bulged with an unusually large amount of cargo, including mail, foodstuffs, and even art treasures.

The executive staff of the Collins Line was handsomely represented in the sailing list: Mrs. Edward Knight Collins, wife of the general manager, and their two young children, Henry and Mary Ann; two daughters of James Brown, president of the company—Millie and Grace (Mrs. George Allen)—a son, William, his French-born wife, and two grandchildren of the senior Brown.

James O. Luce, forty-nine-year-old captain of the *Arctic,* had brought along his crippled son, Willie, eleven, in the expectation that the voyage might improve his spirits.

On the twenty-seventh of September, three days out of New York, the sidewheeler was some forty-five miles south of Cape Race in a dense fog. She was, however, steaming at her normal thirteen knots.

Luce himself was down in his cabin working out the noon position when he heard the officer of the deck cry:

"Hard starboard!"

The master had barely gained the deck when he "felt a crush forward and at the same moment saw a steamer under the starboard bow."

The strange ship smashed against the *Arctic,* virtually demolishing the entire starboard side of the bow, then drifted off astern.

When Luce recovered his balance from the heavy shock and his vessel returned to an even keel, he gained the impression that the *Arctic* was "comparatively uninjured." He ordered a boat put over to assist the other ship.

The bow of the "other," which was the small French steamer *Vesta,* had been almost completely torn away. Two boats were lowered, containing both passengers and crew, and were rowed frantically toward the *Artic.* She seemed the only hope of the occupant's salvation.

One boat came under the churning starboard paddle wheel of the Collins liner and was immediately swamped. Everyone on the frail craft was lost. The second was swallowed up by the fog —forever.

Meanwhile, the first officer of the boat Captain Luce had put over to assist the ship that had hit the *Arctic* noticed that his own steamer was "leaking fearfully" and immediately reported the damage to the captain. Luce ordered maximum steam pressure on the pumps and a course set due north which should bring the *Arctic* to the nearest land. The four deck pumps were worked by the huskiest male passengers, while others of the travelers joined crewmen in lashing together into crude rafts the yard arms, doors, barrels, and anything else that floated, in anticipation of the sinking of the badly damaged ship.

The carpenter organized a gang of seamen to help him put canvas from the sail loft over the gaping hole in the *Arctic's* bow. Passengers struggled at the same time to remove impeding crates and barrels of cargo.

But even as they worked, the men heard water "rushing in." Soon, the cold Atlantic, black with the filth of coal dust and bilge accumulation, surged upward until the second deck was awash.

The fires went out with a hiss. The *Arctic* lost all headway and began to list to starboard.

No one—surely not the captain—had kept track of time. However, it was at least two or three hours after the accident when all hope was abandoned and discipline became nonexistent.

Terrified from watching the ocean slowly coming up over their footboards, the "black gang" from the engine room rushed the boats and succeeded in getting away in one of the six the *Arctic* carried.

One of their number was seen brandishing a revolver as a swimmer tried futilely to clamber aboard.

"Let the passengers go in the boat!" Luce yelled in a voice audible to many on the decks over which the waves were now sloshing. The panic was spreading to the male travelers, one of whom was grabbed by Luce as he fought for the second lowering boat.

The captain was left holding a torn portion of the man's shirt. Its wearer gained the lifeboat, which was launched so imperfectly that all of its occupants—men, women, children, and crew—were dumped into the sea.

In desperation, Luce seized a small ax and threatened other onrushing men. It was useless. The mob, like the French storming the Bastile, could not be controlled. The scene was one of utter chaos with men leaping twenty feet from the top of the rail, pushing and maiming those who had already taken refuge in the boat. His account follows:

My attention was then drawn to the other quarter boat which I found broken down but hanging by one tackle. A rush was made for her, also, and some fifteen got in and cut the tackle and were soon out of sight.

I found that not a seaman or carpenter was left on board, and we were without any tools to assist in building a raft, as our only hope.

39

The only officer left was Francis Dorian, the third mate, who aided me with the assistance of many of the passengers. We had succeeded in getting the fore and main yard and two topgallant yards overboard and such other small spars and materials as we could collect when I was fully convinced that the ship must go down in a very short time. Not a moment was to be lost in getting the spars lashed together to form a raft.

There was, however, one last lifeboat which the captain hoped to fill with the remaining women and children. Dorian was ordered not to allow its oars out of his sight.

The little cluster of passengers with the captain heard him say, at least once, hoping to give them courage, "The fate of the ship shall be mine." They felt he would not abandon them as had others of the staff and crew.

There was not much more time. Making a final inspection of what little of the deck was not already awash, Luce discovered a Negro stewardess whom he recognized as Anna Downer, still bending over one of the hand pumps. He told her she had better come with him and get in the last boat. However, Anna kept on working the wooden handle up and down, and that was the last he ever saw of her.

The *Arctic* had been afloat, remarkably enough, longer than four hours when her settling rate abruptly accelerated. Luce ordered the lifeboat away so hurriedly that Dorian had no chance to toss in the oars.

Walter Peter McCabe, a twenty-four-year-old Irish crewman, on his first voyage, jumped onto the paddlebox. He described the experience in this fashion:

> We sprang on the saloon deck and in an instant were engulfed in the surging waters which soon closed over our heads. Down, down, we sank, with our noble vessel into the bosom of the ocean and the terrible thought took possession of my mind that I was drowning.

A passenger, Paul F. Grann, heard "one fearful shriek . . . from that agonized company as they were swept forward against

40

the smokestack, and then all was over." The shattered vessel plunged down, stern first.

Captain Luce soon found himself on the surface after a brief struggle with his own helpless child in his arms, then again felt himself impelled downward to a great depth. His account continues:

> Before I reached the surface a second time I had nearly perished, and lost the hold of my child. As I again struggled to the surface of the water, a most awful and heartrending scene presented itself to my view—over 200 men, women and children were struggling together amidst pieces of wreck of every kind, calling on each other for help, and imploring God to assist them. Such an appalling scene may God preserve me from ever witnessing again.
>
> I was in the act of trying to save my child when a portion of the paddle box came rushing up edgewise, just grazing my head, falling with its whole weight upon the head of my darling child. Another moment I beheld him lifeless in the water. I succeeded in getting on to the top of the paddle box, in company with eleven others; one, however, soon left for another piece, finding that it could not support so many. Others remained until they were one by one relieved by death. We stood in water, at a temperature of 45 degrees, up to our knees, and frequently the sea broke directly over us.

McCabe, contrary to his fears, did not drown. He later wrote:

> I retained my consciousness all the time I was under the water, and it was with a feeling of intense joy that I found, after about half a minute, that I was rapidly rising towards the surface. It was all darkness before me, but now I could see a dim light above me, and in a few seconds I was on the top of the water, struggling for life. Being a good swimmer, and having, besides, the support of a life preserver, I succeeded in reaching a door, which was floating a few feet from where I rose. I looked around me, but there was no trace of the vessel except a few loose timbers and the rafts which were floating about, some with and others without passengers.

41

Finding I could not retain my hold of the door with safety, I left it and swam to a barrel which lay a few feet from me, and from this again I swam to the large raft, to which some seventy persons were clinging. The sea, though not strong, was rough, and the waves, as they dashed remorselessly over the raft, washed away a portion of its living freight.

It was an awful scene—a multitude of human beings, in the midst of the ocean, without the slightest hope of assistance, while every minute one by one was dropping into a watery grave, from sheer exhaustion. Those who had life preservers did not sink, but floated with their ghastly faces upwards, reminding those who still remained alive of the fate that awaited them.

The raft at one time was so crowded that many had to hold on by one hand. Very few words were spoken by any, and the only sound to be heard was the splash of the waters or the heavy breathing of the poor sufferers, as they tried to recover their breath, after a wave had passed over them. Nearly all were submerged to their armpits, while a few could with great difficulty keep their heads above the surface. The women were the first to go; they were unable to stand the exposure more than three or four hours. They all fell off the raft without a word, except one poor girl, who cried out in intense agony, "Oh, my poor mother and sisters."

Luce, atop the paddle box, passed the night in similar agony and suspense, expecting every hour would be the last for himself and his few hardy companions. His account of the ordeal goes on:

At last the morning came, surrounded with a dense fog—not a living soul was to be seen but our own party, seven men being left. In the dense fog of the morning we saw some water casks and other things belonging to our ship, but nothing that we could get to afford us any relief.

Our raft was rapidly settling, as it absorbed water.

About noon, Mr. S. M. Woodruff, of New York, was relieved by death. All the others now began to suffer very severely for want of water, except Mr. George M. Allen and myself. In that respect we were very much favored, although we had not a drop on the raft. The day continued foggy, except just at noon, as near as we could judge, we had a clear horizon for about half an hour, and nothing could be seen but water and sky.

42

Night came on thick and dreary, with our minds made up that neither of us would again see the light of another day. Very soon three more of our suffering party were relieved by death, leaving Mr. Allen, a young man, and myself. Feeling myself getting exhausted, I now sat down for the first time, about eight o'clock in the evening, on a trunk, which providentially had been found on the wreck. In this way I slept a little throughout the night, and became somewhat refreshed.

About an hour before daylight—now Friday, the 29th—we saw a vessel's light near to us. We all three of us exerted ourselves to the utmost of our strength in hailing her, until we became quite exhausted. In about a quarter of an hour the light disappeared to the east of us.

Soon after daylight a bark hove in sight to the northwest, the fog having lightened a little—steering apparently for us; but in a short time she seemed to have changed her course, and again we were doomed to disappointment; yet I felt hopes that some of our fellow sufferers may have been seen and rescued by them.

Shortly after we had given up all hopes of being rescued by the bark, a ship was discovered to the east of us, steering directly for us. We now watched her with the most intense anxiety as she approached. The wind changed, caused her to alter her course several points. About noon they fortunately discovered a man on a raft near them, and succeeding in saving him by the second mate jumping over the side, and making a rope fast around him, when he was got on board safely, this man saved proved to be a Frenchman who was a passenger on board the steamer with which we came in collision.

He informed the captain that others were near on pieces of the wreck; and, going aloft, he saw us and three others. We were the first to which the boat was sent, and safely taken on board about 3 P.M. The next was Mr. James Smith, of Mississippi, second class passenger. The others saved were five of our firemen.

The ship proved to be the *Cambria,* from Glasgow, bound to Montreal.

McCabe became the sole survivor of the seventy persons he estimated were clinging to his raft. The last to die had been a man apparently of some wealth, judging from his silk, oil-soaked coat. The young crewman held onto his final companion while he

43

promised, between gasps, to "reward" him "handsomely" when they reached New York. A wave finally snatched him from McCabe's grasp.

The durable Irishman was rescued, by chance, the second evening as the third officer's boat drifted by. Without oars, Dorian had fashioned paddles from planking and seats.

This boat was picked up by the steamer *Huron*. Two others came ashore on the Avalon Peninsula, seventy miles south of St. Johns, Newfoundland. The remaining three lifeboats were never seen again.

Of the estimated 435 who sailed, 85 lived through the ordeal. Only 24 were passengers.

Not one woman or child survived. Collins had lost his wife and two children; Brown, five members of his family. All in all, it was a bleak hour in chivalry.

It would have required an older and far more sturdily established steamship enterprise to outlive this calamity. When a sister ship, the *Pacific,* disappeared two years later, with all 190 aboard —possibly as the result of hitting an iceberg—doom was sounded for the Collins Line. In February, 1858, its three remaining vessels were auctioned, and the company was wiped off all nautical ledgers.

Captain Luce did not again directly dare the vicissitudes of the sea. He remained only on its fringes, in the marine insurance business, surviving into his seventy-fifth year.

If there was any good—paradoxical as that possibility appeared—to emerge from the fate of the *Arctic,* it lay in the embryo glimmerings of Atlantic steamer "tracks." A young American naval navigator, Lieutenant Matthew Fontaine Maury, appalled at the sacrifice of life, recommended the next year, in 1855, the observance of passenger sea lanes between the new world and the old.

These should run twenty to twenty-five miles apart, the Europe-bound steamers plying the southern fringe, the westbound ships to the north. And seventeen years later, in 1872, the United States Hydrographic Office strongly suggested these ocean highways in a pamphlet. No country, however, then or thereafter possessed the powers of traffic policeman on the open oceans.*

Meanwhile, there was also the sea itself, and the weather. In September, 1857, the steamer *Central America* foundered in a gale within 150 miles of the east Florida coast. Of the estimated 592 aboard, 170 were saved. The shock of bereaved next of kin as well as of the press appeared to be magnified since the elements had manifestly proven mightier than the self-propelled liners.

And in this fatal decade there still would be, as *Leslie's Illustrated Newspaper* exclaimed, "another of those appalling massacres of steamship passengers . . . perpetrated upon the high seas."

Just four years after the *Arctic* vanished beneath the cold, gray swells of the North Atlantic, another well-advertised and "elegant" steamer, the 2,334-ton *Austria,* of the New York and Hamburg Line, was nearly one thousand miles east of Nova Scotia, nine days out of Southampton.

Collision, however, did not enter into her own peculiar date with destiny. The most meticulous navigation, conceivably, by all the ships plying the Atlantic Ocean could not save the *Austria.*

The German vessel, on her second voyage, with six hundred aboard, was endeavoring to make up time lost in bucking headwinds all the way westward. Slightly longer and more rakish than the *Arctic,* the *Austria* sustained the tradition of her sailing forebears with a carved Austrian eagle glowering from her overhanging prow.

Weighing anchor from the Solent Estuary, below Southampton, on September 8, 1858, the liner encountered the voyage's first jinx. The capstan suddenly spun out of control, hurling one sailor overboard, who was drowned, and seriously injuring two others.

*The United States Coast Guard has no power to regulate sea lanes in deep water, although hydrographic charts continue to strongly recommend such observance. United States passenger vessels—such few as there are today—must observe recommended tracks, with obvious penalties: the suspension or revocation of a master's license.

"From the time the ship was laid on her course," recalled Chartres Brew, a government employe of London, "we experienced strong westerly winds. On the 12th, the weather was more favorable and on the 13th a speed of 11 knots had been attained. All were in high hopes of reaching New York by the 18th."

The mood, as the shores of America neared, had belatedly become as "merry as a marriage bell," in the opinion of Henry Smith, of Chelsea, Massachusetts.

"Passengers," he found, "were amusing themselves in various ways. Some, gathered in groups, were telling stories, cracking jests, narrating anecdotes. Others were engaged in shuttlecock and other games."

On this second day of milder skies, Monday, the thirteenth, the master, Frederic A. Heydtmann, was so pleased at what other passengers described as "genial weather" and prospects of "an agreeable termination to the voyage" that he decided to make his command quite literally shipshape, and also pleasant to the sense of smell.

Following tradition, he would start at the bottom, in the crowded, odorous steerage and work up. Again, in accordance with accepted procedure the boatswain, accompanied by the fourth officer, was ordered to heat a heavy chain until it glowed and dip it in tar. The resulting clouds of smoke presumably would fumigate the hold.

That day the bos'n had allowed the iron to become nearly white-hot its entire length. With a scream of pain, he dropped the links, which upset the tar pot. A rush of air swept through an open hatch. . . .

At this moment, about 2:30 P.M., according to a New York City music professor, Theodore Glaubensklee, many of the passengers, filled with an ample Sunday dinner, were distributed about the decks, basking in the unaccustomed sunshine when the cry of "fire!" drilled into their consciousness like a lightning bolt.

Glaubensklee turned to see flames already bursting skyward through the middle deck and "men, women and children running to and fro in despair and uttering the most heart-rending cries."

The steamer was still heading directly into prevailing westerly winds. All hatches and portholes—the number of which was a boasted feature of the *Austria*—had been temporarily opened to ventilate and "fumigate" the below decks area. As a consequence, she soon was transformed into a mass of crackling flames from stem to stern. Her beautiful mahogany veneer and dazzlingly varnished bulkheads had hastened, like so much tinder or powder trains, the headlong dash of the flames.

Chartres Brew, who was a summertime Thames River sailor, ran to the man at the helm and told him to put the ship "with her side to the wind." But the sailor understood no English.

Brew then raced to the nearest lifeboat to try to assist with its lowering. Panic had already taken over. So many people were seated or standing in the small boat that it could not be lifted off its blocks.

Some were persuaded to step out. The boat was swung over the side. All rushed back, yelling, pushing, and clawing. Again, overloaded, the craft plummeted into the waters, spilling dozens of its hysterical occupants overboard.

Captain Heydtmann himself was not setting the most inspiring of examples, as he struggled with the falls of a port side lifeboat.

"We are lost!" he was heard to yell. "Oh God—we are all lost!"

In the next instant, as the boat started to descend, Heydtmann was seen by a Hackensack, New Jersey, traveler—Philip Berry—shinnying down a rope toward it, but "attempting to rest his feet on one of the seats of the boat as it swayed about in its dangling position, he missed his mark. He suddenly let go his hold and sank."

Whether or not the helmsman had understood Chartres Brew became academic. The former himself abandoned the wheel as flames licked at his feet. Anyhow, the crackling tar had streamed down open vents and ladderways into the engine room, firing other combustibles and, presumably, suffocating all of the personnel of that hapless "black gang."

The *Austria* continued, brightly afire, in one long, circling course, pilotless, at diminishing speed.

Albert Vezin, of Philadelphia, who had already lost sight of his mother and two young sisters in the fire and smoke, managed to haul six people to safety up through a broken skylight. Another passenger, trying to assist occupants topside by rope was not so deft. A steward appeared at the end of his rope, already strangled. Brew put his impressions of the disaster in writing:

> At this time, the scene on the quarter deck was indescribable and truly heart-rending. Passengers were rushing frantically to and fro—husbands seeking their wives, wives in search of their husbands, relatives looking after relatives, mothers lamenting the loss of their children, some wholly paralyzed by fear, others madly crying to be saved; but a few perfectly calm and collected.
>
> The flames pressed so closely upon them, that many jumped into the sea. Relatives clasped in each other's arms leaped over and met a watery grave; two girls supposed to be sisters, jumped over and sank kissing each other. A missionary and wife leaped into the sea together, and the stewardess and assistant steward arm in arm followed.
>
> One Hungarian gentleman with seven fine children, four of them girls, made his wife jump in, then blessed his six eldest children, made them jump in one after the other, and followed them with an infant in his own arms. I, about this time, was standing outside the bulwarks holding on by the davits, leaning out to avoid the flames, which were leaping towards me. I saw a swamped boat under me, spinning by a rope still attached to the ship.
>
> As the oars were tied in her I thought, if I could get to her, I would be enabled to save myself and some others. I let myself down by a rope passing over a man who was clinging to it, but who refused to come with me. I took out a penknife to cut the tackle; the large blade broke, and I then severed it with the small blade. The ship passed ahead. As the screw approached I found the boat drawn towards it.
>
> I tried to keep the boat off, but the screw caught and capsized her over me. I dived away from the ship and came to the surface near a boat which was keel upwards. I got on her, and

48

by pressing on one side with the assistance of a wave she righted, but was still swamped. The oars had been knocked out by the screw.

The only thing I could find in her to paddle with was some laths nailed together as a sheathing for the sides. When I looked around, the ship was a quarter of a mile away from me. I could see ladies and gentlemen jumping off the poop into the water in twos and threes, some of the ladies in flames. Several hesitated to leap from the burning ship until the last moment, as the height was 22 feet.

The spectacle was now that of a ship aflame, but not sinking, plowing ahead without directing hands.

Finally, the engines stopped. At 5 P.M., there still were living souls aboard, including Professor Glaubensklee, huddled at the bow, standing upon or holding onto the chains leading to the bowsprit, beside the Austrian eagle. In fact, one agile male passenger crouched atop the carved bird.

Just before sunset, the French bark *Maurice* hove to nearby and sent two boats over to the burning *Austria*. Two hours later the bark also brought aboard those in Chartres Brew's lifeboat.

One man was pulled from the water after having clung to a spar for six hours. Another, Second Officer Bernard Hartmann, had saved himself by alternately treading water and floating on his back the same length of time.

The Norwegian bark *Catarina* completed rescue operations in the early morning hours, plucking some twenty-one men from yardarms, hatches, and other wreckage.

The ill-fated *Austria* was abandoned to burn herself out, a gutted hulk and, presumably, to sink. None ever knew. She could have become a charred Flying Dutchman of the North Atlantic.

Not until sixteen days later when the survivors were landed in Halifax was the fate of the overdue *Austria* communicated to anxious families and friends and—to the world.

Of the six hundred aboard, only ninety-one survived. In this disaster, only seventeen of the crew were rescued. The percentages, however, remained heavily in favor of the males—only six women lived to recall their afternoon of terror.

Paradoxically, the *Austria* had fallen victim not only to carelessness with combustibles but to the very ventilation system which was an advertised asset of the German liner. It spread flames like a bellows.

5.

The SULTANA

THE 1850s HAD NOT BEEN KIND TO SEA VOYAGERS. BUT IN THE
first half of the sixties, news of far more immediacy relegated
shipwrecks to back pages of newspapers or totally submerged
such items. The death and disaster wrought by the Civil War
commanded all the limited space the dailies or weeklies could
offer.

Scarcely had the ink dried on the surrender terms at Ap-
pomattox before the nation was stunned by the assassination of
President Lincoln, on April 14, 1865. As the funeral train inched
west, halting at every station or whistle stop to afford the sorrow-
ing multitudes a last look at the bier, printers "turned the rules"
to solemnize their columns with black borders. Day after day,
there was little to read but the progress of the dead Emancipa-
tor's remains on the journey back to Springfield, Illinois.

Then, starkly, a ship seized prime attention once more. This
was not at sea, but down the Mississippi, not very far from the
farmland soil in which Abraham Lincoln was newly at rest.

"Calamitous Accident on The River," headlined the New
Orleans *Times* of May 1, 1865.

Other papers about the country, some newly sworn to de-
fend the Union, reacted with equal shock.

On April 21, the St. Louis and New Orleans packet, the

51

seventeen-hundred-ton, two-year-old *Sultana* had cleared New Orleans for Cairo, Illinois. While her desirability as a passenger sidewheeler was not subtly hawked to river travelers, she was running this trip almost exclusively for the Army.

Emaciated, weary, half-sick federal prisoners of war had assembled at Camp Fisk, on the environs of Vicksburg, Mississippi, from the pest holes of Andersonville, Macon, and Castle Morgan (Cahaba, Alabama) prisons. At least 1,866 of them—$5 a head for enlisted men and $10 for officers—piled aboard the *Sultana* at wharves that had been wrested less than two years previously from their Confederate defenders.

There was also a small group of "reb" POWs on board, plus two infantry companies to guard them and to protect the *Sultana* from diehard bands of guerrillas still lurking along some sections of the western shore of the river.

In addition, twelve ladies of the Christian Commission, who had served as nurses in the Vicksburg hospitals, were aboard, on their way back north.

Still, this wasn't all. The skipper, J. Cass Mason, who doubled as a part-owner of this sidewheeler, found space for 236 civilians, paying full passenger fare.

In the holds were stowed 150 horses, cows, and pigs, also 100 hogsheads of sugar. The latter was partially for ballast since the steamer, like all of her sister ships on the river, was topheavy. A huge manifest of passengers only worsened the boat's stability, since travelers had a distressing affinity for suddenly shifting from side to side in large, impulsive groups.

The count of people on board became capriciously inaccurate. No one, much less the skipper, was told for sure if the Confederate prisoners were included in the federal POW count, or indeed if the category "soldiery" encompassed infantrymen. And, again, were the women from the Christian Commission listed among the regular passengers?

Curiously, none of the bulging load was shared with two other steamers also docked at Vicksburg.

Something was wrong with one of the four new-type high

52

pressure boilers. This occasioned a slight delay in the port won so recently by General Grant.

Finally, the *Sultana* sailed, discharging some of her cargo at Helena, Arkansas, 175 miles north of Vicksburg, and then at Memphis, Tennessee.

Among the "Johnny Yanks" was twenty-one-year-old Chester Berry, from South Creek, Pennsylvania; P. L. Horn, the same age, and Otto Barden, twenty-four, both of Wooster, Ohio; as well as an Indiana lieutenant, Joseph Taylor Elliott.

Their berthing was varied. Berry and Elliott had been assigned cabins, although individual space was at a premium. Elliott was not able to lay claim to a cot until he had threatened physical violence.

Barden slept atop a grating directly above one of the greasy, noisy steam pistons, but he didn't care. He'd seen some tough fighting—in fact, he had been captured by General Nathan Bedford Forrest's hard-riding cavalry. Now, any kind of accommodation looked good to him.

Horn, recent survivor of a prison train wreck, stretched his bedroll on an upper deck and dozed, oblivious to a light drizzle continuing into the first minutes of Thursday, April 27.

Those who were not asleep watched the street gas lights of Memphis fade astern in the night's damp gloom.

The *Sultana* passed the mouth of the muddy Wolf River and neared Paddy's Old Hen and Chickens Islands in a two-mile-wide stretch of the river, somewhat more than three miles north of the city. An ironclad, the USS *Essex,* at anchor just below the grubby islands, logged the sidewheeler's passage.

Considering the overcrowding and the resulting slightly rolling motion, the evening had not been entirely unpleasant. Berry, a prisoner since the fighting at Fredericksburg, sang hymns in chorus until after midnight, concluding with the always popular, "Sweet Hour of Prayer." Until Memphis, where they had disembarked, a troupe of opera singers had led the harmonizing.

Just after two o'clock, when the *Sultana* was abeam of the

53

first island group, something happened. The officer of the watch on the *Essex* noticed it, and at once raced to awaken his executive officer, shouting:

"A steamer's blown up!"

Aboard that steamer, sleep should have been over.

Otto Barden, close as he was to the engine room, survived what apparently had been a tremendous blast of the leaky boiler that had been patched up in Vicksburg. Some of the details of the accident, as he recalled them, follow:

> Hot steam, smoke, pieces of brickbats, and chunks of coal came thick and fast. I gasped for breath. A fire broke out that lighted up the whole river. I stood at this hatch-hole to keep comrades from falling in, for the top was blown off by the explosion. I stood here until the fire compelled me to leave. I helped several out of this place.
>
> I tried to get a large plank, but this was too heavy, so I left it and got a small board and started to the wheel to jump into the water. Here a young man said to me, "You jump first. I cannot swim."
>
> This man had all of his clothes on. I had just my shirt and pants on. I said to him, "You must paddle your own canoe. I can't help you." Then I jumped and stuck to my board.

Berry was struck on the head by a stick of cord wood. He was sure it had fractured his skull, noting:

> The first thought I had was that while the boat lay at Memphis someone had gone up the river and prepared such a reception for us. I lay low for a moment, when the hot water soaking through my blanket made me think I had better move. I sprang to the bow of the boat, and turning, looked back upon one of the most terrible scenes I ever beheld.
>
> The upper decks of the boat were a complete wreck and the dry casings of the cabins, falling in upon the hot bed of coal, were burning like tinder. A few pails of water would have put the fire out, but, alas, it was ten feet to the water and there was no rope to draw with; consequently the flames swept fiercely through the light wood of the upper decks.

He might have added that all the wooden buckets were themselves burning like torches.

Lieutenant Joseph Elliott, who had been dreaming that he was "in the regions of eternal torment," noticed that many men remained asleep after the explosion. His later account of his experiences is graphic and horrifying:

The thought came to me that I had the nightmare, and in that condition of mind I turned around and made for the stern of the boat, hardly knowing what I was doing. The ladies' cabin was shut off from the men's cabin only by curtains, and I pushed back a curtain and started through, when I was confronted by a lady, who I supposed was in charge of the cabin, with: "What do you want in here, sir?"

I paid no attention to her, but went ahead, saying that there was something wrong with the boat.

I went on through the cabin to the stern of the boat and climbed up to the hurricane deck. Throwing myself across the bulwark around the deck, I looked forward toward the jackstaff. The boat's bow was turned toward the Tennessee shore, one of the boat's chimneys was down, and all the men were in commotion. As I started back, realizing that it was not a dream, I heard the men calling: "Don't jump; we are going ashore."

I answered, saying that I was going back to where I came from. On getting back and looking down into the river, I saw that the men were jumping from all parts of the boat into the river. Such screams I never heard—twenty or thirty men jumping off at a time—many lighting on those already in the water —until the river became black with men, their heads bobbing up like corks, and many disappearing never to appear again. We threw over everything that would float that we could get hold of, for their assistance. . . .

About this time one of the Tenth Indiana Cavalry boys came to me, asking:

"Have you seen my father?"

I said, "I have not; but I know the stateroom he occupied," and started with him to go into the ladies' cabin.

As we entered the door, we met his father who was coming out. They threw their arms around each other, and as they embraced I looked up to the ceiling and saw the fire jumping along

55

from one cross-piece to another in a way that made me think of a lizard running along a fence.

The fire was moving even faster than a lizard. Nothing could be done to contain it. After one of the stacks split in two and crashed, killing at least one soldier in its path, those aboard the fiery packet began jumping and dropping over the sides in large groups. The first cutter from the *Essex* rowed close by and picked up several struggling in the wet dark of predawn. When the Navy crew attempted to deposit these survivors ashore, sentries from Fort Pickering challenged them, threatening to shoot if they landed.

The soldiers belonged to Company A, Third U.S. Colored Artillery (Heavy). Because there was still a concern about guerrillas, they were interpreting all too literally their night orders to "shoot at anything that moved" on the river.

The cutter continued looking for another place to come ashore, while in the background others close to drowning were "imploring us for God's sake to save them; they couldn't hold out much longer."

P. L. Horn, like many, clung to the sides of the burning derelict as it floated downstream. At one time, he and others were pushed away by a mule kicking out blindly in its desire to gain the shore.

One woman was seen to rush on deck and place a life preserver around a child in her arms. In an instant she tossed the infant overboard, then jumped herself and grabbed the child from beneath the surface.

Daniel McLeod, a soldier crippled from the fighting at Shiloh, cried out, "Throw me overboard! I'll burn to death here!"

Captain Mason and another officer complied. The former prisoner of war floated clear.

At Fogleman's Landing across the river John Fogleman himself shook neighbors out of bed and they worked like men possessed to knock together a crude raft. With it they soon were

56

hauling survivors aboard. Ultimately they pulled forty people out of the river.

As the *Sultana* sank lower, nearly hidden by the boiling flames and pyrotechnics resulting from explosions of paints and other combustibles, Captain Mason was seen tearing shutters off the windows and hurling them into the water for use as rafts.

Chester Berry had listened to "such swearing, praying, shouting and crying I had never heard." Then he jumped. He struck out for the shadow of willows along the bank, illuminated by the burning steamer.

Elliott encountered difficulties when he jumped. His underwear slid down around his feet. Fortunately, he was a good swimmer. As he sank down into the muddy blackness of the river, he held his breath. Finally, he pulled his drawers free.

Surfacing again, he found the torn-off staircase which had led to the wheelhouse. He hauled himself onto this odd perch, which also was sanctuary for one other survivor.

Chester Berry found a board and kicked vigorously, trying to propel himself through the water. When he was nearly exhausted and began to despair of attaining the nearby shore, a river steamer, the *Pocahontas,* attracted by the huge blaze, rescued him.

William Norton, of Summit County, Ohio, hung onto a mooring ring, jutting out from the side of the *Sultana.* It proved a satisfactory handgrip, safely removed from the cauldron of the fire, except that another man grasped him around the neck in his struggle for the same ring.

While Norton was fighting free a third and fourth survivor became embroiled in a similar death combat.

From his staircase, Elliott watched the *Sultana* drifting along, not far off, burning lower and lower toward the waterline. Those afraid to take to the river were "singed off like flies," it seemed to him.

Most of those who did "take to the water" were just as frightened once the muddy, clammy river was all about them.

They screamed and flailed out as they fought for possession of a single planking.

Then, with a "hissing," the nearly incandescent *Sultana* partly vanished beneath the river. Since her paddles had stopped with the explosion, she had floated like a derelict almost two miles back downstream. In moments, only the flaming fagots of her superstructure cast their ghastly, flickering shadows over the horror still being enacted upon the predawn surface of the "Father of Waters."

Elliott's account continues:

> One man who passed us was bobbing up and down in a way that reminded me of the frog in the game of leap-frog. As he came within a few feet of us, I asked him what he was on, and he answered me: "Don't touch me; I am on a barrel." He actually was astraddle a barrel, holding on to the rim.
>
> We finally came up with a man who was on the end of a large log. With his consent we joined forces, one of our men throwing himself partly on the log and partly on the steps. The other man then crawled over onto the log and I crawled up on the steps, where I was when I was picked up. We made no further exertions to get on shore, but floated on down the river with the current.
>
> I must have become unconscious or only semi-conscious, as I have no recollection of how the steps got separated from the log. I remember passing Memphis, and seeing the gas lights burning in the streets. Then it is all blank until I heard the splash of an oar, and tried to call for help, but my voice seemed to have left me. It was some such feeling as when one tries to call out in a nightmare.

Otto Barden, who had clung to a tree, was rescued by the same steamer, as was Horn.

Daniel McLeod, too, was found in a tree, half-submerged on the river bank. (He made a full recovery after the amputation of his right leg.)

Nate Wintringer, the chief engineer, had saved himself by hanging onto a plank. A little girl, barely clinging to other

58

flotsam but splashing with her free hand, vanished beneath the murky waters as a boatman vainly grabbed at her.

Only one woman was known positively to have survived, although there were rumors that one other had come ashore at the foot of Beale Street, after having lost hold of her child. The deliverance of the sole identified lady was unusual. Mrs. Harvey Ennis, who had just boarded at Memphis, rode in plunging fashion to shore on the broad back of a mule. Her husband, a lieutenant in the federal Navy, her child, and a sister all were drowned.

Some, including Norton, were rescued by canoeists, as an heroic if motley fleet paddled, poled, and oared its way out from both shores, daring the dark, swift currents and all the perilous bars and islands.

The *Sultana* had come to rest. The charred hulk settled in a depth of twenty-six feet, her jackstaff showing. At low water, bones, some skulls, a scorched shoe, a blackened rifle muzzle were visible within the wreck. None cared to visit the gruesome spectacle.

Bodies continued to wash ashore for weeks down the snaking course of the Mississippi to New Orleans. The body of the captain was never located, and thus a $200 reward for J. Cass Mason was never claimed.

None would ever be able to count the loss of life that fiery early morning on the river. Including the crew, there were at least 2,200 on board when the *Sultana* poked upstream from Memphis. Officially, 1,238 soldiers perished and no less than 200 passengers and crew.

The totals could have been even higher. It was, by any count, the worst river disaster in American history—an unenviable record which is yet to be exceeded.

Several years later, a diehard Confederate in Vicksburg boasted he had placed a bomb in the *Sultana*'s coal bins. He was not taken seriously. An imperfect patch on a leaky boiler enabling it to explode under pressure, made much more sense to river men and all others who sorted the grim evidence.

One hundred years later, mine detectors and selective drillings failed to summon the twisted skeleton that lies in the mud and silt supposedly across from Memphis' Civic Center in the old river channel. Furthermore, it is believed to be in or close to the shallow inlet known as Hopefield Chute.

Just upstream, pilings sunk for a new bridge in 1969 also did not encounter any obstruction resembling a steamer's wreck.

Somewhere in the muddy bed of the Mississippi—along with the *Sultana*'s rotting, rusting remains—are a rumored $18,000 in gold and the ghosts of hundreds who survived the worst torments of prison camp and had almost, but not quite, made it home again.

6.

The COSPATRICK

THE CIVIL WAR SOON WAS RELEGATED TO STATUARY, PLAQUES in village churches, and wearisome, oft-told tales as yesterday's boys in blue and gray recalled the most poignant moments of their lives. There were organizations, complete with ladies' auxiliaries, aplenty.

The nation now plunged into the industrial revolution, marveling at one scientific achievement after another, and before the 1870s were out, the incandescent light as well as the telephone were realities. Electric machinery, as well as motors for cumbersome vehicles such as trolley cars, approached the manufacturing horizon, as did the internal combustion or gasoline engine, and, wonder of wonders, inside plumbing!

Ocean travelers had reason to expect somewhat improved and more certain fortunes than had been the lot of their predecessors. However, as it turned out, the ability to weave cotton faster and better, or to illuminate a city's streets more brightly did not necessarily presuppose superior navigation or general shiphandling.

The *Atlantic,* of the White Star Line, for example, was essentially a postcivilization creation, a handsome iron-hulled steamship, 420 feet over-all, with a capacity of one thousand passengers and crew. She was half again the length of the *Arctic.*

On her crossing from Liverpool, in March, 1873, with 931 aboard, the *Atlantic,* even as the *Austria*'s, had bucked implacable headwinds. Her progress was so impeded that Captain James W. Williams took out pencil and paper to come to the inescapable conclusion he could not possibly make New York with his remaining supplies of coal.

He resolved to put into Halifax and replenish his almost empty bunkers. And he almost did, except that he neglected to order soundings. The *Atlantic* smashed hard onto the ledges of Mars Head, off the mouth of Halifax harbor.

Within a relatively few yards of the rocky coast, the White Star Liner foundered and more than five hundred souls were lost.

This tragedy of April 1, 1873, appeared to be needless, attributable solely to carelessness—and in this decade of technical advances!

The nation had barely forgotten the disaster at the approaches to Halifax when the French packet *Ville-du-Havre* put New York astern, on November 15, bound for the port of her name. Considerably more ornate than the *Atlantic* but of about the same dimensions, the 5,100-ton steamer carried 135 paying passengers, 6 stowaways, and a crew of 172, plus a large cargo of wheat and cotton.

She was not many hours east of Ambrose Channel, however, when shaft trouble caused Captain Marius Surmonte to stop the engines and rely on sails. Although repairs were seemingly effected, one of the propeller blades broke three days later, during a heavy storm.

Nonetheless, vibrating all over, the *Ville-du-Havre* throbbed ahead, with virtually all on board ill from a combination of high seas and an off-balance propeller. Six days out of New York, in —paradoxically enough—the calmest, clearest weather of the voyage, the liner collided at two o'clock in the morning with a barque, the *Loch Earn* of Glasgow.

The effect, according to a passenger, the Reverend Nathaniel Weiss, of Paris, was like "two terrific claps of thunder."

Ville-du-Havre sank within ten minutes. Of the 313 persons she carried, only 87 were brought aboard the *Loch Earn*. And all but 28 of these were officers and crew. Every passenger had to jump into the water since the two boats that had been launched were both packed to the gunwales with ship's company.

While the captain himself was rescued, along with his two daughters, his wife was among the missing.

All in all, considering how the big new passenger liners were behaving, to say nothing of the deportment or lack of deportment of the crews, it was not altogether surprising that those contemplating sea voyages should consider, once again, the slow, old-fashioned sailing ships. And that is what 429 immigrants—all farm laborers and their families—did when they sailed, on September 11, 1874, from Gravesend, The Thames, England, bound for Ausland, New Zealand.

Their choice was the majestic, twelve-hundred-ton, teak-built *Cospatrick,* embarked upon her second voyage under the flag of the Shaw Savill Line. It required a crew of forty-four to tend the ample acreage of canvas billowing from the three-master. The 190-foot-long, eighteen-year-old wooden ship had formerly carried troops to India and coolies to various ports.

Captain Alexander Elmslie, with a brother in another Shaw Savill ship, had walked the quarter deck of the *Cospatrick* under her previous owners. Seamen, signing aboard, felt a special confidence, believing if any master should know this big vessel, Elmslie should.

He also maintained a "tight" ship, especially in the observance of fire regulations. There was a stationary water pumper, for example, in the fo'c'sle which could produce considerable pressure in the coils of canvas hose. Every hatchway was illuminated at night by a locked battle lantern so none could light up a pipe unnoticed. Smoking below decks was absolutely forbidden. Further, a fire watchman or "constable" had to be appointed for each fifty or so passengers, from among their ranks to act as a sentry through the hours of darkness.

The ship's physician, Dr. Cadle, conscientiously made his

daily rounds. While he could spot early hints of plague or scurvy and deliver babies, he was helpless to combat seasickness. And this voyage, running into winter, was an exceptionally rough and also a protracted one.

More than two months after leaving the Downs, at the mouth of the Thames Estuary, *Cospatrick* had not yet rounded the tip of Africa. She was, on November 18, butting into the gray, hostile swells three hundred miles south southwest of Cape Agulhas, just east of the Cape of Good Hope. Everyone was sick, including the wife and four-year-old son, Alexander, Jr., of Captain Elmslie. Two other children, young girls, had been left at home in Gravesend.

At twelve-thirty that early morning, there suddenly rang out and was repeated from throat to throat the cry, "Fire!" Henry MacDonald, the second mate, who had just retired after turning over his watch, raced out of his cabin and toward the fo'c'sle from which clouds of smoke billowed.

They seemed to issue from the bosn's locker where rope, oakum, paint, and varnish were stored. However, this was not the entire contents of the tinder box area. Nearby were also several casks of fat, kerosene, seventy tons of coal, and forty tons of "spirits."

Now, Elmslie gave orders that any good shiphandler would have duplicated in such an emergency:

"Haul her about!"

That is, he would try to run the *Cospatrick* before the wind. With the wind behind her, the flames would not so easily sweep the length of the ship. Perhaps the conflagration could be confined in the forepeak long enough to be extinguished. This was a routine procedure that had worked effectively in the past.

Several immediate circumstances, however, militated against the master. The sailors faced an almost impassable obstruction in getting to their yards. Panic had spread equally as fast as the flames. The decks were a seething mass of terrified, screaming people.

And those who did succeed in reaching the rope ladders to scramble aloft found the breeze was too light to bring the lumbering vessel around. Within fifteen minutes, flames were licking upward from the now abandoned forward hatch.

The pump could not be manned since it was in the fo'c'sle, the seat of the inferno. Bucket brigades were attempted. This was far too slow since the buckets had to be lowered and filled each time with seawater.

At least two of the lifeboats, as old and dry as the *Cospatrick* herself, crackled like kindling from their davits, finally crashing into the ocean when the falls burned through.

An aft starboard lifeboat had been filling with men, women, and children, until more than eighty—twice its capacity—seethed and cowered inside. Swung over the side, it appeared to be the farthest area from the ever-mounting flames.

There was soon a creak and a rasp. The badly overweighted davits bent lower and lower, then snapped altogether. The screaming horde was dumped into the sea to drift astern along with the hissing, smouldering fagots from the ship.

Now, the chief mate, Charles Romaine, took position by the port quarter boat, under orders from the master, and shouted above the growing roar of the flames:

"No one touches her, unless myself or the captain!" He turned to his assistant, MacDonald, "Shoot anyone who tries. Smash 'em!"

One by one, the three masts, starting with the foremast and ending with the mizzen, astern, snapped off, and crashed in a shower of sparks and fiery splinters across the decks. Many more lives were lost when they were caught under the crushing impact of the falling masts.

Now Captain Elmslie threw his wife overboard and jumped himself. Dr. Cadle took the captain's son in his arms, and followed, hoping to find some floating bit of wreckage that was bouyant and not red hot.

Two boats got away, one commanded by the chief mate, the

other by the second, MacDonald. There was no food nor water aboard. If there had been jury masts or sails for them they had been lost in the hysterical confusion.

While the survivors in the two boats, thirty-nine in one, forty-one aboard the other, watched, an explosion blew out the stern of the doomed ship. It was the end of the *Cospatrick*.

"Thirst," MacDonald, commanding the boat with the forty-one persons, ultimately would testify, "soon began to tell severely on all of us. Bentley, who was steering, fell overboard and was drowned. Three men became mad that day and died. We threw the bodies overboard."

There were no women in the party. However, someone produced a girl's petticoat which was rigged upon an oar for a sail. Soon MacDonald's boat was alone, having been separated from the chief mate's by a storm. He later described their plight:

> On the 24th, four men died. . . . We were so hungry and thirsty that we drank the blood and ate the livers of two of them.
> On the 25th, we were reduced to eight, and three of them were out of their minds. Early in the morning of the 26th, a ship passed close to us. She was a foreigner. We hailed her but got no reply. She must have heard us. One more died that day.
> On the 27th, it was squally all around, but we never caught a drop of water, though we tried. Two more died that day. We threw one overboard but were too weak to lift the other body.
> There were only five of us left—two able seamen, one ordinary, one passenger and myself. The passenger was out of his mind. All drank sea water.
> We were dozing when the madman bit my foot. I woke up. We then saw a ship bearing down on us. She proved to be the *British Sceptre*, from Calcutta to Dundee.

Only three of the 473 who had sailed on the *Cospatrick* survived. In addition to MacDonald, they were Quartermaster Thomas Lewis and an eighteen-year-old seaman, Edward Cotter. The second boat, under Chief Mate Romaine, never was seen again. Nor was so much as a charred spar from the wreck washed ashore, anywhere.

They had drifted westward, nearly six hundred miles toward St. Helena. In fact the trio were ultimately debarked at that lonely island off the West African coast to which Napoleon had been banished for the second time.

The point of sinking of the *Cospatrick,* off Cape Agulhas, was not far from the site of the loss of HMS *Birkenhead* in 1852 when 454 drowned. The stoic manner in which British infantrymen, many of them Scots, met their deaths inspired the phrase "Birkenhead Drill."

Unlike the Collins Line, Shaw Savill robustly survived this unfortunate tragedy. The "down under" company served the kingdom in peace and battle. In World War II, it lost thirteen of an existing fleet of twenty-six ships, including three in the ill-starred Malta convoy of August, 1942. The heroic *Jervis Bay* was sunk by the pocket battleship *Admiral Scheer* on North Atlantic convoy, November 5, 1940.

Captain Fogarty Fegen, commanding the fourteen-thousand-ton armed merchant cruiser, deliberately challenged his formidable adversary in order to give the thirty-seven escorted ships time to disperse. He saved all but four, although he lost his cruiser, his life, and 198 of a crew of 263 in this most courageous and dramatic action at sea. He was posthumously awarded the Victoria Cross.

In the 1970s, Shaw Savill's two twenty-thousand-ton queens, the *Northern Cross* and *Southern Cross,* provide the luxurious service to New Zealand which sailing vessels such as the *Cospatrick* couldn't even approximate in the 1870s.

7.

The PORTLAND

A QUARTER OF A CENTURY AFTER THE HORROR OF THE *Cospatrick,* elegance had come even to coastal shipping: plush furniture and heavy carpeting in the saloons, electric lights, sometimes electric steering, even telephones together with hot and cold running water.

In fact, the sidewheeler *Portland,* of the Boston and Portland Steam Packet Company, pampered her passengers with all of these luxuries. The 2,300-ton, 281-foot-long night boat was one of two such operated, as travelers better knew it, by "the old granny line."

The sobriquet had been earned because of the extreme if not possibly excessive caution of the captains. The least blow tended to send the lumbering vessels scurrying to port, if indeed they weren't already warped safely to one of the numerous docks between the Bay State and Maine.

A far more comfortable mode of travel between Down East and Massachusetts than the dirty, noisy steam trains, the sidewheelers were especially in demand before and after large social or business affairs in either state. The annual Mechanics Fair in Boston was one such event. In 1898, this important merchants' convocation was ending the Thanksgiving weekend and those who dwelt one hundred or more miles to the north of the Hub City sought, in customary throngs, to follow the sea route home.

Saturday, November 26, however, had not brought the best weather. In fact, the forecast was somber:

"Heavy snow and warmer tonight. Sunday, snow and much colder. Southeasterly winds shifting by tonight to northwesterly gales."

Captain Hollis Henry Blanchard, fifty-five-year-old master of the *Portland,* decided, however, that this wintry evening the Boston and Portland Steam Packet Company could *not* be. called "granny." When Captain Alexander Dennison, of the sister *Bay State,* phoned from Portland to announce, "It's blowin' like sixty down here!" Blanchard snapped back that *he* would sail.

For one consideration, the crusty Blanchard wished to be present at a family reunion Sunday at his home in Yarmouth, just north of Portland. Yet, Dennison's was not the only suggestion that Blanchard hold hawsers taut. John Liscomb, manager of the line, sick with a cold in Portland, had telephoned Charles F. Williams, passenger agent in Boston, saying that the *Portland* should wait until 9 P.M. for a weather report.

There remained doubt, however, that Blanchard ever received this message.

Captain C. J. Leighton, a Rockland passenger and friend of the master, had decided at the last minute that he wanted no part of the voyage.

"By George," he told the skipper of the *Portland,* "I don't think this is a fit night to leave port!"

And with that Leighton picked up his luggage and walked back onto India Wharf. Snowflakes already were slanting past the old pier shed. They were thick enough so that for the first time there was a note of uncertainty in Captain Blanchard's voice as he called to the wharf's watchman: "Keep an eye out for me. I might come back!"

The sidewheeler cast off her lines and pushed out across the choppy waters. A few minutes later, she was logged passing Deer

Island light at the harbor entrance. Next, the shadowy silhouette of the steamer *Kennebec*, plying between Bath, Boothbay, and other Maine ports, hauled by, and blew her whistle. She was returning to port.

Several other vessels, including a tugboat struggling for refuge, also observed the *Portland* paddling for the open sea.

Just after 9 P.M. she had thumped past Gloucester, about three miles offshore. Captain Bill Thomas of the schooner *Maude S.*, recognized her "dim white form." Then she was noted by Thatcher's Island lightkeeper, partly obscured by mountainous waves breaking over her.

By 11 P.M. at least two fishing vessels could attest that the *Portland* was still off Gloucester. One, the *Grayling*, believed the night boat was "pitching and rolling badly." The master of the little craft shot off a flare to warn her away.

Nearly at midnight, the schooner *Edgar Randall* glimpsed the *Portland* off Eastern Point Light, not far from the reef of Norman's Woe, apparently trying to make Gloucester Harbor. Captain D. J. Pellier thought the superstructure was damaged.

If the sidewheeler were endeavoring to steam into harbor the winds kept beating her back. Also, in the confusion of the wild night the master just might have been uncertain whether Gloucester's long breakwater stretched out from the southerly or easterly coast. Other ships, unaware that it was to the east, had smashed hard onto the formidable rocky peninsula.

The gale, meanwhile, mounted in violence. The wind reached, then exceeded a velocity of sixty miles per hour and the snows became more dense. The steamship *Ohio*, inbound from England, missed Boston harbor's entrance and drove hard and high onto narrow Spectacle Island, coming to rest incongruously on an even keel.

The tug *Cumberland* arrived at her moorings in South Boston, minus her barge and three men aboard which she had towed out of Baltimore.

By 5 A.M. the storm, gone mad—belatedly listed as a "blizzard of hurricane intensity"—was ripping up trees and poles and tearing off roofs from Martha's Vineyard Island north to Wiscasset, Maine. There, a two-master was smashing against the rocks. Surfboat crewmen found it impossible, at the moment, to reach her.

While New York City's storm was not equal to that of '88, heavy snows had already checkmated any attempts at motion. Long Island Sound was strangely deserted of any shipping.

As dawn broke over the Cape Cod area, a white, bone-chilling frozen desert was revealed under the roaring gales and snow still slanting down from a leaden sky. Lobster boats in every cove had sunk or been swamped at their moorings.

At least six vessels were in distress off Race Point: the schooner *King Philip,* heavy with eighteen hundred tons of coal, in command of Captain A. A. Duncan, of Portland; the *Pentagoet,* of the Manhattan Line, and former Civil War gunboat, bound for Bangor; the small schooners *Ruth M. Martin, F. R. Walker,* and *Addie E. Snow,* and—the steamer *Portland,* which seemingly had been blown all the way back from Gloucester.

About 7 A.M. that Sunday, Michael Hogan, master of the *Ruth M. Martin,* which had lost her sails, boats, and anchor, spotted "a big sidewheeler" through a rift in the clouds.

Hogan thought the vessel was "drifting with the wind but keeping her head with the storm, indication that she was under steam." Curiously, Hogan was trying to reach the "big sidewheeler," in the belief the latter offered greater refuge.

Then, by an incredible act of fate, a series of giant waves swept his schooner over Peaked Hill Bar, off the tip of Cape Cod, and onto the beach at Provincetown.

Samuel O. Fisher, the keeper of Race Point Life Saving Station, who was clocking winds at ninety miles per hour, heard four blasts of a whistle that seemed to come from a large steamer. He rang the station bell and shot up rockets. But he heard or saw nothing more.

Sunday wore on as the gale and snows finally abated. In the

71

dim light of evening, a surfboat crewman, John J. Johnson, spied a life preserver half a mile east of Race Point. On it was the printing, "Steamer *Portland* of Portland."

Nearby was an accumulation of wreckage. Then, along the beaches on both the Cape Cod Bay and seaward sides of Cape Cod body after body—children and adults—most clad in night garments, washed ashore.

Among them lay the mortal remains of Oren Hooper, owner of a house furnishings store and one of Portland's wealthiest citizens. Hooper, accompanied by his fourteen-year-old son, Karl, had chosen the night boat because he possessed a pass on the Boston and Portland Steam Packet Company.

Thus he would save the few dollars' train fare for himself and Karl.

Before dawn, Monday, an incredible backwash from the *Portland,* as well as from other wrecked ships, was strewn along Cape Cod's barren, frosty beaches: piano keys, barrels of lard and sausage, mahogany table legs, door locks, chandeliers, stairways, rag dolls, even the entire helm with the electric controls still dangling from it as if in mockery of this wondrous, modern way to steer a steamship.

Whether the *Portland,* obviously disabled ever since her sighting off Gloucester, had broken up under the fury of the storm, and struck a sandbar, or had collided with the coal schooner *King Philip,* whose debris was mixed with that of the sidewheeler's, was a matter of speculation.

At Orleans, a morgue was set up in Mayo's blacksmith shop. Carpenters were summoned from all over the cape and South Shore to knock together makeshift coffins.

Shipwrecks were expected off Cape Cod but never in living memory had there been such mass death.

Those who had waited Sunday morning on Portland's snow-swept Franklin Wharf had long since gone home when the news finally reached Maine's major port city late Tuesday afternoon. The delay was caused by the fact that all communication lines

72

from Cape Cod had been knocked down by the hurricane winds and ice.

The Boston *Herald's* headline was to the point, if grim:

ALL PERISHED!
The Steamer *Portland* carried 140 souls to death on Cape Cod!

None, however, really knew how many were aboard.

The Portland *Press* added its own bit of understatement:

GRIEF HAS STRICKEN OUR CITY.

In nearby Lewiston, Nora Metcalfe, a newlywed, was baking chicken, impressed by the curious fact that somehow an unusual number of cats were lined up atop the snowdrifts outside her kitchen window, watching. Her twenty-seven-year-old husband, Lewis, was expected home on the night boat after a job hunt in Boston. The lumber mill in Lewiston, where he had worked, had recently shut down.

She did not know which trip he would be on, but she was certain he'd be cold and hungry when he did crunch through the ice to their plain little country home. Then, down the path she saw a neighbor, approaching her front door.

He carried a newspaper under his arm, and he appeared to have a "very curious expression" upon his face. . . .

Thursday night was choir rehearsal for the First Parish Church, Portland. But Miss Emily Cobb would not be present. She had sailed on the *Portland*.

Daniel Rounds, a cobbler in the same city, did not possess the heart to open up his shop, all week long, or the next. His wife Anna and their young daughter, like Emily Cobb, could never come home again.

Another Sunday was coming. New England pastors tore up their scheduled sermons, inspired to new fervor and oratory by nature's ravages and this watery slaughter of the innocents.

In Orleans, on the Cape, numbed by the tragedy, the Reverend E. Leishof, of the Universalist Church, chose a topic of "hope" which he believed would "lighten the grief of the relatives of the unfortunates."

But whether or not any of his confreres of the cloth could assuage anyone's despair or dry a single tear, the *Portland* had sailed from old India Wharf for the last time. She had left in her violent wake a sorrow and an emptiness which would dwell a lifetime in too many New England hearts.

Those who had waved bright little flags earlier in the same year to departing soldiers and sailors for the battlefields in Cuba and thrilled to martial band music had unexpectedly but acutely learned the shock of abrupt death and intimate loss.

8.

The GENERAL SLOCUM

How, EAST COAST SKIPPERS ASKED THEMSELVES, COULD CAPTAIN Blanchard knowingly have steered his *Portland* out into the teeth of a gale?

True, 150 ships had been wrecked in the great blizzard which came to be known as "the *Portland* storm." The damage to many types of property, to telephone lines and other communications totaled at least $10 million.

Most of the lost vessels, however, were caught en route and had no choice. The master of the sidewheeler did not have to sail; or, at least, he could have come about for safety before it was too late.

The loss of the *Portland* with all on board was especially confounding to cautious oldtimers who had guided sidewheelers in and out of America's waterways for a quarter of a century or more. One such was Captain William H. Van Schaick, whose three-decker *General Slocum* was among the largest excursion boats to ply the waters surrounding Manhattan Island.

Built in 1891, the sidewheeler, owned by the Knickerbocker Steamboat Company, was 250 feet long, just thirty feet shorter than the *Portland,* and had a capacity of more than two thousand passengers. She bore the name of General Sherman's 20th Corps commander in the Atlanta campaign—Major General Henry W.

75

Slocum, an able if rather nondescript officer, who had died in 1894.

Captain Van Schaick, slender, bearded veteran of the rivers, was sixty-one years old when the *Portland* was torn to pieces. He did not face the challenges to which Down East masters were regularly accustomed. The weather was invariably good since no one went on excursions in the winter.

In fact, the *General Slocum* had never poked her prow so much as a foot out of New York harbor, or nearby Long Island Sound. This was one sidewheeler, Van Schaick could confidently predict, which would never break up in a gale.

That Wednesday, June 15, 1904, was an especially bright summery morning. All the Sunday school children and their mothers from St. Marks German Lutheran Church, at Sixth Street near First Avenue in Manhattan's "Little Germany," figured themselves extremely fortunate to be embarking upon their annual outing in such warm weather. After their cruise up the East River and into the Sound the church group would go ashore at Locust Grove, Long Island.

The Reverend George Haas, pastor of the church, himself led the singing as the steamer cast off, late, 9:40 A.M., from a pier at Third Street, on the East River. He was joined by 1,357 other passengers in a chorus of *"Ein Feste Burg ist Unser Gott"* ("A Sturdy Fortress is Our God").

"I have worked hard to make this better than any excursion we have had before," Haas exclaimed in his pronounced German accent.

The children waved little American flags and their picnic baskets in time to the music. In fact, the band on the upper deck was still tootling away and the youngsters were "frolicking about and having a fine time," according to a passenger, John Eiell, twenty-one, as the sidewheeler passed Astoria and headed for Hell Gate. This was an area of swift currents.

On the shore, John E. Ronan, a Dock Department employe, took the pipe out of his mouth and remarked to a companion:

"Look at the *Slocum*. Don't you hate to work when you see a crowd having as good a time as that?"

About ten o'clock, opposite Ninety-Second Street, however, less than a quarter of a mile farther on, another watcher, William Alloway, a dredge captain, glimpsed sudden evidence that all was not so happy. He saw a "burst of smoke" from the lower deck, just forward of the stacks.

At once he blew four blasts on the dredge's whistle.

Aboard the excursion boat at the same moment, Eddie Flanagan, the mate, who was mingling with the passengers, felt a deckhand tugging at his shoulder.

"Mate," he cried, "there's a fire forward! It's got a pretty good headway!"

Lillie Mannheimer, nine, exclaimed to her aunt, Millie Mannheimer, seated beside her:

"I think the boat is on fire, Auntie. See all the smoke?"

"Hush," whispered Aunt Millie, "you must not talk so. You may create a panic."

The deckhand was referring to a so-called "second cabin" forward, just back of the crew's quarters and under the main deck where paint, oil, and gasoline for the lamps were stored. It was in the same relative area and serving much the same purpose as a similar fo'c'sle on the *Cospatrick*.

The dredge's whistle was repeated by tugs and other nearby river craft before three blasts were finally sounded on the *Slocum's* whistle.

The realization of an emergency if not an awareness of the fire itself loosed panic throughout the crowded sidewheeler. Passengers and crewmen alike fell instant victims to hysteria. A steward, heating a tureen of clam chowder over a gasoline stove in the galley, just aft of the "second cabin," stormed out, knocking over the lamp as he jumped.

John Coakley, a ticket collector, rushed into the cabin and tried to beat the fire out with a burlap bag. This only fanned it. In moments, flames spewed out of the small compartment, sizzled

77

along the deck and joined the blaze already crackling in the galley.

The conflagration was already beyond control.

The sidewheeler, nonetheless, lunged ahead at more than twelve knots, driven by the incoming tide and Van Schaick's desire to beach his command in shallows through which anyone should be able to wade ashore. He had thought momentarily of heading into one pier when he noticed someone on its end waving him off.

After all, with the tar and dry planking on a wharf, a blazing ship warping alongside could create considerable havoc and pierside fires.

On the stricken *Slocum* careened, past 130th Street where, on June 28, 1880, the excursion steamer *Seawanhaka* had burned with a loss of sixty-two lives.

Since the fire was forward, the wind fanned the flames aft, licking down the dry decking and uprights with increasing acceleration. Van Schaick and his pilot, Edward Van Wart, stuck to the wheelhouse even though smoke and sparks were now blowing in.

Eddie Flanagan, the mate, and Daniel O'Neill, a deck hand, had run a hose toward the fire and valved on the pressure. The hose burst. No more attempts were made to fight the blaze. Fire buckets were left hanging from their rusty hooks to await the encroaching holocaust.

A policeman, Charles Kelk, on duty near the band shouted: "Be calm, folks!"

Flanagan made similar efforts, soon beating the flames away from his own trousers as he shouted and implored.

It was already too late to keep calm. In fact, there was no place of refuge left on the crowded, burning steamer.

People were beginning to jump, not having any idea where they were, or even caring if they could swim a stroke.

"Frieda!" came the piercing, anguished cry from someone on the hurricane deck. *"Meine Frieda!"*

Frieda, her little girl, was already lost in the swirling wake. . . .

Other mothers themselves tossed their children over the sides, thinking the waters somehow less a menace than the conflagration.

Those of the twenty-five thousand lifejackets that could be torn loose from the almost unyielding slats and wiring in the overhead above the decks fell apart in the grasping. The canvas-cotton covers seemingly had long since rotted through. Much of the cork filling had itself crumbled.

"The river surface," one of the picnickers reported, "was white with cork dust as though it had been covered by an avalanche of talcum powder."

Those few who actually girdled their waists with the belts watched them disintegrate and "melt away."

The Reverend Mr. Haas paused in handing out of the worthless belts to sink to his knees.

"Dear God!" he cried. "Have mercy on us!"

His wife Anna and twelve-year-old daughter, Gertrude, jumped. They were at once swept under the still churning paddles.

"They all rushed to the after part of the ship," continued John Eiell, "in a stampede that carried those who were near the rail overboard against their will. . . . It seemed to me as if the women and children were pouring over the sides like a waterfall."

From shore the passage of this flaming excursion steamer, whistle blowing all the while, had been an unbelievable spectacle, something out of Dante's *Inferno*. Tugs, racing after her, were unable to overtake the *Slocum*. One yacht, pennants gaily fluttering, did not even try. She kept on down toward the Battery.

The sidewheeler had been plowing forward little more than three and a half minutes when she hove close to North Brother Island, opposite 145th Street, the location of the Health Department's Isolation Hospital.

The *Slocum* "came for the beach," according to one incredulous doctor, "like a flaming meteor."

People on the river and ashore were spurred into frantic action. Most had already been alerted by the very sight and sound of this "meteor." Doctors, nurses, even patients hot with fevers,

79

a motley assemblage, streamed through the doors as well as first-floor windows of the institution and raced toward the flats on which the sidewheeler was grounded.

Across the water, on the Manhattan side, the 150 employes of a marble works dropped their hammers and chisels, commandeered anything which floated—even half-awash, abandoned skiffs—and started for North Brother.

From half a mile down the river, the fireboat *Zophar Mills* was surging ahead under full steam, laying down a screen of inky black coal smoke in her wake. Those who earned their livelihood on or by the river would swear they had never heard so small a vessel blow its whistle with such shrill insistency.

Of the tatterdemalion fleet converging on the sidewheeler, now burning like an exploded Texas oil well, the *Goldenrod* was the first to reach the *Slocum*.

The passengers, according to a deckhand on the tug, "came headfirst, sidewise, hitting the planking, crashing against the railings . . . in a rain of bodies."

Many who landed on the *Goldenrod* in this manner died instantly of broken necks.

Michael Graham, the excursion boat's steward, grabbing a bag containing $1,000 in silver, jumped from the stern—into deep water. He went down, down, then had to let go of his precious trust which was promising to drown him.

He floated up through the murky water, breathless, and struck out for shore, keeping as far away from the blazing hulk as he could.

A policeman, Hubert Farrell, working from the schooner *Bayliss,* which like so many other river craft had cast off moorings and arrived with incredible speed, dove in. Stroking along the surface of the river toward an ever-growing mass of struggling survivors, he look and saw "above us . . . a furnace of flame."

In a few moments' time he had saved eight lives.

People were quitting the glowing derelict as fast as they could, any way they could.

Miss Marie Krieger, caught on an upper deck, slid down

a pole to the water and managed to grasp a rope dangling beside the boat. She had to relinquish this, however, in short order because the flames began to shoot out of the portholes right above her. Suddenly, she found a little boy beside her, frantically holding onto a life preserver.

Then a coal barge slid close to them and a deckhand threw a rope and pulled them on board.

A little boy of about six did not fare anywhere near so luckily. He climbed the flagstaff on the stern of the *Slocum* to escape the flames, then fell into them as the pole burned through.

Peter Wingenter, fifteen, proved as strong and resourceful as any boy on board. He rescued four small children apparently abandoned on an upper deck, victims of the mingled panic and cowardice of the moment. He sought to go back for more but was restrained from doing so.

The hurricane deck aft collapsed just after he had brought the last of the four to safety. This caused further loss of life, on board and in the water.

Tugs, the fireboat *Zophar Mills,* lighters, row boats—all sorts of craft—were now surrounding the *Slocum. Tug No. 7* of the New York Central Railroad bravely rammed into the port paddle box. Crewmen leaped atop the smoldering housing and passed people down to the deck.

One of those saved by *Tug No. 7* was a little girl, Lizzie Krieger, who was crying plaintively:

"Mama is all burned up. . .!"

The tug *Walter Tracy* steamed off, her decks overflowing with the rescued, the dead, and the dying—about one hundred in all.

George W. Johnson, mate of the *Franklyn Edson,* kept diving off the Health Department boat to retrieve people in the water. On his final trip, he held onto a boy by the hand while a woman was sprawled across his broad, muscular back.

Two prisoners from adjacent Riker's Island, where the steamer *Chester W. Chapin* had gone aground the night before, grabbed a skiff and started rowing like possessed creatures toward

North Brother Island. A workhouse guard close by looked the other way.

An assistant nurse, identified only as Miss O'Donnell, of the Isolation Hospital, dragged more than half a dozen persons out of the water before she became too breathless to go in again. Attendants now were herding patients back to the wards. They were blue and shaking with their fevers and from the wildness of the moment.

Early in the afternoon, Clara Hartman, about eleven, pushed aside the tarpaulins covering her in a morgue established in the Alexander Avenue Police Station to blurt:

"I wasn't dead, was I?"

When attendants were able to listen to the girl they realized she had not only been brought there under the mistaken impression she was dead, but actually had been hauled through the water behind a rowboat as if she were just another corpse. She had lost her mother and sister.

As the day drew toward a hushed close, Captain Van Schaick, his hair, moustache, and eyebrows all but singed off and his eyes injured, sat dazed in a hospital ward, repeating:

"My ship, my beautiful ship . . . oh, all those people. Oh, God, the people. . . !"

The way he looked and the way he spoke carried the same air of unreality as the immensity of the tragedy itself.

By 10:30 P.M., 415 corpses had been tagged, although not necessarily identified. Others were in many improvised morgues and funeral parlors on either shore of the East River.

As next of kin from "little Germany" and elsewhere in the New York boroughs joined survivors in shuffling through the dimly lit morgues, looking for relatives and friends, it became apparent that one particular group had sustained the greatest toll of all.

Henry A. Kohler, an insurance man, had lost his own life. With him perished his wife and ten-year-old son, Henry, Jr., cousins, sisters-in-law, brothers-in-law, and other relatives—twenty-nine in all.

82

It was also apparent that the congregation of St. Mark's Lutheran Church had been virtually obliterated. The Reverend Mr. Haas survived, without family or much of his parish flock.

When police investigators and those of the United States Department of Commerce and Labor had finally finished their recapitulation, they estimated that 955 had died and 175 were injured out of 1,358 who had been aboard the *General Slocum.* In other words, only 228 had survived, and 75 of those would later succumb to their burns and injuries.

Out of a crew of 30, two were killed and five were injured.

"This great loss of life," noted the Department, "a percentage of death of 70.39—over 7/10th—is obviously abnormal and extraordinary."

Strong as the observation was, it still rang with understatement.

The United States Department of Justice then charged the master, the pilot, the Knickerbocker Steamboat Company, and its directors with misconduct, negligence, and inattention to duty. Van Wart, the pilot, it turned out, wasn't even a licensed officer.

It was not the first steamboat to be destroyed by fire in the East River or Long Island Sound, but this statistic held small comfort for the bereaved. The *Lexington,* for example, burned off Norwalk on January 13, 1840, with the loss of 122 lives.

Nor was the *Slocum* the last ship disaster in this month of June, 1904. On the twenty-eighth, the 3,318-ton *Norge,* of the Scandinavian-American Line smashed onto Rockall Rock, west of St. Kilda, in the New Hebrides, with the loss of 654 immigrants, en route to America.

Van Schaick did not go to trial until nineteen months after the tragedy, in mid-January, 1906, the same day, by coincidence, on which the Carnegie Hero Fund Commission rejected the latest nominations for awards in connection with *Slocum* rescue operations. Unofficially, it was learned that the Commission members had concluded there were "no heroes," but only victims and survivors.

The captain opened his defense in United States Circuit

83

Court by asserting that he had carried nearly thirty million passengers without a fatality in his long years as a navigator. He swore that he had remained in the pilot house until the blazing sidewheeler was beached and had been the last to leave this control station.

He observed that he could not have steered for shore sooner than the mile distance the blazing *Slocum* traveled since there were sunken rocks on one side of the river, oil storage tanks and lumber yards on the other. There was little he could say of the hoses, other than to maintain they were of generally the same type as carried on other ships.

Before all the testimony was concluded, the coastal steamer *Valencia,* en route from San Francisco, to Vancouver, went on the rocks off Cape Beale, British Columbia, on January 23. All but 35 of the nearly 160 on board were lost. A group of those plucked off the hurricane deck by a surfboat were found huddled together singing, "Nearer My God to Thee."

On January 27, a verdict was rendered in the *Slocum* case. Van Schaick was found guilty of failing to train his crew at fire drills and to keep his fire apparatus in shape. The jury was unable to agree on other, perhaps more serious, charges involving specific losses of life.

His sentence of ten years to a federal prison brought almost universally sympathetic cries of "scapegoat" from the nation's press and from many of the survivors themselves. No American merchant captain had ever before received such punishment for offenses involving the performance of his duties.

Much of the public compassion for the old master—a mood that represented a reversal of sentiment from that expressed in the weeks subsequent to the disaster—was occasioned by the fact that the officers and directors of the Knickerbocker Steamboat Company had not themselves been brought to trial. The case against a steamboat inspector had ended in a mistrial. Charges against others involved had been dropped in toto.

To most Americans, in 1906, the handling of the matter did not seem fair at all.

With all appeals exhausted, Van Schaick entered Sing Sing Prison in 1908.

His friends in marine circles did not forget him. It could, each one reasoned, have been *he,* save for kinder fate and greater luck.

There was one particular staunch friend with a zealot's desire to free the tired little man—his wife, Grace. She had been a nurse at the time of the disaster and, in fact, treated the burns of many of the survivors. She had married Van Schaick while he was freed under bond and awaiting trial.

By 1911, the remarkable number of a quarter of a million signatures had been collected, asking Executive clemency for this white-haired, frail, onetime steamship captain, already past seventy years of age. In 1912, President William Howard Taft granted Van Schaick that pardon.

"In this thing about the *Slocum*," he murmured to reporters as he walked out through the gates of Sing Sing. "I did the best I could. I always did the best."

It was his own catechism. He had said it many times before.

Almost blind, partly as a result of the fire, the master of the ill-starred excursion steamer died just one day after his ninetieth birthday, on December 8, 1927, at the Masonic Home in Utica, New York.

Curiously, Rev. George Haas had predeceased him by just nine weeks. And by the thirties, most of the members of the *Slocum* survivors society had themselves passed on.

9.

The WARATAH

ON THE OTHER SIDE OF THE WORLD, FIVE YEARS AFTER THE *General Slocum*'s name had been added to the growing list of the world's ship disasters, the large and well-appointed *Waratah* was completing her second round trip from London to Australia.

She cast off from St. Paul's Wharf, Durban, South Africa, Monday, July 26, 1909, as a uniformed band on Quayside Road struck up "God Save The King." The 9,339-ton queen of Lund's Blue Anchor Line slowly put the bluffs of "The Point" to port and poked her blunt prow toward Natal Roads.

Soon the little knots of bon voyage wishers were blurs through the smoky gloom. Even the dominating Town Tall Tower blended into the evening's background.

At thirteen knots, the black, twin-propellered, 465-foot-long *Waratah* (named for Australia's favorite wild flower) offered the fastest service between London and Australia, for traveler and shipper alike. She had left Melbourne only on July 1. Although her capacity was 128 persons in first class and 160 in third, in addition to a crew of 144, the *Waratah* booked approximately 100 passengers on this return voyage to England.

For the great distance she must traverse, the liner was amply fitted with refrigerators, dry food bins, and a distilling system geared to fifty-five hundred gallons of fresh water daily. Broad decks and roomy lounges, designed to ease the tedium of long voyages, attracted families to the liner.

On this passage there were upwards of twenty children aboard, including infants in arms. The Turners, of Durban, whose five sons and daughters ranged in ages from three to fourteen years, easily earned the distinction of being the largest family group. Their nursemaid was one of several occupying the *Waratah's* comfortable staterooms.

That the vessel was deep with sixty-five hundred tons of cargo, loaded at Melbourne, Sydney, and Adelaide seemed in itself to insure stability, especially around the stormy Cape of Good Hope. She drew thirty-five feet of water.

Included in the manifest were seventy-eight hundred bars of lead, four hundred bales of wool, hundreds of flour sacks, one thousand boxes of butter, frozen carcasses, leather strips, and timber. Topside, around her bridge, rested three hundred tons of bagged coal—common stowage to help provide a safety margin of fuel.

The diverse freight was insured for nearly $700,000. This approximated the cost of the vessel when she was launched at Glasgow in 1908, the year Captain Van Schaick had entered Sing Sing.

There seemed every reason to anticipate a pleasant, easy, and profitable remaining journey, first to Cape Town, then up the coast of West Africa to London. In the event of the improbable, the *Waratah* carried sixteen lifeboats, with capacity for eight hundred persons.

However, even under most halcyon conditions, no passenger ship can make port without at least one prophet of gloom. The Jeremiah this trip had been a Cape Town executive, Claude Sawyer, to whom the entire passage from Sydney had been an unrelieved nightmare. He thought the *Waratah* had "listed and snap-rolled" in heavy or medium seas to a degree that appeared far beyond reasonable tolerances.

Several days out of Durban, Sawyer awoke sweating from a nightmare—a man "in bloodstained armor" and brandishing a sword had been chasing him around the promenade deck. This was too much. He forfeited the remainder of his fare and went ashore where he checked in at the Metropole Hotel, planning to continue to Cape Town by rail.

The other passengers, especially a South African priest, Father Fadle, found Sawyer quite droll. Especially to the *Waratah*'s master, J. I. Ilbery, Sawyer was worse than absurd. But, then, Ilbery, after forty years at sea and soon to retire, had seen the type before.

Mrs. Nora Connolly, of Dublin, had herself evinced apprehension. The widow of a coal miner, she had amassed considerable savings. Before sailing, she had cabled most of it—the equivalent of $5,000—to the National Bank of South Africa in London.

About 9 P.M. the *Waratah* confirmed by blinker light to the signal tower atop the darkening heights of Cape Natal, to starboard, that she was "standing out to sea."

Late that night the large steamer *Guelph,* inbound, exchanged identifications with her. "HNGM" was the *Waratah*'s code. Both vessels were then one hundred miles south of Durban.

At 9:30 A.M., Tuesday, the freighter *Clan MacIntyre* passed the *Waratah* close by, off the Bashee River. If the former correctly identified her, the Lund's liner must have been averaging eighteen knots. The mouth of the Bashee was 220 miles down the coast from Durban. Boosted along by the four-to-six knot Agulhas Current, sweeping down the southeast shores of Africa, the *Waratah* was capable of this considerable speed.

Then, that same evening, about seven-thirty, Captain A. J. Bruce, of the 4,212-ton *Harlow,* another British freighter, en route from the Philippines, observed what he took to be the mast top lights and red port running light of a ship somewhere close to the horizon. He estimated his position to be about 20 miles east of Cape Hermes, 160 miles south of Durban.

Suddenly, there was a flash of light, followed by bright flames towering a thousand feet into the night skies by the guess of the master of the *Harlow*. This was followed by two explosions during the next half hour.

Captain Bruce, even so, made no effort to investigate an apparent sea disaster. He figured he would file a routine report when he docked in Newport News two weeks later. However, the *Waratah* had been placed sixty miles further south of this position that morning by the *Clan MacIntyre*. Had she been afire off Cape Hermes, she would have reversed course hours before and bucked the current.

On Wednesday, the *Clan MacIntyre* ran into a northeast gale, tossing her onto her beam ends. The *Bannockburn,* en route from New York to New Zealand, was wallowing past the southernmost coasts of Africa, encountering the same storm, of "unprecedented violence." Most of her deck cargo, including coal, was washed overboard.

The *Waratah* was expected in Cape Town, nine hundred miles west of Durban, no later than Thursday. The day passed, as did Friday without a sign of the liner. On Saturday, five days after the ship's sailing, worried agents for Lund's Line ordered the steamer *Fuller* and a tug out to search the coastal waters eastward.

"Have you spoken to the *Waratah?*" their mates called, through megaphones, to passing ships.

But they did not "hallo!" long. They were compelled to put back to port because of continuing foul weather.

The Royal Navy was advised. Officers, agreeing there was cause for concern, dispatched HMS *Forte* from Durban, as well as the cruiser *Hermes* and a patrol vessel from Cape Town.

Not until August 6 were fears for the liner's safety confided to the newspapers. A week later, two coastal steamers passed what resembled bodies floating off the mouth of the Bashee River. Vultures wheeled overhead. Lookouts, however, reported the surface of the sea too rough to make positive identification of the bobbing objects.

In early September, Lund's chartered the Union Castle ship

Sabine with orders to search the South African coast commencing at Durban, with special emphasis on the densely jungled shores of the Bashee River. From the Bashee it was seventy miles farther south to the nearest beachhead of civilization, East London—a jungle route where survival would have been difficult if not impossible.

Then, the *Sabine*'s orders were expanded to sweep south to the Crozets, Prince Edward Island, and Kerguelen, barren extrusions of land in the desolation of the Indian Ocean. Kerguelen, an icebound French possession of doubtful value situated as an outer rampart of Antarctica, itself lay thirty-five hundred miles southeast of Durban.

While the *Sabine* was poking around this lonely, austere ocean, Lloyd's, on December 15, "posted for inquiry" the *Waratah*. This was preliminary to declaring the liner officially lost in order that insurance claims could be considered. The families of the approximately 220 on board, including the crew faced a bleak Christmas, with scant hope at all of finding even one soul alive.

Early in February of the following year a chartered steamer, the *Wakefield,* together with two smaller vessels, hauled up their anchors to retrace the route of the *Sabine,* now safely back in port. She had found no hints of the *Waratah*, nor any other ships that might have "spoken" the missing liner.

In March, timbers, a hatchway, and a cushion marked with the letter "W" were found floating in Mossel Bay, east of Algoa Bay, 450 miles west of Durban. They could have been part of the *Waratah*. But were they?

July, 1910, was the first anniversary of the disappearance of the queen of the Lund's fleet of nineteen liners and freighters. All search vessels were home, all clues had been sifted and dismissed as inconclusive. Had she collided with a sailing vessel, one of the number that were missing every year? Had there been a subterranean earthquake or waterspout that capsized the *Waratah?*

Might the liner have fallen victim to the severe storm reported by the *Bannockburn* and other ships? She was well loaded. Even though passenger Sawyer was not pleased with her stability, or lack of it, it seemed as though the *Waratah* should have been able to recover from any roll or convulsion caused by wind and waves.

Hers was a mystery baffling to sailor and landlubber alike. Even assuming that the *Waratah* had been smashed or burned into wreckage, something of unmistakable identity should have been washed ashore. And yet, no "clincher" had been found along much of the great length of the Agulhas Current and the unfriendly shores it washed.

Oldtimers in South African nautical circles began to recall other wrecks and mysteries in these waters. In 1818 for example, the East India sailing vessel, *William Pitt,* with all seventy aboard, had vanished off the Cape of Good Hope en route to Bombay. This disappearance was followed in the succeeding eight years by the loss of the sloop *Julia,* out of Durban, the schooner *Bridekirk,* and the twenty-gun frigate HMS *Martin.*

Casualties continued off this storm-tossed graveyard of the South Atlantic throughout the nineteenth century. Mariners, shippers, underwriters, and even passengers came to assume a fatalistic attitude toward this attrition. On a broad scale, Lloyd's totaled up its lengthening ledger sheets and discovered that in the twenty years ending in 1909, no less than 2,420 steam and 5,911 sailing ships of United Kingdom and colonial registry were lost. These figures include ships that foundered, were stranded or involved in collisions, were listed as missing or lost through other established causes. The net tonnage lost was 1,935,596 tons in steam vessels and 1,281,762 tons in sailing vessels. A grand total of 23,274 people lost their lives in this interval—12,309 in steam ships and 11,235 in sailing vessels. This is a rate of approximately 416 ships a year.

The disappearance of the *Waratah* was now retreating into the limbo of probate courts, with upwards of 244 last wills and testaments to be opened, read, and conceivably disputed. The search for heirs commenced. As a typical example, who would inherit the $5,000 Nora Connolly, of Dublin, had prudently cabled to a London bank?

91

Finally, on December 15, 1910, in London's historic Borough of Westminster, a formal inquiry was convened by Magistrate John Dickinson. During the five-day session, it was suggested that the *Waratah,* even as nervous passenger Clarence Sawyer had believed, was prone to "a slow majestic roll with a deep pause at the extremity," as well as a pitch.

The Court, after "careful deliberation" became certain that the liner had sunk "in the gale of July 28, 1909, which was of exceptional violence," off the Bashee River, in perhaps six thousand feet of water. Those who sifted the evidence were "on the whole inclined to the opinion that she capsized . . . but what particular chain of circumstances brought about this result must remain undetermined."

Scant weight was accorded the sighting of the "explosion" by the master of the *Harlow.* The keeper of Cape Hermes Lighthouse had noticed nothing unusual that night. The freighter's mate had contradicted the testimony of Captain Bruce, reporting that he himself had observed numerous brush fires in the jungle.

However, even the announced finding was tainted with a contradictory ring since the court agreed that the *Waratah* "was in proper trim for the voyage she was about to undertake," upon clearing Durban. In other words, she was well and carefully loaded. If, indeed, she were topheavy—steaming without full cargo and coal bunkers or unballasted—this would not have been true on her last voyage.

A seaman who identified himself as "Nicholson" testified that when he was about to sign on the *Waratah,* Chief Officer Owen had warned, "If you can get anything else, take it, because this ship will be a coffin for somebody."

It was, for Owen, just as he predicted.

Further allegations at the hearing were to the effect that the master and at least one of the ship's engineers had not been fully satisfied with the stability of the new liner or her metacentric characteristics—that is, her center of buoyancy. It was suggested that Lund's Line had brought pressure upon Captain Ilbery to keep his criticisms to himself.

92

Whether owners or builders were to blame, Lund's no more than Collins Line could sail on after so prominent a tragedy. The shipping company sold all remaining eighteen vessels to the Peninsula and Oriental Line and removed the old name plaques from the world's ocean forwarders.

But the *Waratah's* memory would not fade as rapidly as that of the company that had operated her. There was a report that in the summer of 1932, in a hospital in Ontario, Canada, a sick old seaman, John Noble, called a nurse to his bedside and whispered that he had something to tell her.

The man had, according to the story, been a crewman on the *Waratah* when she was struck by a fierce storm. He explained that "among my mates were some ready to mutiny. I refused to join them."

He then told how the ship suddenly rolled over and sank with all aboard except for himself and "a ten-year-old girl of a wealthy English family." Her description could have been that of one of the Turners of Durban.

Noble continued that he assisted her in the water and both finally struggled ashore at East London.

Why had he not reported their presence at once? Supposedly, the old sailor succumbed in the hospital before he could finish what might have been just another fo'c'sle yarn. Indeed, no hospital in the Oshawa area of Ontario, where Noble was said to have died, can find records substantiating either the existence of the person or his narrative.

In 1939, timbers were found off the Bashee River which were vaguely identified as belonging to the missing Lund's liner. In the early 1950s, a pilot with the South African Air Force thought he saw the silhouette of "a large ship" lying on her side atop a reef but just under the surface. The position corresponded closely to that considered by the formal inquiry to be the *Waratah's* final resting place.

Patrol vessels, armed with good coordinates and bearings from the pilot, conducted a careful search which finally revealed nothing.

Then, in 1954, Frank Price, an Englishman, told of how a Boer, one Jan Pretorius, had been illegally prospecting for diamonds near the Bashee River that fateful last week of July, 1909, when he saw a ship wallowing inshore during a bad storm. Pretorius, however, kept the information to himself until years later since he did not want to be caught in violation of strict diamond laws.

And Price averred he had been sworn to secrecy not to reveal the old Boer's secret until after his demise.

These stories, possibly fables, tended only to deepen the mystery of the *Waratah*. Someday, her secret—surely not cracked at the trial which could only surmise—may yet be revealed. Until then, the ghostly image of the *Waratah,* like that of the *Flying Dutchman,* must sail on through the world's stormy and uncertain seas.

10.

RMS TITANIC

BY THE FIRST DECADE OF THE TWENTIETH CENTURY IT APPEARED past time to build a true superliner: one, unlike the *Waratah*, that wouldn't simply disappear; one, unlike the *Portland,* impervious to all gales; one, unlike the *Slocum, Cospatrick, Sultana,* and far too many others which would be fireproof; one, it went without saying, that could not be "stove" even by the largest whale; one, in sum, which would prove unsinkable.

In 1908, the Cunard Steamship Line had inaugurated service with the 32,000-ton *Lusitania,* the first of her size to be driven by steam turbines instead of reciprocating pistons. At the remarkable top speed of twenty-seven knots, or thirty-one miles per hour, she had captured the Atlantic Blue Riband, crossing the ocean in four and a half days.

The directors of the highly competitive White Star Line had to admire *"Lusy's"* performance as well as that of her equally swift sister, the *Mauretania.* But were either of these two greyhounds quite big or luxurious enough, or truly unsinkable?

Corporately speaking, White Star decided the answer was No. So they set marine architects to designing one that should answer each and every dream of transatlantic magnitude and extravagance.

The line's answer was found first in the *Olympic,* then in her yet larger sister, the *Titanic,* 883 feet over-all, the largest and gaudiest vessel ever conceived, a Victorian palace afloat. She featured deluxe suites, Turkish baths, and period furniture.

With sixteen strong watertight compartments, the liner was supposed to float with any two of them flooded. She also displaced an unheard of 66,000 tons.

"Everything," the London *Times* editorialized, "had been done to make the huge vessel unsinkable, and her owners believed her to be so."

It was not surprising that the *Titanic* attracted names familiar to society and business pages for her first voyage in 1912. None but the wildest imaginations could nurture apprehensions about this maiden, springtime crossing of the North Atlantic.

Colonel John Jacob Astor, one of the wealthiest men in the world; Isidor Straus, the department store founder; George Widener, Philadelphia financier; Major Archibald "Archie" Butt, President Taft's military aide; Benjamin Guggenheim, the financier-philanthropist; and Francis Millet, the artist, were among the 1,315 passengers—about half the liner's capacity—who had embarked on the *Titanic*.

There were 324 in first class, 285 in second, and 706 in third, also known as "steerage." The crew accounted for 885 additional people making the total on board 2,201.* The "one" was the captain: sixty-year-old Edward J. Smith, completing forty years at sea and scheduled to retire after this voyage. A white-bearded patriarch with an easy smile and friendly manner, "Smitty" Smith was described as "born to command."

Joseph Bruce Ismay, chairman of the board of White Star, had personally requested Smith's transfer from the slightly smaller sister ship, *Olympic*. "Smitty" Smith's newest command was not fast by the measure of the fastest. Her curiously old-fashioned "up and down" reciprocating engines worked two of

*This number is taken from the British Board of Trade records. Due to inaccurate pier totals at sailing time, last-minute embarkation, crew changes, infants in arms—having no ticket or passport—and the fact that the purser's true count went down with the ship, it is impossible to arrive at a completely accurate figure. For example, the *World Almanac* states that 2,207 people were aboard, while the *Encyclopaedia Britannica* lists the total as 2,224.

her propellers; a steam turbine drove the third screw, between the others. Those combined could drive the liner at a maximum eighty revolutions, the equivalent of about twenty-three knots, or twenty-six and a half land miles an hour, about five below *Lusitania's* potential.

Thus, neither Ismay nor Smith could hope for more than to arrive in New York "on time." That would be Wednesday, April 17, just one week after her departure from Southampton. She had called at Cherbourg and Queenstown.

Records were out of the question.

It had been a pleasant, routine passage ever since the new liner put the Old Head of Kinsale—the last Irish headlands—astern and swept out into the Atlantic. Not until Sunday, the fourteenth, was there a hint that conditions in the westbound steamer track might be other than propitious: Ice, as the Navy's Hydrographic Office in Washington had been aware for several weeks, was drifting southward from Greenland and eastward from Newfoundland, in large fields.

Some of the ice warnings for the Hydrographic Office were radioed by ships directly to the Marconi wireless stations at Cape Race, Newfoundland, or Long Island, if their transmitters were powerful enough. Smaller steamers attempted to relay their sightings by way of large vessels, such as the *Titanic*.

The first alarm crackled into her radio room at 9 A.M. Sunday, the fourteenth, from Captain James Barr, of the Cunarder *Caronia,* directly advising the *Titanic* "westbound steamer reports bergs, growlers [icebergs with most of their bulk under water] and field ice in 42° N from 49° to 51° W April 12. Compliments."

The position given was only a few miles north of the big liner's course and half a day's steaming distant.

The message was acknowledged by *Titanic*.

At 11:45 A.M. the Hamburg-American liner *Amerika* informed the *Titanic* that she had just passed "two large icebergs" in a position slightly south of that noted by the *Caronia*. The *Titanic* relayed this information along to Cape Race.

97

At 1:42 P.M., the White Star liner *Baltic* "called" the *Titanic* with a long report:

> Have had moderate variable winds and clear fine weather since leaving. Greek steamer *Athenai* reports passing icebergs and large quantities of field ice today in 41° 51' N 49° 52 W.
> Last night we spoke German oiltank Steamer *Deutschland* Stettin to Philadelphia. Not under control. Short of coal, Lat. 40° 42' N Longitude 55° 11' W. Wishes to be reported to New York and other steamers. Wish you and *Titanic* all success.
>
> Commander

The *Athenai's* sighting would have put the ice directly onto the *Titanic's* course.

Although Ismay would later swear that matters concerning navigation were "absolutely" out of his "province," since he was "not a navigator . . . simply a passenger on board the ship," this radiogram experienced a curious circulation. Captain Smith showed the warning to the White Star managing director who then shoved it into his pocket.

At 6:30 P.M. Radioman Cyril Evans, of the small Leyland liner *Californian*, en route from London to Boston, tapped out to another ship of the line, the *Antillian*, "three bergs five miles to southward of us. Regards, Lord [Stanley Lord, master of the *Californian*]."

The position given put the ice a bit to the east of the apparently larger field already reported, but almost on the *Titanic's* course.

The *Titanic* broke in during the transmission simply to indicate she had overheard the communication.

Ismay, during the afternoon, showed the *Baltic's* warning to two women and remarked casually that the vessel would be in ice that night. Not until 7:10 P.M. by Ismay's watch did the captain encounter him in the smoking lounge and ask, offhandedly, "By the way, sir, have you got that telegram I gave you this afternoon?"

When Ismay pulled it out of his pocket, "Smitty" Smith declared, "I want it to put up in the officer's chart room."

At 7 P.M., just before Captain Smith remembered the iceberg warning, the ocean temperature dropped to 32 degrees. It had been 56 at noon. The drop in air temperature had followed an almost parallel graph, from 50 degrees to 30.

While it was true that the sea temperature was being meticulously recorded, this had been routine, every two hours since leaving Southampton. There was also scientific basis for doubt as to whether cold or warmer water in these areas would be more suspicious. There was the confusing presence of the Gulf Stream combined with the eddies of hot and cold currents that masses of ice necessarily arouse.

At 9:40 P.M. the steamer *Mesaba* radioed the *Titanic,* "Much heavy pack ice and great number of large icebergs. Also field ice. Weather, good, clear."

Jack Phillips, first Marconi operator on the *Titanic,* took the warning down, then laid it aside.

At eleven, Captain Lord, who had decided to stop his ship entirely, asked Evans to advise the *Titanic* that the *Californian* was hove to in the ice fields, very close to the big liner's position.

Evans tapped out at five after eleven, "Say, old man, we are stopped and surrounded by ice."

Phillips by this stage of the voyage was already exhausted from the volume of chit-chat messages he was radioing for his paying passengers. He flashed back, angrily:

"Shut up, shut up! I am busy. I am working Cape Race."

Phillips penciled nothing of the transmission.

Evans, the only operator aboard the six-thousand-ton *Californian,* was also weary. He drew off his earphones, switched off his set, and went to bed.

Aside from his unusual activity in the radio shack, it was just a quiet Sunday night at sea. The devotion services, ending with customary Church of England prayers for the well-being of the King, had been over for some hours. A few passengers strolled the decks one final lap before turning in. Little knots of men were playing cards.

Most of the ship was bunked in for the night, including those members of the crew not on watch.

It was cold, calm, starry but moonless. Many on watch had never observed the ocean so flat and mirrorlike. For this reason, it was all the more unbelievable to Frederick Fleet, a twenty-five-year-old lookout high up in the crow's nest, when suddenly at about 11:40 P.M. he saw a "black mass" ahead. Since he had been to sea four years, he was salt enough to realize that the object, with no moon to illuminate it, was doubtless an iceberg, black or not.

Fleet rang three bells, a signal of danger. He telephoned the bridge.

"What did you see?" came a calm voice, presumably that of William M. Murdoch, the first or chief officer.

"An iceberg right ahead!"

Fleet "kept staring ahead."

Murdoch ordered "hard a-starboard! Engines full astern!"

On a vessel of the bulk of the *Titanic,* the rudder could not answer "hard a-starboard" or "hard a-port" for at least thirty seconds. There was this lapse of time before the ship could start to turn.

At approximately twenty-two knots, it required nearly four minutes to stop her, even with propellers churning wildly in "full astern." She would travel half a nautical mile in those four minutes.

The liner clipped the iceberg with "a slightly grinding noise," as it sounded to Fleet. Even though he saw some ice chunks and shavings tumble onto the forecastle and weather deck, the lookout still thought the collision was no more than "a close shave."

Fourth Officer Joseph Boxhall was aware of merely "a slight impact." (A "slight impact" which nonetheless would be estimated by the U.S. Hydrographic Office as equal to a force of nearly 1.2-million-foot-tons, or "energy enough to lift fourteen

100

monuments the size of the Washington Monument in one second of time.")

C.E. Henry Stengel, a leather manufacturer from Newark, New Jersey, had just retired when his wife called him. He had been moaning in his sleep.

"Wake up, you are dreaming," she said.

As he opened his eyes, he heard "a slight crash." He "paid no attention to it until I heard the engines stop. When the engines stopped I said, 'There is something serious, there is something wrong. We had better go up on deck .'"

Mrs. Catherine E. Crosby, of Milwaukee, accompanied by her husband, Captain Edward G. Crosby, a Great Lakes shipmaster, and her daughter, Harriette, had been slightly edgy since she watched seamen taking the temperature of the Atlantic during the afternoon. They had explained to her that the liner "was in the vicinity of ice fields."

She had not "retired long when I was suddenly awakened by the thumping of the boat." Her husband hurriedly dressed, ran out, then returned with the curious observation, "You will lie there and drown. The boat is badly damaged."

Colonel Archibald Gracie, of Washington, D.C., former Army officer and sometime historian, was awakened by what seemed to be "the blowing off of steam." He partially dressed, even though he could not perceive any commotion in the passageways and went on deck.

"Presently," Gracie would recall, "along came a gentleman . . . who had ice in his hands. Some of this ice was handed to us with the statement that we had better take this home for souvenirs."

Mr. Ismay, of Liverpool, got up, strode hurriedly along the passageway and met one of the stewards and said, "What has happened?"

The steward replied, "I do not know, sir."

Ismay then returned to his room, put on his coat, and went up on the bridge where he found Captain Smith and asked him what had happened.

"We have struck ice," the captain answered.

"Do you think the ship is seriously damaged?" Ismay asked.

"I am afraid she is," answered Smith.

Meanwhile, First Officer Murdoch informed the captain that the watertight doors had been closed.

Boxhall, the fourth officer who, like his fellow mates on the bridge had "no knowledge" of icebergs or that the liner "was so near the icefield," was ordered below. Although his inspection of living space was hurried and cursory, omitting cargo and engine areas, he found no evident damage.

Stopped and blowing off steam to relieve boiler pressure now that she had been halted in her headlong passage and was dead in the water, the *Titanic* was quite obviously in trouble. In ten minutes, she had taken ten feet of water in her bilges, maybe more in some of them. In twenty minutes, the mail room floor, twenty-four feet above the keel, was awash. The pumps could not begin to keep up with the inward rush of icy water.

Thirty minutes after the collision, Captain Smith decided it was time to call for help. He had been poring over blueprints in the chart room with Thomas Andrews, the managing director of Harland Wolff Shipyard, builders of the *Titanic*. "Smitty" Smith had been convinced that the great vessel had sustained a three-hundred-foot gash at least, on her starboard side well below the waterline. This was apparent from the number and positions of the boiler rooms and holds that were flooded.

She could not possibly float much longer.

About 12:05 P.M., the captain entered the radio shack and unemotionally told Operator Phillips, "We had better get assistance."

"Yes, at once," Phillips replied.

Harold Bride, the smooth-faced, twenty-two-year-old second Marconi operator who had been awakened, although not by the crash, heard Phillips sparking out the letters "CQD!" the international call for assistance, followed by "MGY," the *Titanic*'s own identification.

The North German Lloyd *Frankfurt* was the first to acknowledge. But she was 140 miles to the southwest. Something of a tub, she could make no more than twelve and a half knots, straining every boiler rivet. That meant she was half a day's steaming distant.

In quick succession, the 6,600-ton Canadian Pacific *Mt. Temple*—fifty miles to the west, and just as slow as the *Frankfurt* —the Allan liner *Virginian,* and the Russian tramp freighter *Birma* replied.

So disbelieving of the message was the officer of the watch aboard the *Virginian,* 170 miles east of the *Titanic,* that he physically shoved the hapless radio man down the ladder away from the bridge, advising him against any further "jokes" that night.

Determined, nonetheless, and desperate, the Marconi operator literally kicked in the door to the cabin of the captain, who had been asleep, and showed him the plea for help. The *Virginian* was headed, at seventeen knots, toward the sinking White Star liner.

The *Mt. Temple,* fifty miles west, answered, but its transmission was muddled by static. Phillips replied:

"Can not read you, old man, but here my position. . . . Come at once. Have struck berg."

Now the *Mt. Temple* turned around and started toward the icefield and the *Titanic.* She could probably cover the distance in four hours.

The *Frankfurt* then commenced a curiously wordy conversation, finally causing Phillips to inquire:

"Are you coming to our assistance?"

Again, from the *Frankfurt:*

"What is the matter with you?"

"We have struck iceberg and sinking please tell captain to come."

"O.K. will tell the bridge right away. O.K., yes. Quick."

At twelve thirty-five, just half an hour after Phillips had begun calling for help, Harold Cottam, the sole wireless operator aboard the *Carpathia,* fifty-eight miles southeast of the *Titanic,* politely called the big White Star liner to say that there were a number of commercial messages waiting for her at Cape Race.

When Phillips replied, Cottam's shock was almost as profound as that of the master of the *Virginian*.

Captain Arthur Rostron, of the *Carpathia*, "had just turned in" when the first officer arrived, breathless at his door. He later reported:

> I gave the order to turn the ship around and immediately I had given that order I asked the operator if he was absolutely sure it was a distress signal. I asked him twice.
>
> I picked up our position on my chart, and set a course to pick up the *Titanic*. The course was north 52 degrees west true fifty-eight miles from my position.
>
> I then sent for the chief engineer. In the meantime, I was dressing and seeing the ship put on her course. The chief engineer came up. I told him to call another watch of stokers and make all possible speed to the *Titanic,* as she was in trouble. He ran down immediately and told me my orders would be carried out at once.
>
> After that I gave the first officer, who was in charge of the bridge, orders to knock off all work which the men were doing on deck, the watch on deck, and prepare all our lifeboats, take out the spare gear, and have them all ready for turning outboard.
>
> Immediately I had done that I sent for the heads of the different departments, the English doctor, the purser, and the chief steward, and they came to my cabin, and then I issued my orders.

On the *Titanic* the water continued to rise and the people were taking to the boats—"women and children first," for the most part.

Stengel, the leather manufacturer, later recalled that he

> put on what clothes I could grab, and my wife put on her kimono, and we went up to the top deck and walked around there. There were not many people. That was where the lifeboats were. We came down to the next deck, and the captain came

up. I supposed he had come up from investigating the damage. He had a very serious and a very grave face. I then said to my wife, "This is a very serious matter, I believe."

I think Mr. Widener and his wife—I think it was Mr. Widener—followed the captain up the stairs, and they returned, and I presume they went to their staterooms. Shortly after that the orders were given to have the passengers all put on life preservers. I went back to my stateroom and put a life preserver on my wife, and then she tied mine on. We went back up to the top deck. Then I heard the orders given to put all the women and children in the boats and have them go off about two hundred yards from the vessel.

Of course I was a little bit agitated. . . . While they were loading the lifeboats, the officers or men who had charge of loading the lifeboats said, "There is no danger; this is simply a matter of precaution." After my wife was put in a lifeboat she wanted me to come with them, and they said, "No; nothing but ladies and children."

After the five boats, I think it was, or the boats as far as I could see on the starboard side, were loaded, I turned toward the bow. I do not know what led me there, but there was a small boat that they called an emergency boat, in which there were three people, Sir [Cosmo] Duff Gordon [the wine merchant], and his wife and Miss [Laura] Francatelli [his secretary]."

I asked the officer . . . if I could not get into that boat. There was no one else around, not a person I could see except the people working at the boats, and he said, "Jump in."

The railing was rather high—it was an emergency boat and was always swung over toward the water—I jumped onto the railing and rolled into it.

The officer then said, "That is the funniest sight I have seen tonight," and he laughed quite heartily. That rather gave me some encouragement. I thought perhaps it was not so dangerous as I imagined.

After getting down part of the way there was a painter on the boat, and we were beginning to tip, and somebody hollered to stop lowering. Somebody cut that line and we went on down.

Just as I jumped into the boat someone else, a man named A. L. Solomon, appeared. I do not know where he appeared from, but he asked to get in and jumped in the boat with us. There were five passengers and, I understand, three stokers and two seamen; that is, five of the crew.

105

Captain Crosby, meanwhile, had returned to the deck and now was back again in his stateroom, No. 22.

"He said to my daughter," Mrs. Catherine Crosby recalled,

"the boat is badly damaged but I think the watertight compartments will hold her up." I then got up and dressed, and my daughter dressed, and followed my husband on deck. She got up on deck, and the officer told her to go back and get on her life preserver and come back on deck as soon as possible. She reported that to me, and we both went out on deck where the officer told us to come.

I think it was the first or second boat that we got into. This was on the left-hand side where the officer told us to come, and it was the deck above the one in which our staterooms were located; our staterooms were located on the B deck, and we went to the A deck where the officers and lifeboat were. We got into the lifeboat that was hanging over the rail alongside the deck, men and women with their families with us. There was no discrimination between men and women.

[There were] about thirty-six persons . . . in the boat [just about half the capacity].

There were only two officers; the rest were all first-class passengers. My husband did not come back again after he left me. . . .

There were absolutely no lights in the lifeboats, and they did not even know whether the plug was in the bottom to prevent it from sinking . . . no lanterns, no lights, nothing at all in these boats but the oars. One of the officers asked one of the passengers for a match with which to light up the bottom of the boat to see if the plug was in place.

The officers rowed a short distance from the *Titanic*.

Meanwhile, Colonel Gracie, from Washington joined his friend, Clint Smith.

"We did notice a list but thought it best not to say anything about it for fear of creating some commotion," he later stated. "Then we agreed to stick by each other through thick and thin if anything occurred, and to meet later on. He went to his cabin and I to mine. I packed my three bags very hurriedly. I thought if we were going to be removed to some other ship it would be easy for the steward to get my luggage out.

"As I went up on deck the next time I saw Mr. Ismay with one of the officers. He looked very self-contained, as though he was not fearful of anything, and that gave encouragement to my thought that perhaps the disaster was not anything particularly serious.

"Presently I noticed that women and men had life preservers on, and I thought it was rather previous."

After "Smitty" Smith had informed Ismay that he thought the ship was seriously hurt, the managing director of White Star went down below where he encountered Mr. Bell, the chief engineer, who was in the main companionway.

Ismay later stated, "I asked if he thought the ship was seriously damaged, and he said he thought she was, but was quite satisfied the pumps would keep her afloat.

"I went back onto the bridge. I heard the order given to get the boats out. I walked along to the starboard side of the ship, where I met one of the officers. I told him to get the boats out. . . . I assisted, as best I could, getting the boats out and putting the women and children into the boats.

"I stood upon that deck practically until I left the ship in the starboard collapsible boat, which is the last boat to leave the ship, so far as I know. More than that I do not know."

Second Officer Charles H. Lightoller, hurrying the people along into the boats, remained almost deafened by the noise of the steam surging out of eight exhaust pipes. This was necessary because the engines were stopped. It would, he thought, "have dwarfed the row of one thousand railroad engines thundering through a culvert."

Even so, he was amazed at the general calm and patience of the passengers, for whom all he could in honesty manage was a "cheery smile of encouragement."

Mrs. Isidor Straus steadfastly refused to enter a boat without her husband. There were other women of similar mind, including Mrs. Lucien P. Smith, of Philadelphia and Cabell County, West Virginia. However, Mrs. Smith later related:

"My husband insisted, and, along with another lady, we went down. After staying there some time with nothing seemingly going on, some one called upstairs saying they could not be lowered from that deck, for the reason it was enclosed in glass. That seemed to be the first time the officers and captain had thought of that, and hastened to order us all on the top deck again.

There was some delay in getting lifeboats down. In fact, we had plenty of time to sit in the gymnasium and chat with another gentleman and his wife. I kept asking my husband if I could remain with him rather than go in a lifeboat. He promised me I could. There was no commotion, no panic, and no one seemed to be particularly frightened; in fact, most of the people seemed interested in the unusual occurrence, many having crossed fifty and sixty times.

However, I noticed my husband was busy talking to an officer whom he came in contact with; still I had not the least suspicion of the scarcity of lifeboats, or I never should have left my husband.

When the first boat was lowered from the left-hand side I refused to get in, and they did not urge me particularly; in the second boat they kept calling for one more lady to fill it, and my husband insisted that I get in it, my friend having gotten in. I refused unless he would go with me. In the meantime Captain Smith was standing with a megaphone on deck. I approached him and told him I was alone, and asked if my husband might be allowed to go in the boat with me.

He ignored me personally, but shouted again through his megaphone, "Women and children first."

My husband said, "Never mind, Captain, about that; I will see that she gets in the boat."

He then said, "I never expected to ask you to obey, but this is one time you must; it is only a matter of form to have women and children first. The boat is thoroughly equipped, and everyone on her will be saved."

I asked him if that was absolutely honest, and he said, "Yes." I felt some better then, because I had absolute confidence in what he said. He kissed me good-by and placed me in the lifeboat with the assistance of an officer. As the boat was being lowered he yelled from the deck, "Keep your hands in your pockets; it is very cold weather." That was the last I saw of him; and now I remember the many husbands that turned their backs as that small boat was lowered, the women blissfully innocent of their husbands' peril, and said good-by with the expectation of seeing them within the next hour or two.

By that time our interest was centered on the lowering of the lifeboat, which occurred to me—although I know very little about it—to be a very poor way to lower one. The end I was in was almost straight up, while the lower end came near touching the water. Our seaman said, himself, at the time, that he did not know how to get the rope down, and asked for a knife. Some person in the boat happened to have a knife—a lady, I think—who gave it to him. He cut the rope, and we were about to hit bottom when someone spoke of the plug.

After a few minutes' excitement to find something to stop up the hole in the bottom of the boat where the plug is, we reached the water all right. The captain looked over to see us, I suppose, or something of the kind, and noticed there was only one man in the boat.

Major Godfrey Peuchen, a manufacturing chemist from Toronto, was then "swung out" into the boat as a needed male. Other men, who were in no way shoving to board the lifeboats, also found themselves being lowered with the women and children for the same reason.

James B. McGough, a department store buyer from Philadelphia who had already noticed a ship-wide reluctance to trust the flimsy-appearing boats, was actually "caught by the shoulder" by an officer and "pushed" into a boat with the admonition:

"Here, you are a big fellow. Get into the boat!"

He then rowed hard, hoping to get away from "the suction" if the *Titanic* sank.

Ismay, however, whom some had reported lingering wistfully around other boats as they were being loaded, finally stepped into one without urging.

"No passengers were on the deck," he would recall. "So . . . I got into it."

It was now slightly more than an hour after the *Titanic* had struck the iceberg and Jack Phillips had raised the *Olympic*. Five hundred miles east and bound for Europe, she was turning about and pouring on coal in an effort to race to her crippled sister in time.

At about five minutes before one o'clock, Phillips switched to the new distress call, "SOS," with the wry observation from Bride that it might be his "last chance to send it."

Rockets now were fired at intervals.

Ship by ship, they began responding to the *Titanic's* plea. The *Carpathia* was already driving hard at seventeen knots. Boats were ready for rapid lowering, lines were coiled in readiness to go over the sides, even "derricks topped and rigged and steam on winches." Shortly, rockets would be fired at regular intervals to advise of her approach.

She expected to be in the disaster area at 4 A.M.

The *Mt. Temple* hoped to be there close to 6 A.M. However, she was confronted with what was, perhaps, the thickest portion of the icefield. It was so bad at one time that Captain Henry Moore stopped the *Mt. Temple* and "had a man pulled up to the masthead in a bowline, right to the foretopmast head" to seek a clear channel.

The Russian freighter *Birma*, confronted with the same ice barriers, could theoretically be near the *Titanic* by 7 A.M.

The *Virginian*, under way, might be at the scene slightly after 9 A.M.

The garrulous *Frankfurt* finally announced, "Our captain will go to you!" At thirteen knots, however, she was eleven hours away.

The *Baltic*, too, had swung about. However, the relatively swift White Star liner was 370 miles to the east.

The *Californian*, hove to perhaps twenty miles north of the *Titanic*, was doing nothing since she had switched off her wireless for the night. After all, how many times did the Marconi man Cyril Evans have to be told to "shut up!"

There had been a disturbing sighting of lights and rockets

110

during the early morning hours by Second Officer Herbert Stone, of the *Californian.*

The fact remained, nonetheless, that the Leyland Line freighter did not proceed to investigate, or at least arouse her radioman.

None of those ships who were responding, however, were close enough. The *Titanic* was going fast.

On the tilting deck, the band stoically played what survivors would identify as the Episcopal hymn, "Autumn."

Phillips tapped the message, which was to be his last, at 2 A.M., "Come quick, our engine room flooded up to the boilers."

He lit candles in the radio shack and switched on the battery-powered emergency transmitter. He wouldn't have a chance to use it.

Lightoller then watched "the sea . . . rolling up in a wave, washing the people back in a dreadful huddled mass."

Bride was apparently the last one to see the captain, who "jumped overboard from the bridge when we were launching the collapsible lifeboat." "Smitty" Smith looked "all right" to the second radio operator.

As Lawrence Beesley's boat pulled off, "a sense of loneliness" came over him. The former science master at Dulwich College had jumped into a boat after the loading officer found no more women to answer his call. Two ladies, however, did leap as the craft was being lowered from its davits.

Soon, Beesley would recall, "in the distance the *Titanic* looked enormous. Her length and breadth were outlined against the starry sky. Every porthole and saloon was blazing with light. It was impossible to think that anything could be wrong with such a leviathan, were it not for that ominous tilt."

Catherine Crosby's boat "must have rowed quite a distance, but could see the steamer very plainly; saw them firing rockets and heard a gun fired as distress signals to indicate that the steamer was in danger. We continued a safe distance from the steamer, probably a quarter of a mile at least."

111

As Lawrence Beesley watched, the *Titanic* "slowly tilted straight on end. . . ."

Those left aboard who had been swarming toward the stern as less and less of the great ship was left out of water clung desperately to deck houses, ventilators, stanchions, the deck railings, anything in one final desperate bid for security and—life. They clung and did not jump.

"The lights in the cabins and saloons," Beesley continued, "which had not flickered for a moment since we left died out, flashed once more and then went out altogether. Others in his boat heard the chorus of terrible calls for help."

The doomed liner hung perpendicularly, her three monster propellers plainly visible. As everything inside her, from furniture and cargo to the very engines themselves tore loose, a din like thunder rolled across the eerie stillness of the night. The angle was so steep that the forward funnel toppled loose.

Then the *Titanic* settled aft slightly, picked up speed and slid rather quietly under the black waters of the North Atlantic. Lightoller heard a hushed gasp from those in his boat:

"She's gone!"

The time was 2:20 A.M. Monday, April 15, 1912. The *Titanic* had just left Lloyd's registry of world shipping.

Colonel Gracie, one of only some dozen to be washed from the plunging liner and live, would tell of "a sort of gulp as if something had occurred behind me, and I suppose that was where the water was closing up, where the ship had gone down; but the surface of the water was perfectly still, and there were, I say, this wreckage and these bodies, and there were the horrible sounds of drowning people and people gasping for breath.

"While collecting the wreckage together I got on a big wooden crate, some sort of wooden crate, or wood of that sort. I saw an upturned boat, and I struck out for that boat, and there I saw what I supposed were members of the crew on this upset boat. I grabbed the arm of one of them and pulled myself up on this boat."

Not until Phillips was standing atop an upturned boat did

112

he remember, in Lightoller's hearing, the warning from the *Mesaba* which might have saved the *Titanic* but which only the radioman had heard or seen.

"I put the message under a paperweight at my elbow" Lightoller heard Phillips say. He had meant to show it to the captain after he cleaned up some of the commercial traffic that had bedeviled him the whole voyage.

The first radio operator apparently slipped from the boat, because Lightoller never saw him again.

Shortly after 3:30 A.M., Henry Stengel saw a rocket, two lights, then another green light and urged the men with him to keep pulling at the oars.

The *Carpathia* had arrived.

She was in time to save only seven hundred souls out of the 2,201 who had been aboard. Thus 1,501 had perished (though because of late embarkations and crew changes the figure would be subject to slight variations).

The worst toll had occurred in steerage where only 25 per cent of the passengers had been saved. Only 24 per cent of the crew lived. Paradoxically, another seven hundred could have left in the boats, most of which rowed off half full. There had been a widespread reluctance of the passengers, especially the older ladies, to leave the liner.

Dead were these big names: Colonel Astor, Major "Archie" Butt, Guggenheim, Millet, Mr. and Mrs. Straus, George Widener and his son, Harry; also the lesser names such as Captain Crosby, who had weathered many a Great Lakes blow, and Lucien P. Smith. Colonel Gracie would die the same December. Crosby's was among a number of bodies, floating in lifejackets, later recovered by "funeral ships."

Pilloried for the rest of his life for leaving his ship with so many still on board, Bruce Ismay would wish he had not survived.

Perhaps the sacrifice had produced a safer Atlantic Ocean. The International Ice Patrol was born out of the disaster. Stricter rules were enforced by nations and shipping companies as to the number of lifeboats carried. The *Titanic* had hung from her davits enough boats to accommodate only 50 per cent of the people on board: sixteen standard and four collapsible boats—testament in itself to the owners' belief that their ship was unsinkable.

Liners were compelled forever afterward to carry sufficient radiomen for a twenty-four-hour watch.

The major question of why the *Titanic* was plunging at maximum speed through known icefields could never be answered. The captain had gone down with his ship. The suspicion would persist, nonetheless, that Smith himself had come to believe the deadly myth that his command was indestructible.

The major mystery was the purported presence of the "other ship." The *Californian,* hove to in the icefield some ten to twenty miles distant, was not necessarily observing the *Titanic.* Lights, distances, and, certainly, shapes in the vastness of the North Atlantic especially on a flat night are extremely deceptive and sometimes downright illusory. The author, on wartime convoy duty in these bleak waters, can himself vouch for this.

Not one survivor from the *Titanic* could swear that he or she had seen anything resembling the *Californian*— until she, like the *Carpathia,* was on the scene the next morning. Nor could anyone on the *Californian* swear that he had seen the sinking White Star liner that fateful night.

The *Californian* had been stopped approximately an hour before the *Titanic* rammed the iceberg. She was bound to drift since the currents of the sea, even in a seeming flat calm, are never wholly at rest. She could have been and probably was well over the horizon from the maiden voyager.

The "other ship" has become a legend in her own right, and one scarcely happier than the *Titanic*. The assumptions that successive generations have made are not quite of the gossamer texture of old wives' tales. But neither can they be traced back to unequivocal fact, and they surely do disservice to the memory of a sturdy salt of the early years of the century, Captain Stanley Lord.

11.

The Storms of 1913

THE LOSS OF THE *Titanic* DISCOURAGED TRANSATLANTIC TRAVEL no more than had the loss of the *Norge,* the *Ville du Havre, La Bourgogne,* the *Arctic*—all before the White Star maiden voyager which had sailed, Wagnerianlike, so impressively into oblivion.

The near-saturation of news space devoted to the tragedy approached, then rapidly exceeded the bounds of morbidity. An immediate but quite unintended result was to guide the public's focus onto the steamship company as well as the *Titanic's* slightly smaller sister, *Olympic.* Requests for passage on her exceeded all earlier demands. It was very much like sightseers frenziedly visiting the scene of a sensational crime. Passengers appeared anxious to share, if only vicariously, in the experiences of the ill-fated men and women who had been aboard the *Titanic.*

For even the slightly imaginative, it was not difficult to stand on the boulevardlike decks of the *Olympic* and muse, "Isidor Straus and Mrs. Straus must have been about here," or "Bruce Ismay stepped into this lifeboat. . . ."

A latter-day male traveler could ask himself, "Would I have nonchalantly lit a cigarette and gone down with the rest. . . .?" A woman might wonder, "Would I have fought to stay at the side of my husband?"

The funerals were still being solemnized in the United States, Canada, and Great Britain for those bodies that had been recovered when the International Mercantile Marine Lines, encompassing all major transatlantic companies, published amidst the daily sailings the following bulletin:

> All steamers of the undermentioned lines will follow the new southerly course eastbound and westbound, thus avoiding all possibility of meeting ice, and each steamer will have boat and life raft capacity for every person on board including both passengers and crew.

It scarcely seemed too soon or too much to offer—a century after the Savannah had inaugurated steamship service between the new world and the old.

A year passed. Liners, adhering more or less to the "new southerly course," proving a rather narrow street for two-way traffic, slowed their propellers on the first anniversary of the *Titanic's* loss, in order to strew flowers in their wakes.

Spring, 1913, turned into summer. There existed an uneasy feeling in the Balkans, within earshot of the saber-rattling from Berlin. Imperial Germany, desiring, as Kaiser Wilhelm barked, "a place in the sun," had built a formidable fleet since the turn of the century. Not in the same naval league as Great Britain, Germany nonetheless had entered the teens with thirty-three mighty battleships or dreadnoughts.

As the sea strategist and historian Sir Julian Corbett observed, the Royal Navy now faced "a first-class naval power" for the first time since the Dutch wars of the seventeenth century.

But American tourists were not deterred. When June's flurry at Newport, Pride's Crossing, and Southampton subsided, the social registry joined businessmen and more mundane family groups in a lemminglike quest of the Thames Embankment, the Place de la Concorde, Unter den Linden, any number of spas, the funicular up Mont Blanc, and assorted palazzios farther south. . . .

Summer had come. And it was a sellout as well as a safe one for transatlantic travel, whatever might be fulminating in the purlieus of Potsdamer Platz.

116

Autumn was another story. As early as October, a rough winter was heralded. In the first week of that month, the 3,600-ton *Volturno,* out of Rotterdam, chartered from the Canadian Northern Steamship Company, was wallowing in monstrous seas, twelve hundred howling miles east of Halifax.

The small vessel carried 564 passengers, largely Polish, Balkan, and Levantine immigrants, destined for Ellis Island, New York. In her holds were oils, wines, gin, burlap, rags, peat moss, chemicals, and yet other items of a quasi-floating general store.

The entire time at sea had been an unrelieved hell for the small, overcrowded *Volturno.* Everyone was sick. It would have been rough sailing even for veteran salts, and many of the passengers had never seen a body of water larger than a river or lake.

At 7 A.M., Thursday, October 9, Captain Francis Inch was confronted with something yet more disturbing—smoke began issuing from a forward hatch. Inch, a young Samson, immediately seized an ax and smashed a hole in the tarpaulin and wooden planking large enough to allow a fire hose to be unwound into the depths of the hot cargo hold.

This was orthodox procedure. The salt water in this case, however, mixed with items of the cargo for an unorthodox explosion. Now the hold blazed furiously, more like a Vesuvius than the ship's actual Italian namesake—a river.

Inch, the man of action, indulged no more hopes of extinguishing the fire, especially since he could not turn on the flood valves. He feared the additional water would sink the liner, already well below the Plimsoll, or normal load line. He ordered an "SOS," the distress call dramatized the past year by the *Titanic.*

Eighty miles distant, the Cunarder *Carmania* instantly replied, "Hold on, chaps, we're coming!"

Whipped by the gale, the flames leaped upward, scorched the masts, then burned through the antenna connections. An officer climbed up through fire and smoke to rig the wireless back in place.

A lurch of the ship threw him down onto the deck. Badly hurt and shaken, the plucky officer nonetheless stood up and limped to the bridge.

Passengers, swathed in lifejackets, surged onto the decks. Inch, uncertain that rescue would arrive in time, ordered one lifeboat over the side. Commanded by the chief officer and containing about twenty-four passengers, mostly women, it capsized just as it touched the water. All in it were lost.

The second lifeboat was launched successfully, but it sailed out of sight.

The third also reached the water, only to be swept aft and smashed by a comber which brought the stern of the ship down upon it. More than one hundred now had died. Captain Inch ordered a halt.

At noon, the *Carmania* hove to, in sight. She tried for half the afternoon to put a boat alongside the burning *Volturno*. Each time one neared, swells tossed boat and rowers back. The attempt was for the moment abandoned.

Before dusk, three German vessels were on the scene—the freighter *Seydlitz,* the *Grosser Kurfuerst,* and the *Kroonland.* They proved as helpless as the *Carmania.*

There appeared to be only one chance left: to summon a tanker that might dump oil to blanket the seas long enough to bring off the surviving passengers and crew.

In response to Captain Inch's latest plea, the Anglo-American petroleum carrier *Narragansett* acknowledged with a jaunty:

"Will come with the milk in the morning!"

As explosion after explosion from the *Volturno* lit the stormy night, even "the morning" did not appear soon enough for the "milk."

At 2 A.M., the tenth of October, Captain Inch radioed:

"For God's sake, do something!"

By dawn, a rescue fleet of half a dozen freighters and passenger ships circled the *Volturno.* Boats had been put over by most of them, including the *Grosser Kurfuerst,* whose coxswain

118

shouted in halting English to the silhouettes of huddling passengers:

"Jump! *Gott in Himmel,* jump!"

None had the courage to do so except C. J. Pennington, the junior wireless operator. The radio shack had been reduced to cinders.

Pennington sank down, down until he was certain he would never surface again. Then he bobbed up, well past the *Grosser Kurfuerst's* lifeboat, to be hauled over the gunwales by the next, that from the *Kroonland.*

In the murky gray light of a new day, the *Narragansett* dipped in through the spindrift and started pumping out her oil, just as promised. Other vessels kept appearing from over the dark-green horizon until eleven were hove to. Their small boats dotted the seas, partly flattened by the oil.

There was no space on the *Volturno* away from fire, smoke, or blowing cinders. At last the survivors commenced leaping into the water. Those too old, weak, or sick to do so were aided by crewmen who formed human ladders down the sides of the ship to pass them to the nearest boat.

In the best traditions of the sea, Captain Inch was the last to leave.

Of the 657 aboard, including crew, when the *Volturno* sailed from Rotterdam, 133 had died. Even so, the tragedy could have been much worse.

The weather that fall vented its fury inland as well as upon the open seas. Exactly one month after the ordeal of the *Volturno,* another storm howled across the often unruly Great Lakes and spewed its venom impartially on sailor and landlubber alike.

Many residents of Cleveland, Ohio, barely made it home from church Sunday, November 9, as the snows blew in. The temperature tumbled and the cold was so paralyzing that pedestrians banged on the doors and windows of already stalled trolleys for the sole privilege of shelter. Then, once inside, they were threatened with suffocation, and ultimately many had to be rescued by policemen or firemen.

119

The latter faced their regular duties as well. They hauled half-frozen equipment through the drifts and then struggled to coax pressure out of the hydrants to fight a fire that leveled a four-story rag factory.

By nightfall, nothing moved in Cleveland, properly tagged by one reporter, "a city of splendid isolation." All that could be seen beneath the lattice-work of toppled utility poles and their web-tangle of wires were white, ever-accumulating mountains of snow—almost twenty-two inches high. People were afraid to cross the streets—even if they somehow could—for fear of electrocution.

Heating plants of all descriptions failed as pipes froze and coal trucks were imprisoned in their sheds. There was hardly any drinking water. Faucets that could be turned at all yielded but a muddy, slushy fluid. The copydesk man on the *Plain Dealer* who wrote that Monday morning CITY STAGGERS UNDER LASH OF EARLY BLIZZARD knew whereof he spoke.

Crack trains, including the *Twentieth Century Limited* from New York to Chicago, were halted by giant drifts on a lonely right-of-way. Engineers couldn't even see their signal towers, much less nearby farmhouses, as the Midwest was isolated by the thick white fury of the storm.

Cattle caught in the fields froze where they stood.

In Chicago, uprooted trees together with acres of glass shards from blown-out store fronts made the loop virtually impassable.

Uncomfortable and inconvenient as it was along the shores of the Great Lakes, very few inhabitants succumbed. On the waters, upwards of two hundred vessels struggled blindly for port. The lakes were still open for navigation.

The Weather Bureau's warning did not wholly prepare either sailor or landlubber for the winds ahead. On Friday, the seventh, the forecast had read, "Brisk to high southwest winds this afternoon, shifting to northwest Saturday on upper lakes," followed by a "P.S." on Saturday concerning "high northwest winds."

The press on Sunday interpreted these advisories to mean

120

"local snows and colder. Monday fair and slightly warmer. Brisk winds."

They proved "brisk," indeed.

Without radios, some ships were caught in the middle of the lakes. A number of captains heeded the forecast to remain moored to their docks; others shrugged and put out from port anyhow.

Among the latter was the *Henry B. Smith,* with a gross weight of more than sixty-six hundred tons. Her master, James Owen, did not see why he couldn't buck the gale. He loaded ore at Marquette and sailed into Lake Superior about 5 P.M. Sunday.

Watchers ashore saw her characteristic long hull outside of the breakwater, rolling heavily, and apparently attempting to come about—even as the *Portland,* fifteen years previously, had tried to do off Gloucester. Then, the dense snow hid her. With her crew of twenty-three, she was never seen again. Not a trace washed ashore, not so much as a life ring or identifiable spar.

When the storm somewhat abated on Monday, those individuals whose thoughts had been centered around their own survival began to think of the waters on which they were dependent for economic well-being.

Mounting anxieties were lent further substance when a door panel from *Lightship No. 82* washed ashore at Buffalo. She had been stationed astride the channel leading into that busy Lake Erie port. Scrawled upon the sliver of wood was this message from Captain Hugh M. Williams:

"Goodbye, Nellie. Ship is breaking up fast. . . ."

The 105-foot lightship was gone, with all six aboard. Nellie Williams was only the latest of an accumulating number of widows this second week of November, 1913.

The storm peaked Sunday evening over Lake Huron, which, by the same measure, experienced the greatest carnage. Among the few who survived to chronicle his ordeal was Captain James Watts, carrying a load of soft coal on the *J. F. Durston* up the lake toward the Straits of Mackinac. His ultimate destination was Milwaukee on the lower west shore of Lake Michigan.

121

Late Saturday and early Sunday, the weather was building up until, Watts would note, "by noon it was blowing a hurricane." All hands were exhausted by evening from trying to balance against rolls nearing the horizontal, as well as from the terror of the experience.

The howling of the winds was itself deafening and demoralizing as though the elements were venting a personal, willful malice upon each and every man aboard ship. Ice was forming so rapidly in layers that most hatchways were sealed as if they had been welded.

The crew of thirty-two was already exhausted when the worst of the storm hit, shortly before 10 P.M. Sunday, spearheaded by ninety-mile-an-hour gusts—"real blowing," in the laconic estimation of the *Durston*'s hard-bitten skipper. She was wallowing slowly ahead, with enough steerage way so that the seas wouldn't smash broadside and flood the engine space and cause her to founder.

However, the veteran of more than thirty years on the lakes kept pushing northward. Watts knew the folly of attempting to turn toward one of the many ports along the shores. He was certain that he could not bring her about and remain afloat. The captain wrote about the *Durston*'s ordeal:

> The waves broke over our bow with a thunderous force that was terrifying, crashing over us from both starboard and port. They met in the center of the deck and rushed wildly down the deck, hellbent for the engine house, breaking over it with a roar and a boom like hundreds of cannon.
>
> Then they curled up—often above the ridge of the smoke stack—and sped over the stern of the ship . . . they were like mountains. All the lifeboats, life rafts and life belts in the world wouldn't have been worth a tinker's damn.

When dawn broke, the *Durston* "looked like a ghost ship," covered by "about a thousand tons of ice," in Watts's estimation.

The coal-laden *Howard M. Hanna* was swept onto rocks off Pointe aux Barques, on the west shore of Lake Huron as she tried

122

(U.S. COAST GUARD PHOTO)

The Italian liner *Andrea Doria* in the last stages of sinking after collision with the Swedish-American liner *Stockholm* in fog approximately 205 miles east of New York and 55 miles south of Nantucket Island on July 25, 1956.

The Swedish-American liner *Stockholm* as she appeared before the tragic collision with the *Andrea Doria*.

One "fearful scene" was "being enacted — men leaping from the top of the rail 20 feet, pushing and maiming" those already in the boats or in the water. So it seemed to the hapless captain in the last moments the *Arctic* was afloat.

The explosion of the steamer *Sultana* in the Mississippi River on April 28, 1865.

The 1,200-ton emigrant ship *Cospatrick,* built of teak wood, caught fire on a voyage to New Zealand in 1874. Only 3 of the 474 aboard survived.

Captain Alexander Elmslie, of the *Cospatrick* (right), Mrs. Elmslie (left), and 4-year-old Alexander Elmslie (center).

The magnitude of the tragedy when the excusion steamer *General Slocum* burned in the East River off Manhattan Island on June 15, 1904, defied comprehension. More than 1,000 were sacrificed, primarily children and their mothers.

The trouble with the immigrant ship *Volturno* was that she wasn't fireproof.

Empress of Irelar
sunk May 29th 19
930 Lives Lost.

Collier STORSTAD
which rammed the
IRELAND
showing damaged
Bows

When the collier *Storstad* rammed the *Empress of Ireland* on May 29, 1914, 930 lives were lost.

Captain Turner enjoyed a hearty chuckle before the *Lusitania* sailed from New York: "The best joke I've heard . . . this talk of torpedoing."

Fred Hanson, a Swedish pantryman, snapped this photograph of the *Vestris'* last moments. It was one of the most dramatic moments the camera ever caught. The man leaning against the superstructure is George Bogg, a steward, both of whose arms had been broken. Because of the solicitude of his fellow crewmen, he arrived safely aboard the *American Shipper,* almost helpless though he was.

Ed Johnson snapped this bow view of the *Vestris* in extremis — her last hour before she sank.

Ed Johnson today with Mrs. Johnson at their Scarsdale, New York, home.

Who set fire to the cruise liner *Morro Castle*?

The 83,000-ton luxury liner *Normandie* rests at Pier 88, North River, in New York City on February 9, 1942, with fire raging thoughout her thirteen decks, and water from firefighting vessels streaming down her side. The liner was undergoing conversion to a troop transport when the fire occurred.

The cruise liner *Yarmouth Castle* as she appeared in port prior to the fire that subsequently ravaged her on a trip from Miami to Nassau in the Bahamas.

Carole Pendleton. She survived the *Yarmouth Castle* disaster.

The *Marpessa*, 208,000-ton tanker belonging to the Royal Dutch Shell Company, sinks off the West African coast following an explosion. Other supertankers, including two of her sisters, have been involved in accidents. On her maiden voyage, the Japanese-built *Marpessa* gained the dubious honor of being the largest vessel ever to be lost, in peace or war.

to make nearby Port Austin. No amount of power would afford the low-in-the-water carrier any steerage.

"Water poured into the engine room," according to Paul Hallwass, a fireman, "and the firemen could not keep steam up. We all went on top to find that the cabin had been washed away."

The entire engine compartment was waist deep in sooty, icy water. The chief engineer described his domain as a "damn mess."

"Great waves broke over us," Hallwass continued, "and we stayed in the mess room and the kitchen, the only places that were left. Twice the lifesavers from Port Austin tried to reach us, but their boats were smashed and wrecked and they had to give up the attempt.

"For thirty-six hours we were completely at the mercy of the heavy sea. Every moment we expected the vessel to go to pieces."

Not until Tuesday could the shore group, whose dock and rescue station was itself in splinters, slog through to the *Hanna*. The men were using a surfboat they had dug out from under drifts of frozen sand.

Among the twenty-five rescued crewmen was the stewardess, Mrs. Sadie Black, who had tried vainly to prepare hot food in the half-awash galley. By the time the ore boat was abandoned, Mrs. Black was dog-paddling between the stove and the long mess table.

Her heroism would not be forgotten. Before the week was out, she was presented with a loving cup, properly inscribed, from her shipmates. Thus, Mrs. Sadie Black joined other "unsinkable" female immortals of the oceans and inland seas, such as Mrs. Bates, from gold rush days, and Anna Downer, of the *Arctic*— all the plucky ladies who themselves shared and personified the creed, "Don't give up the ship!"

As a matter of fact, Sadie Black did not alone represent her sex on the Great Lakes. Most of the carriers numbered a woman in the "housekeeping" or culinary departments. If not, the steward or one of the officers often brought his wife along for the voyage.

Finally, the full casualties of the storm were known: nineteen ships lost, fifty-two others stranded or damaged, 248 crew

123

members dead, representing a total vessel and cargo value in excess of $10 million. Lake Huron took the most severe beating. Of all the ships on the lake during the blizzard, twenty-four sank or were wrecked and 80 per cent of those on board lost their lives.

Marine casualties were no rare visitor to the Great Lakes. The steamer *Erie,* for example, had burned on her namesake lake, August 12, 1841. At least 250 persons perished. Nine years later, the *J. P. Griffith* also caught fire, with a loss of two hundred lives.

Nothing, however, had ever exceeded the total physical damage wrought by the great storm of 1913. It has not yet been approximated, as a dwindling band of oldtimers on the shores of those inland seas still attest.

12.

EMPRESS OF IRELAND

SIX MONTHS LATER, SOME 275 MILES NORTHEAST OF LAKE
Ontario, another of the frequent ocean liner sailings from the port
city of Quebec took place. This time, what otherwise would have
been a routine departure had been solemnized with religious
overtones.

As the 14,191-ton *Empress of Ireland,* ornate queen of the
Canadian Pacific Line, pushed off from her pier below Chateau
Frontenac promontory, a Salvation Army band of forty-three
musicians on deck struck up: "God be with you till we meet
again."

It sounded a fitting bon voyage for the 171 delegates and
families leaving Canada on May 28, 1914, for the Salvation
Army's international congress in London. It would be the largest
ever held.

This contingent, led by David Rees, the elderly and ailing
Canadian Commissioner of the Salvation Army, was among the
1,479 persons who sailed that Thursday at 4:30 P.M. The crew
accounted for approximately 420 of the total. Because of usual
last-moment replacements and absentees the muster roll would
not be wholly accurate until several days out of port.

It was a typically mild, calm, late spring afternoon on the
St. Lawrence River although more smoky than normal from a

125

forest fire somewhere in the vastness of northern Quebec Province. When the travelers had their fill of the passing fishing villages along the shore and the rough but undulating panorama of hills and dark green bluffs, they went below to dinner or to rest in their comfortably appointed cabins.

"The ship was as still as a dish on a shelf," it seemed to R. A. Cunningham, longtime professor at the Manitoba Agricultural College, among the delegation to the London conference. "I could hear the splashing of the water from the bow and every little while a sort of crash as a bigger wave rose and hit her on the nose. She was a pretty ship. . . ."

Captain J. E. Dodd, an editor of the Salvation Army's *War Cry,* scribbled a last dispatch that would be posted at Rimouski, a city of two thousand inhabitants, 180 miles down river from Quebec. Not only a mail and pilot station, Rimouski, with its stores, cafés, and also a large convent, was an outpost of civilization.

Just east, at Father Point, which docked the pilot boat, a ferry connected with Baie Comeau, Saguenay, leading into the wilderness of northern Quebec Province.

"We were on our way to the congress in a deeper sense than ever before," concluded Dodd, "and the next stop was Liverpool."

For the youthful correspondent the voyage was also honeymoon.

To others on board, the Salvationist's religion was a bit too heavy, surely too solemn. In the Victorian lounge, M. D. A. Darling, an Englishman returning from a visit to Shanghai, glanced over the selections with which the ship's string ensemble would tonight honor their special guests. His attention paused momentarily at one: "The Funeral March of a Marionette." At least a few were more lighthearted.

Before the stewards commenced clearing the mirrored first cabin dining salon, there had been repeated champagne toasts at one long table. It was assigned to the Shakespearean actor Laurence Irving and his wife, Mabel Hackney, returning with their company after a successful Canadian tour. Laurence was the son of the yet more illustrious Sir Henry Irving.

Hymns were finished, the final nightcaps had been tossed off when Captain Henry George Kendall, the ship's master, shook hands with Pilot Adelard Bernier and ordered the *Empress* stopped.

At thirty-nine, Kendall had been a ship's officer for slightly more than twelve years, and a master with the Canadian Pacific for half of that period. This was his first voyage as commander of the *Empress of Ireland.*

The time was 1:20 A.M., Friday. The liner had just passed the yellow lights of Rimouski and was standing off the pilot station at Father Point.

The muted ringing of the engine signals had awakened no one. Bernier, carrying his little satchel, swung down the rope ladder to the tug *Eureka,* waiting almost motionless. Only the sailors saw the pilot off. No cameras were present to click as passengers, often wistfully, observed this symbolic departure.

Bags of mail were exchanged between the *Empress* and the launch *Lady Evelyn,* running for the postal service. Then, Kendall signaled the engine room, "Start."

Already the river had widened to thirty miles. The Gulf of St. Lawrence and the Atlantic lay ahead this clear, bitter night. The thermometer had dropped to a degree or two above the freezing mark.

At 2 A.M., Cock Point gas buoy, the first channel marker for vessels inbound to Rimouski, winked ahead. In the last few minutes, however, wispy fog had sent grayish cotton blobs across the river. This came as no surprise to Captain Kendall, since the cold ocean winds mixed about here with the warmer inland currents.

Then, dodging in and out of the fog patches, the master picked up the starboard running light of another ship, possibly two miles distant. While there seemed sufficient leeway for the vessels to pass, starboard to starboard, Kendall ordered the

Empress, which had been clipping fifteen knots, stopped again.

He had good reason. The green light of the approaching vessel had vanished in the murk as suddenly as it had materialized.

Kendall's worry was augmented. He ordered "full speed astern," since the momentum of the heavy liner was carrying her forward at several knots despite the fact that her twin propellers were not turning.

On the other vessel, the Norwegian collier *Storstad,* low in the water with ten thousand tons of coal—making her gross seventeen thousand tons—Chief Officer Alfred Toftenes had seen the *Empress'* lights, but figured he would pass the stranger to port.

As the Canadian Pacific steamer slid by Cock Point buoy, even though her propellers were churning the water in reverse, Kendall still had not seen the approaching mast or bridge wing lights a second time. He ordered three prolonged blasts, meaning:

"I am going full speed astern!"

Toftenes heard it. A phlegmatic sort, he now experienced a teasing concern: the blackness of the river, its currents, the nearby shore, fog, another ship somewhere ahead, the tremendously deep draft of the *Storstad* and its disturbingly great inertia. How would he ever stop the collier, if he had to, *in a hurry?*

He figured he couldn't. However, to widen what the chief officer believed was the margin of safety between the two vessels he ordered a course change slightly to the right—to starboard— believing the other ship to be off to port—to the left.

It was a game of blind man's buff. Lost momentarily in the fog, the *Storstad* was actually aiming straight at the *Empress'* starboard.

In any case, Toftenes decided—too late—that he had best summon the master, Thomas Andersen, just awakened and dressing in preparation for greeting the pilot at Father Point. This voyage, the heavyset veteran captain had brought along Mrs. Andersen, also up and preparing to go on the bridge.

When Andersen arrived at the helm he saw nothing. Neither did he hear a whistle. Not especially apprehensive, the master

128

nonetheless read the wrinkled look upon his chief officer's face and understood the tone of his voice.

"Full speed astern!" the captain called down to his engineer.

Kendall, on the *Empress,* heard "one prolonged blast" ahead, although he saw nothing. The unidentified ship must, he estimated, be no more than "four points upon my starboard bow." In other words, she was close, not head on, but with an equal potential of peril.

"Full speed ahead!" Kendall ordered, hoping to pick up more maneuverability. He also instructed the helmsman "hard a-port!"—an acute turn to the left.

Then, the captain of the *Empress* saw the bow of the *Storstad* finally break through the wispy rolls of fog, hardly more than one hundred feet distant.

Kendall raced to the bridge wing and shouted through a megaphone: "Go full speed astern!"

Andersen, who thought the *Empress* was steaming "at great speed, eight to ten knots," obeyed. But it did not matter. The heavy collier smashed into the starboard side of the liner, amidships, between the two funnels, all but cutting her in two.

Sparks cascaded brilliantly around the point of impact, like those from braked trolley wheels.

The very impact had swung the *Storstad* out of the great gash. She glided past the *Empress* to be once more swallowed by the fog, like a bandit who has struck in the night and made good his getaway.

Lieutenant Alfred T. Keith, twenty-two-year-old bandsman, experienced a "first impression that the boat which was removing the pilot from the liner was bumping the side of the *Empress.*" When he heard people shouting, he continued, he "jumped out of bed and saw water pouring into the passageway porthole. I sensed something was wrong."

Keith awakened his three cabin mates.

Ensign* E. Pugmire, a financial officer with the Salvation Army in Toronto, felt no shock, hearing only "a grazing sound as

---

*Ensign is his first name.

if we were touching a berg." When this noise continued, he hurried up on deck "to see what was wrong."

Plenty was wrong, in addition to the expected confusion of half-dressed and freightened people awakened from sleep. For one consideration, he found the *Empress* "already listing over dangerously."

At once, Kendall knew his command was doomed.

"Prepare to abandon ship!" he ordered as he opened the signal whistle wide. "Close the watertight doors!"

In moments, Chief Engineer William Sampson called back to the bridge: "No steam!" Now, there was no hope of beaching the vessel, two miles offshore.

The wail of the siren had in seconds subsided into a fast dying lament.

"The engines are gone!" Sampson shouted once more to the bridge through the brass speaking tube.

One watertight door, between the engines and the after boiler room, banged shut. Then all controls became inoperative, even as electricity flickered out, plunging the length and depth of the ship into blackness. . . .

At the Great Northern Telegraph office, on Father Point, manager John McWilliams, who had helped prepare the *Empress'* outgoing mail, was aroused by the clanging of his bedroom alarm bell. He at once "rushed downstairs in his night clothes," to be advised by the Marconi operator, William James Whiteside, what he had picked up from the *Empress of Ireland*.

"SOS—in collision!"

A quick look at the operations blackboard informed McWilliams that the *Lady Evelyn* had already docked at Rimouski. The *Eureka* was still inbound. McWilliams picked up the phone to the postal boat's berthing slip and yelled:

"The *Empress* is sinking! Go to her assistance! Rush!"

The *Evelyn* cast off and churned back down Rimouski Roads. At best, the tender wasn't fast. And the scene of the accident was seven miles eastward.

The *Eureka* was contacted as she neared her Father Point pier and turned herself around.

Ninety miles east, the steamer *Hanover* was hauling in, preparing to pick up a pilot shortly after breakfast. Marconiman Whiteside tried to raise her in the hopes she could hurry upriver under forced draft.

It was no use. Apparently, like the wireless watch on the *Californian,* the Marconi shack atop the steamer *Hanover* was shut down for the night. On the other hand, several ships, five hundred miles at sea, heard the call and came about westward.

Other things were shut down. Kendall himself, in anticlimax, had spoken his final orders to William Sampson:

"Finished with engines!"

The chief engineer, accompanied by two assistants, then "climbed the ladder on the side which really was a ceiling now, like the flies on a wall. . . ."

Firemen and trimmers followed as the river cascaded through crushed bulkheads. James McEwen, a junior engineer, drenched with oily salt water and choking on coal dust, attempted to close a starboard door.

A wall of black water hit him.

"I ran for my life, that's what I did," McEwan would explain succinctly.

Although the *Empress* was listing as steeply as Sampson's experience indicated, some passengers reacted slowly to the onrushing danger. James Ferguson, from England, was awakened only by his suitcase floating against his face.

Others with cabins on the same lower deck were swept through doors and even portholes wrenched open by the collision. Those on levels not already awash had barely time to pull robes or coats over their pajamas and night dresses before stumbling out into the passageways.

For the most part, resignation and a sense of being overwhelmed predominated rather than panic. When a Toronto resident, F. E. Abbott, was asked by Laurence Irving if he thought

131

"the boat was going down," the former replied, "It looks like it." Then the actor, who had a cut on his forehead, turned calmly to his wife and suggested: "Dearie, hurry. There is no time to lose."

When Mabel Hackney started to cry, Irving admonished, "Keep cool."

Exceptionally "cool" was Sir Henry Seton-Kerr, a well-known big game hunter, who insisted that another passenger, M. D. A. Darling, who had been reading the concert program, accept his lifebelt. The Englishman returning from Shanghai snapped "no!" A brief argument between altruists was resolved when a second belt was discovered in an overhead rack and each assisted the other into his.

Elderly Commissioner Rees of the Salvation Army was observed on the shoulders of a deputy being carried up a tilting stairway.

George Bogue Smart, of Ottawa, a first-cabin passenger, wandered topsides, "climbed out on the rail and put my arm around the post, then just sat and waited. . . ."

As he did so, he was impressed that the attitude about him was "really marvelous . . . no bad language, no panic to speak of. I never heard people who spoke with such tenderness to each other in that time of great distress and danger."

There were, necessarily, exceptions. John Fowler, from steerage, came upon such a group.

"I tried to quiet the people," he would recall, "by telling them that it was all right and that the boat would right herself."

No one believed that, surely not Captain Kendall. When Augustus Gaade, the chief steward, observed to the liner's master, "Well, this looks to be about the finish," the latter concurred.

"Yes, and a terrible finish, too."

To be sure that no one entertained any illusions, Kendall shouted through his megaphone what he had already called out:

"The ship is gone! Women to the boats!"

Ed Bamford, assistant wireless operator, kept repeating

"SOS." The *Eureka* and *Lady Evelyn* were nearing through the patchy fog. But it appeared that the *Empress of Ireland* couldn't wait.

"Hurry up, there, everybody!" Kendall exhorted, megaphone still in hand. "There is not a minute to lose!"

J. Fergus Duncan, of London, concluded, "It was pretty rotten on deck. We simply stood there. We knew we were going down. There was no question about that from the first and it was no good struggling. The poor women were hysterical but there was no chance to do anything for them."

Within not many minutes, the people were moving along the side of the vessel. They appeared to Dr. James F. Grant, ship's surgeon and a year out of medical school, "as though they were walking down a sandy beach into the water to bathe."

Keith watched for a moment the futile struggle to launch lifeboats "on the high port side." Those that were loosened failed to clear the davits, scraped against the sideplates, and "spilled passengers over the deck and into the water." Keith, a onetime competitive swimmer, "sensed I was going over. I went as low as possible on the port side and dived in head first."

He stayed down a long time, stroking away as far as he could from the sinking ship. Its backwash, he felt, was tugging at him all the while. Finally, breathless, he surfaced and watched "her dying throes as she settled down like a tired duck, and slowly submerged. There were a lot of people and bodies around me."

In her final agony, the *Empress* reminded Cunningham, the professor from Manitoba, not so much of a duck. Rather, the liner "began to turn over like you see a horse rolling in a field. Her great big whitish belly turned slowly upward and I jumped far, because as she slewed over her length of side increased."

Someone had observed Kendall ripping off his coat prior to jumping. He was heard to shout: "Heaven help us because we cannot help ourselves!"

Crewmen, such as Chief Engineer Sampson, walked into the

water along the now horizontal derricks and kingposts. Someone was seen balancing atop the slippery and precarious length of a mast, level with the water, another on one of the twin funnels.

George Bogue Smart, who had quit his erstwhile secure perch on the railing: ". . . went over with her as I was shot out. I went down two times, fully ten or twenty feet, I imagine, and when I came up the second time I saw a dark object in the water. I put forth every herculean effort until I gripped with one hand a deck chair. I hung onto that."

Duncan, of London, "struck out for the rescuing steamer which was standing about half a mile off."

Kenneth A. McIntyre, of the Salvation Army, "heard the dull explosion caused by the water reaching the engines. It was followed by a burst of steam that spread to all parts of the vessel."

Those who had lingered in their cabins, conceivably for warmer and more modest attire or possibly because they were too paralyzed even to move, were doomed. The steam, which McIntyre had observed, as well as smoke, boiled out of opened hatches and ports. Two waves met and swept over the vanishing superstructure.

Suction, which was making a vortex out of the erstwhile placid river, drew hundreds of people down, then expelled them upward again.

Not more than fifteen minutes after the collision, the *Empress of Ireland* was gone.

Chief Engineer Sampson, who had deliberately plunged deep, surfaced the first time in a tangle of ropes and debris. When he bobbed up again, his head hit the bottom of a lifeboat. Although the *Storstad* now had boats on the scene, this was one of the few launched from the *Empress*.

Sampson hung onto the gunwales until, with numbed fingers, he screamed, "If you can't save me, then goodbye!"

One of the ship's butchers finally recognized the chief engineer and aided him aboard the craft. It was already overloaded and awash.

134

Gaade, the chief steward, who could not swim, was sure "it was all over" when he hit the icy river, Then he bumped into an object that turned out to be a corpse encased in a lifejacket. He hung on, and discovered that it was as buoyant as a raft.

Bandsman Ernest Green could think of "nothing but a village suddenly flooded and all the people floating in the water. It was awful to see those faces bobbing up and down with the ship gone underneath, and only water."

The Salvation Army musician had lost his mother, father, and sister.

Seven-year-old Gracie Hanagan, daughter of the group's bandmaster, Edward Hanagan, was very lucky. When she floated up after having gone down "deep, oh so deep," she grabbed a rope dangling from a plank. Gracie hung on to watch her mother and father vanish from sight.

An eight-year-old shipmate, Florence Barbour, of Silverton, British Columbia, rode upon the broad back of a neighbor, Robert Crellin, from home, until both reached one of the few collapsible boats that had been opened up and launched.

Little Florence, whose father had died the year before, was en route to England with her mother and sister. Now, like Gracie Hanagan, she had become an orphan.

None could attain the shore, two miles distant or even discern in the gloom of night just where it was. Even Professor Cunningham who as a boy was known as "the best swimmer in town," was having a hard time.

"I just saw the grayness," he would explain, "and that damned water lapping, lapping like a fool dog . . . it didn't seem wicked or vicious or menacing or cruel, but just foolish like an idiot with a double-barreled shotgun and hopping around and laughing about it. . . ."

George Smart could feel rather foolish himself clinging to his deck chair. When he began to tire he managed to pull it under him in such a position that instead of holding onto it he rested upon it.

Exemplifying the "tenderness" that had impressed Smart

135

was Leonard Delamont, Salvation Army band leader from Moose Jaw, Saskatchewan, who had given his lifejacket to his mother and sister. With it they managed to save their lives.

Keith, the fellow bandsman, clinging to a log, was among the last to be picked up. Curiously, the log had almost finished him off since he had slammed into it while swimming hard. It all but knocked him unconscious.

Only one other of his three roommates was rescued.

Within an hour of the *Empress'* final plunge 120 feet to the river bottom, all who would survive had been picked up. One of the *Storstad*'s lifeboats had made four trips.

"We rowed like demons possessed," said Third Officer John Saxe, in charge of rescue operations from the collier.

"Somehow or other," J. Fergus Duncan continued, "the lifeboats appeared and began picking us up. I was in the water a jolly long time. It seemed like an hour and I believe it was. It was terribly cold."

When the *Eureka,* which had been the first on the scene, deposited its first load at Father Point, the Londoner added, "we were like a lot of red Indians when we got on the wharf, all wrapped up in blankets. I never saw such a big supply from so small a ship."

Aboard the *Lady Evelyn,* a shivering, almost blue-faced man was babbling, as he sipped brandy, "Where's the ship?"

He was Captain Kendall.

Nearby was Charles Spencer, a bellboy, who, he asserted, had been saved by the captain after he "caught hold of me." The youth thought he had been "helped along" in the water by the master for almost twenty minutes.

On a corner of the deck a huddled group managed through chattering teeth a thankful stanza of "God Be with You till We Meet Again."

By the gray, chill light of dawn, with the last load of survivors landed at Rimouski or Father Point, it was already apparent that this was an ocean liner disaster—even if inland—to compare with the *Titanic.*

Of the presumed 1,479 who sailed, 1,012 were dead, or soon would perish from exposure. In other words, only one-third aboard survived. Of the 171 Salvation Army members, only 26 lived. Commissioner Rees, Mrs. Rees, his two daughters, and one son all were drowned. They were among, as one writer phrased it, "the very flower of the Salvation Army in Canada."

Captain Dodd, the correspondent who had written he was on his way "in a deeper sense than ever before," and his bride were not among those saved.

Darling, who had mused over "The Funeral March of a Marionette" and, later, argued politely with the sportsman, Seton-Kerr, about lifejackets, was more fortunate. The latter was not. His jacket did him no good. For that matter, many passengers were fatally injured before they even reached the river.

Laurence Irving, his wife, Mabel Hackney, and the entire troupe were lost. London's theater row would be plunged into deepest mourning.

Almost too heartsick to transcribe what he had viewed, a reporter for the Rimouski paper, *L'Echo du Bas St. Laurent,* wrote: "One of the saddest sights at the pier is the number of children among the dead. . . ."

Someone, perhaps a relative or friend, had scribbled a tag, dangling from one of many wooden coffins rushed into this small community of the St. Lawrence:

"Ne pleurez pas sur moi!"

But how, indeed, could one *not* cry?

Those bodies that came ashore but could not be identified—forty-seven in all—were buried in a small plot at Father Point. The Canadian Pacific promised it would maintain this unusual graveyard in perpetuity.

Solemnity and a preoccupation with divine wrath dominated Canada. A choir was on hand at the Toronto railway station to greet fifteen survivors, including Gracie Hanagan, with the hymn, "Oh, God, Our Help in Ages Past."

In the same city, the Reverend Robert Law, of the Old St. Andrews Presbyterian Church, rationalized, "We may look on it as a rebuke to the inordinate self-reliance of the modern spirit."

Even as the dead were being laid to rest, the crank fringe was explaining it knew all along that a tragedy was brewing. In London, a woman informed the Occult Club of the "strange behavior of the ship's cat." In a vision, she asserted, she saw the feline walking down the gangway before sailing, carrying in her mouth two of her kittens.

The fact that this tabby could not be persuaded to return to the *Empress,* presumably at sailing time, and that later she also emitted "a long and sustained meow"—at the very moment of the liner's sinking—seemed to clinch just about everything.

Captain Kendall, even though he was not a superstitious man, had himself a curious footnote. At this spot on the St. Lawrence in July, 1910, Kendall, as master of the Canadian Pacific's *Montrose*, had aided in the apprehension of the murderer, Dr. Hawley Harvey Crippen. The erstwhile London dentist was fleeing, in disguise, with a young lady, dressed as a boy, aboard the liner.

The alert captain recognized from "wanted" circulars the Michigan-born Crippen, who had dismembered his wife and buried her in the basement of his London home.

For the first time in history, a ship's wireless had been employed to solve a crime. Captain Kendall advised Scotland Yard of his suspicions. Inspector Walter Dew was at once dispatched via a faster vessel, arriving at the Father Point pilot station just ahead of the *Montrose*. He came aboard, pretending he was a pilot, then arrested Crippen and his girl friend.

Some believed that Dr. Crippen, as he stepped up to the gallows, put a curse on Captain Kendall and all vessels on which he might serve.

The steamship line, however, along with the Canadian Rivers and Marine Department, was not especially concerned either with escaped killers, hexes, or, surely not, meowing pussy cats.

"That such an accident should be possible in the river St.

Lawrence," asserted Sir Thomas Shaughnessy, president of the Canadian Pacific Company, "is deplorable."

The Canadian Commission of Inquiry, presided over by Lord Mersey who had sat two years earlier in the *Titanic* hearing, agreed. The *Storstad* was held, unequivocally, to blame. Chief Officer Toftenes' license was revoked for two years, even though a subsequent Norwegian court found both the officer and the collier blameless.

Again, even as two years earlier, this ship disaster of not inconsiderable magnitude did nothing to dampen the ardor for transatlantic commutation, Only a week before the *Empress* sank, the world's largest ship, the 54,500-ton *Vaterland,** of the Hamburg-American Line, had completed her maiden voyage to New York. On May 30, the Cunarder *Aquitania,* seventy-five hundred tons less than the German liner, steamed proudly out of Southhampton on her debut.

Summer came, moved on, and the European war flared into reality, with Allies and Central Powers grappling, in likelihood, to the death.

Back in Liverpool was Frank Tower, an oiler, who had shared a raft with the wealthy Toronto attorney, L. A. Gosselin. His friends around the familar pubs along the Mersey now called him "Lucky" Tower. And this, to say the very least, was apt.

He had survived the *Titanic*.

At first, the young oiler swore he'd never return to sea. Then, as money soon ran low, he thought better. But he'd ship out next time on something bigger and conceivably more watertight than the *Empress of Ireland*.

*The *Vaterland,* interned in Hoboken the same year, was seized by the United States in 1917 and operated during and after the war as the *Leviathan*.

13.

The LUSITANIA

IN LIVERPOOL, THAT LATE SUMMER OF 1914, FRANK TOWER congratulated himself on his good fortune. He'd been able to sign on the Cunarder *Lusitania*. The 32,000-ton superliner still held the Blue Riband for speed, having made a record crossing in 1909 from Bishop's Rock to Ambrose Channel in four and a half days.

She could clock the land equivalent of close to thirty miles per hour, which meant that no merchantman plying the Atlantic Ocean, except for her sister ship *Mauretania,* could catch her. This, now, was no small attribute since England had been at war with Germany and the Central Powers since August 4. "Lucky" Tower, who knew only the sea and engine rooms, much perferred to take his chances on a swift, beautiful liner than in the sloppy, imperiled trenches of France.

That autumn and winter and early spring of 1915, the four-funneled Cunarder bore out the wisdom of Tower's decision. In fact, by May she had become the *only* fast ship on which civilians, with presumably urgent reasons, could cross the Atlantic. The *Mauretania* was being used as a hospital ship, while the larger put ponderous *Aquitania* got into action as a troopship, with both being involved in the monumental debacle of Gallipoli.

On Saturday, May 1, the *Lusitania* sailed from Pier 54, on

the lower part of the Hudson River, in Manhattan. Aboard were 1,257 passengers and a crew of 702.

Among the 157 Americans were such familiar names as Alfred Gwynne Vanderbilt, whose reputed assets of nearly $100 million easily made him the richest young man in the world; Charles Frohman, the celebrated producer; Elbert Hubbard, author of "A Message to Garcia" and founder of the Roycrofters cult, of East Aurora, New York; and others whose names were familiar to the business or society pages.

Hubbard was especially sought after by reporters. He had just written a short essay, "Who Lifted the Lid off Hell?" in which he treated Kaiser Wilhelm not too kindly. The jovial "Sage of Aurora" quipped to his interviewers that it might not be so bad if the *Lusitania* were sunk and he with it since it would be "about the only way" he could "get into the Hall of Fame."

A Royal Navy auxiliary, the Cunarder was not a cargo ship but always carried mail and odds and ends in her limited stowage space. This time, she had topped off with sheet brass, copper, assorted machinery, beef, cheese, lard, bacon, automobile parts, even 205 barrels of Long Island Sound oysters. Her only concession to war's gluttony lay in forty-two hundred cases of small-caliber rifle ammunition and one hundred cases of empty shrapnel shells together with unloaded fuses.

The customary waterfront rumors had it that $6 million in gold bullion was also aboard, locked in the purser's safe. If so, the treasure was not manifested.

There was a bit more stir than usual this drizzly Saturday morning since the German embassy in Washington had inserted a paid traveler's warning in New York newspapers that all vessels sailing under flags of the Allies were "liable to destruction" in waters "adjacent" to the British Isles.

Singularly enough, it was placed next to the Cunard's own departure timetable, the one this day attractively topped by a sketch of the *Lusitania* herself.

News reels turned and reporters talked to passengers and

officers as to their feelings about the impending voyage. Most scoffed at the idea of danger.

"We can outdistance any submarine afloat," asserted Vanderbilt.

Captain William Turner laughed throatily as he rumbled, "Why, it's the best joke I've heard in many days—this talk of torpedoing!"

He did not mention, however, that six of *Lusy's* twenty-five boilers would be cold this crossing. War's needs had resulted not only in a shortage of coal but of stokers as well, many of whom were serving in the armed forces. The great liner's speed was thereby reduced to a maximum of no more than twenty-one knots —still some six knots swifter than any U-boat on the surface,

A lifelong veteran of the sea, having started as a cabin boy on sailing ships, Bill Turner was in his sixtieth year and nearing retirement. As a member of the naval reserve, he was kept closely informed on those military concerns that might affect him or his command. Before he had last left Liverpool, for example, the Admiralty had handed him this confidential advisory:

> German submarines appear to be operating chiefly off prominent headlands and landfalls. Ships should give prominent headlands a wide berth.

Captain Turner wasn't worried. The calm, if rainy and foggy voyage, now nearly completed tended to bear out his *savoir-faire*. As one young lady, Dorothy Conner, from Medford, Oregon, a Red Cross volunteer on the way to the front, summed it up to a fellow passenger:

"It's been such a dull, dreary, stupid trip."

Dorothy had not been able to rouse up more than a bridge game or two. This was her favorite avocation.

On Thursday, May 6, the *Lusitania* was hammering toward her destination at a constant twenty knots. At breakfast time, she was within five hundred miles of the Irish coast. As a routine precaution under war conditions, Turner ordered all eleven lifeboats hung over the sides. These, together with the collapsibles, represented a capacity for more than twenty-six hundred persons, a safety margin of at least six hundred.

Early Friday, May 7, seventy-five miles off Cape Clear, on Ireland's southwest tip, speed was reduced to eighteen knots as patchy fog rolled in. Turner had other reasons for slowing *"Lusy"* down. He wanted to hail Liverpool Bar at exactly 4 A.M. Saturday, high tide, when he would rendezvous with the pilot.

At midmorning, the big Cunarder, by the navigator's estimate, was passing Fastnet Rock, off Cape Clear. Fog prevented an actual sighting.

At eleven o'clock, the fog suddenly blew away. The skies were sunny, the temperature balmy. At eleven twenty-five a wireless was received from the Admiralty, London:

> Submarine active in southern part of Irish Channel, last heard of 20 miles south of Coningbeg Light Vessel. Make certain *Lusitania* gets this.

About noon, a hazy shoreline emerged. Captain Turner was puzzled. He studied his charts, finally decided he was off Brow Head, a promontory fifteen miles northwest of Fastnet Rock.

Something, manifestly, was wrong. Unless the master were in error about the identity of the land, the liner should have passed Fastnet and be on her way along the coast toward Queenstown.

Worried, Turner ordered the engine room to be ready for full emergency steam if called for.

At 12:40 P.M., while the passengers were at lunch, another Marconi dispatch sparked in from the Admiralty:

> Submarine five miles south of Cape Clear, proceeding west when sighted at 10 A.M.

The captain then set a 20-degree course change to the north, which would bring the *Lusitania* closer in to shore. This was contrary to standing instructions, "give prominent headlands a wide berth."

At 1 P.M. a new landfall was identified as Galley Head. Yet, this parcel of Irish headland was sixty miles east of Brow Head. Surely, the liner, fast as she was, could not have steamed that distance in one hour!

At 1:40 P.M., the *Lusitania* was close enough in to make a positive landfall: the Old Head of Kinsale. However, Captain Turner wished to know exactly his distance from the Old Head. Ten minutes later he ordered a four-point bearing—a tedious method of establishing a fix which presupposed a steady course and speed—for forty long minutes.

Now, Turner had violated another procedure of wartime: to zigzag in waters under submarine alert.

At 2:09 P.M., with the four-point bearing about half completed, a few still lingered in the dining saloons. In first class, portly Robert J. Timmins, a cotton dealer from Gainesville, Texas, ordered a second plate of ice cream, as he assured his companion, Ralph Moodie, "We've got time."

In second class, the heaviest booked, with 601 passengers, Archibald Donald, a young Scotch-Canadian en route to officers' training at Edinburgh University, watched one of his tablemates struggle to eat a grapefruit. It struck him as funny.

"Why didn't you order something else?" he asked Miss Lorna Pavey, of Saskatchewan.

Two others joined in the mirth. They were the Reverend H. L. Gwyer, a six-foot, four-inch Episcopalian minister from Calgary, in Western Canada, and his bride of three weeks, Margaret.

In third class, Mrs. Elizabeth Duckworth, a cotton mill employee from Taftville, Connecticut, returning to her native Blackburn, in Lancashire, a world weaving center, pushed back her chair and followed her cabin sharers out of the saloon. They were Mrs. Alice Scott, of Nelson, England, and her small son, Arthur.

Another friend of the voyage, Mrs. Florence Padley, of

144

Vancouver, had just settled herself in a deck chair when she heard someone remark, matter-of-factly, "There's a porpoise."

She stood up to look.

Above her steerage deck, on the promenade, Oliver P. Bernard, scenic director of the Boston Opera House as well as of Covent Garden, in London, paused just outside of the veranda café when something on the sea "impinged on my mental focus." His mind "twanged" like a door slamming.

And in the next second not a door but a torpedo crashed through the seven-eighths-inch-thick steel plates of the starboard side, below and just aft of the bridge. The decks heaved, then settled underfoot as a column of steam and water carrying coal, wood, and steel splinters geysered 160 feet in the air, towering above the radio antenna, then splattered hotly onto the boat deck.

The mighty Cunarder listed to starboard.

Turner ordered the helm hard over. He would try to beach her—the Irish coast, so green and clear under the sparkling afternoon sun, seemed so near. Even so, entertaining no illusions, he ordered Marconi Operator Robert Leith to send:

Come at once. Big List. Ten miles south Old Head Kinsale.

The ammeter needle began to flutter, whispering to him that electricity was going. Leith eyed the emergency generator in a corner of the radio shack.

Down below, in a hissing, billowing cavern of greasy steel gratings and escaping steam, Second Engineer Andrew Cockburn watched his pressure gauges dropping to the zero reading. There was no more power on the propellers, even though the big ship careened ahead under her own momentum.

Approximately half a mile off the starboard bow, youthful Kapitänleutnant Walther Schwieger, of the still submerged U-20, watched in disbelief through his periscope the effects of one torpedo. He was to log:

Shot hits starboard side right behind bridge. An unusually heavy detonation follows with a very strong explosion cloud

145

(high in the air over first smokestack). Added to the explosion of the torpedo there must have been a second explosion (boiler, coal or powder). The superstructure over point struck and the high bridge are rent asunder and fire breaks out and envelops the high bridge. The ship stops immediately and quickly heels to starboard. At the same time diving deeper at the bow. . . .

Florence Padley, who had gone to the rail to watch the porpoise, was still repeating anticlimactically:

"No, it's a torpedo. . . !"

Then she decided she'd better hurry below to her cabin on D-deck. As she approached an elevator, she watched it "go down in a rush." Not knowing whether its cables had suddenly been severed, she abandoned her original intention and started instead for the boat deck, losing a shoe en route.

To Robert Timmins, the cotton dealer who never received his second dish of ice cream, the blow sounded no less nor worse than "a penetrating thrust." Since his cabin was on the high port side he found he was walking up a kind of mountain to reach it. Once inside, he saw the place was an indescribable litter.

In the second-class dining saloon, Archibald Donald had stopped laughing about Lorna Pavey's grapefruit. The towering minister, Gwyer, at once leaned over and suggested, "Let us quieten the people," much as he might have said under other circumstances and in different surroundings, "let us pray."

John Fowler, on the *Empress of Ireland*, had had much the same impulse and had said so in much the same words.

With Donald by his side and the women following, the Reverend Mr. Gwyer strode through the litter of broken china and glasses on the floor, repeating, "It's all right, now . . . there, there . . . no need to hurry, my friends. . . ."

Frightened or not, the diners, it seemed to Donald, moved quickly but orderly. There was no trampling. Only one woman fainted. Her husband and Archie Donald carried her out of the saloon.

Outside, the situation was far worse. Smudged stokers,

oilers, cooks, and others of the crew were piling on deck. To Donald, they appeared like a wild lot.

Wildness, for that matter, had seized hold on many individuals. Elizabeth Duckworth, walking to her cabin with her companions of the voyage—Alice Scott and the latter's little boy, Arthur—had felt the ship shake "from stem to stern." The three, reflexively, started to run. They did not stop until they were on deck, near the bow, which was obviously lower in the water than the last time they had noticed, and now tilting.

Panic seized the trio. The two ladies, clutching Arthur by the hand, then did something they could not have conceived in their most fevered imaginings. They started up the broad rope rigging of the forward mast.

All three were covered with tar and soot when an officer, scrambling up behind them, assured:

"Please come down, now. There's a lifeboat ready."

They complied, although it was hard to tear Arthur loose, who, in his fright, was clinging to the rigging as though he were fastened.

One of the calmest aboard a liner whose assortment of human beings suddenly was illustrating the complete range of emotions was George Kessler, a New York wine merchant, carrying $2 million in securities, helping to load the boats with women. Puffing on a cigar Kessler paused only to shake off the ashes and explain he was acting "only in a spirit of convention" since he had no idea the *Lusitania* would sink.

On the bridge, Captain Turner was reassured by no such illusion. All power was gone. The great liner, listing 15 degrees to starboard, kept moving, under her continuing inertia, in a wide circle.

It was now 2:14 P.M., approximately five minutes after the torpedo had struck, and the Cunarder's SOS's were being answered. The tanker *Narragansett*, which had figured in the rescue of *Volturno* survivors, was thirty-five miles to the southeast. She promised to come at full steam.

147

The small liners *Etonian* and *City of Exeter* were at about the same distance. However, the *Lusitania* had now assumed a list of 20 degrees, and Turner was entertaining grave doubts as to whether his command could last the necessary three hours for their arrival.

Rear Admiral Sir Charles Coke, senior officer of the naval station at Queenstown, dispatched the tugs *Julia, Flying Fish,* and *Warrior.* Commanding the Irish Coast Patrol, Rear Admiral H. L. A. Hood was putting out of the same port aboard the cruiser *Juno,* accompanied by three others of the squadron, *Isis, Sutley,* and *Venus.*

The Royal Navy commander might have been wondering *why* had his patrol been in harbor, in the face of so many submarine warnings in the last days. In fact, only on Wednesday, May 5, the schooner *Earl of Latham* had been sunk off the Old Head of Kinsale by a U-20's deck guns after the crew had abandoned.

It was true, however, that Admiral Hood could not know the same submarine was still operating in his defensive waters.

On board the *Lusitania,* still moving ahead in an uncontrollable arc without engines, no passenger could wait for Hood or any other of the distant rescue fleet. Boats were starting down from their davits, but not in the Birkenhead tradition.

"I always thought a shipwreck was a well-organized affair," ruefully commented Lady Margaret Mackworth, suffragist daughter of D. A. Thomas, onetime Liberal member of Parliament concerned with the Welsh coal miners.

"So did I," said Dorothy Conner, the young lady at her side, who had concluded that the trip was not really so "dull" after all.

Then, before their eyes, a clumsy sailor let the bow line on one lifeboat loose before the stern, allowing it to hang momentarily. Half the occupants were dumped into the water. Others, stronger and with quicker reflexes, saved themselves by hanging onto seats, gunwales, anything until the little craft was leveled again.

148

Lady Margaret turned away, commenting that it was "not safe to look at horrible things." Then she observed to Dorothy that the others, still wandering about the heavily listing deck, reminded her of "a swarm of bees who do not know where the queen has gone."

Not even the master of the liner was proving a good substitute for a queen bee. Turner, observing the confusion from the bridge wing, cupped his hands and shouted:

"Lower no more boats! Everything is going to be all right!"

His not wholly convincing assessment was followed up by a crewman, nattily clad in a double-breasted warm jacket, moving down among the passengers and swinging a revolver. He was waving people away from the boats.

Archie Donald, on the sloping starboard side, now almost awash, watched a fireman poised momentarily on the railing before he dived gracefully into the ocean. The young Canadian, impressed, then decided it was time to follow suit.

First he removed his wristwatch and put it in his left-hand trouser pocket. In the unreality of the moment, it seemed to him the timepiece would not get so wet there.

Before he leaped, his attention was gripped by the actions of several other passengers—first a middle-aged man who meticulously had stripped off the clothing of his wife until she was down to her stockings. Then he folded a lifejacket around her and tied its strings.

On Donald's other side was a familiar man with long gray hair and a big floppy hat. Although Archie Donald did not know him personally, it was apparent that he was Elbert Hubbard, and the woman with him his second wife, Alice.

Donald heard Hubbard politely refuse to be assisted into a boat. It was not out of character in the man who had penned among his voluminous writings and *bon mots,* "We are here now, some day we shall go. And when we go we would like to go gracefully."

Farther down the deck, Timmins, the cotton man, gallantly was assisting a group of women from steerage, who appeared to

149

be speaking in some Balkan language. As he leaned over to kiss one of their hands, he said reassuringly: "All right. All right!"

Momentarily fascinated by the kaleidoscope of types and their reactions to this drama, Archie Donald forgot about jumping.

Oliver Bernard was also distracted, first by the sight of Alfred Gwynne Vanderbilt, dressed in a dark pinstripe suit, dreamily holding what appeared to be a lady's large jewel case. To the opera house scenic artist it was as if the millionaire were waiting "for the next race at Ascot."

In the next instant, Vanderbilt saw that Bernard was observing him, grinned "as if amused by the excitement," then lit a cigarette.

The artist concluded there might not be enough lifeboats to go around. He made his way up to the highest eminence of the ship, the narrow Marconi deck above the boat deck and looked down with a certain detachment on the scene below him, all the more macabre since the background strains of the "Blue Danube" waltz, which the orchestra had played at lunch in first class, still throbbed through his mind.

Aboard the U-20, Schwieger made another log entry:

> Great confusion on board. Boats being cleared and some of them lowered to the water. They must have lost their heads. Many boats crowded, came down bow first or stern first in the water and immediately fill and sink. . . .

The German submarine captain could have no doubt now of his victim, if he ever had, since he hurried a further notation to be incorporated later in his action report:

> . . . in front appears the name *Lusitania* in gold letters.

Certainly, contrary to the U-boat log, not all on board had lost their heads. Charles Frohman, the producer, was heard to say, as he removed his own lifebelt and placed it around a woman nearby who appeared quite hysterical, "Why fear death? It is the most beautiful adventure in life."

Theatergoers would have recognized the philosophy as a line from James Barrie's *Peter Pan*.

Like the *Empress* and all the other passenger ships that developed a list approaching the horizontal, the *Lusitania*'s high side, the port, became useless. Lifeboats hung from their davits against the steel sideplates of the liner as though they had been designed to lie there, securely, defying any attempts to move them farther.

Those that were launched all came from the low starboard. Archie Donald, for one, waited no longer for a boat, on either side. He asked a steward to help him tighten his lifebelt strings, put his money—the equivalent of $40—in the top of a sock, then bent farther to remove his shoes.

The creakings of the ship, the shrillings of people made him realize there might not be time even for this last preliminary to a swim. He jumped, shoes and all.

When he recovered from the first chill of the experience and bobbed back to the surface, he was aware of a "most marvelous revelation," actually an illusion of speed. He stroked almost effortlessly, since the life preserver supplied all the buoyancy, motivated by the single desire to put as much distance between himself and the Cunarder as possible.

Momentarily he paused, amused at the sound and sight of a bedraggled group huddled on a half-sunken raft bellowing, like so many tipplers in a pub, "Tipperary."

James Brooks, an automobile chain salesman from Bridgeport, Connecticut, dove in also without bothering to take off his shoes. To "Jay," a Maine native, the 50-degree temperature felt surprisingly "mild," much warmer than the Androscoggin he had known as a boy had ever been.

It was not quite ten minutes after the torpedoing. In the wheelhouse, Captain Turner saw that the inclinometer measured a list of 30 degrees.

151

"Save yourself!" he ordered his quartermaster, then looked around to see who else might be on the bridge or the Marconi deck.

There were a few, including Oliver Bernard, who watched with a singular sense of remoteness one of the wireless operators—now that there was no more auxiliary electric power—balancing against a rail while holding a small camera.

"What a snap this will make!" he exclaimed.

One of the life boats that had dumped its occupants into the sea floated near, still secured to one davit. The uppermost deck was *that* close to the water. The scenic artist grabbed it, then helped the radioman, D. A. Thomas, the Welsh patron of the coalminers, and others into it.

Someone found an ax and hacked at the rope until the boat swung clear.

The great ship, however, was almost ready for her final plunge. From a distance, Archie Donald wiped the stinging salt out of his eyes, then blinked. The propellers and sixty-ton rudder of the *Lusitania* towered in midair. Some passengers and crew still clinging like steeplejacks to the sternmost deck looked down in fright at the half-sunken ship, the waters dark with people, boats, and debris—all far below them.

There she hung, her bow already on the bottom, three-hundred feet down, compared with the vessel's 790-foot length. Bill Turner, already in the water, believed the liner momentarily "quivered her whole length," in those her very final death agonies.

She did not quiver much longer, as Donald heard an "explosion and rattling of all loose material leaving her deck." The liner settled a bit sideways, her stern pointed shoreward. As she turned over, she dumped more and more of her occupants into the water.

Timmins, the cotton merchant, went below under a Niagara Falls cascading around the superstructure, so deeply that his wet surroundings were "black as the inside of a cow."

Two passengers, a man and Margaret Gwyer, the bride of the Canadian minister, had the incredible experience of being drawn into the funnels as they drew level with the sea, and then hurled out again from the force of underwater explosions.

Margaret sailed into the air, much like a circus performer catapulted from a cannon, and landed in the water near her husband's boat. She survived, as did the other man, who Captain Turner observed to be "swimming like ten men, he was so scared!"

Now, George Kessler, the wealthy wine dealer, turned to look at the frothing circle of water, the clutter of boats, debris, and people. He lay down on his oars, stared for a moment, then murmured:

"My God, the *Lusitania*'s gone."

All others who had survived her death convulsions, less than fifteen minutes in time, were momentarily struck dumb by the same feeling of disbelief: this huge liner, the first of her type to have steam turbines, winner of the Blue Riband, the fastest vessel on the North Atlantic . . . gone like the rustiest, most unseaworthy old tramp steamer.

No more would Turner think that "talk of torpedoing" was much of a "joke."

That one torpedo which had accomplished this Pompeiilike immolation equally surprised the Cunarder's executioner, Kapitänleutnant Schwieger, who was writing a final log entry:

Go to 11 meters and take look around. In the distance astern are drifting a number of lifeboats. Of the *Lusitania* nothing is to be seen. The wreck must lie off Old Head of Kinsale Lighthouse, 14 sea miles distant. . . . The shore and lighthouse are clearly seen.

Those in the "number of lifeboats" were experiencing entirely mixed fortunes:

Lorna Pavey, for one, who had been enjoying her grapefruit when the ship was struck, was helping seamen and others to bail out their little craft, some using shoes. In the excitement of it all, no one had replaced the plug in the keel, normally left

153

out so that rain water wouldn't flood when carried in the davits.

Lorna had had a curious descent into the water, almost parachutelike, after her ample skirt nicely ballooned out. It had been rather fun, she reflected as she bailed.

Archie Donald hauled himself into a partly damaged, collapsible boat, filled to overflowing with a "most motley" assortment of thirty-four persons—passengers and crew, men and women. It was "a most terrible thing to see the people struggling for their lives" and yet not be able to assist any more aboard.

Archie did his best to set a course toward the beckoning, beautiful lighthouse even though no one knew the least about rowing. One occupant was complaining so ceaselessly about his money and his "bonds" that Donald finally tapped him on the head with an oar.

The man then sulked at his gunwales position.

Elizabeth Duckworth, who had been praying, now translated hopes into action when the petty officer in command of her boat indicated they couldn't pick up a swimmer nearby in the water.

"Oh, yes, we can!" snapped the sturdy weaver from Taftville, rolling back her sleeves to expose a pair of formidable biceps.

"Cease rowing!" ordered the officer.

Elizabeth assisted the nearly drowned passenger into the lifeboat, then took an oar herself. Her roommate, Alice Scott, had drowned before her eyes, but Arthur, her son, who Elizabeth had helped into another boat, was well on his way to safety.

Theodate Pope, of Farmington, Connecticut, en route to a spiritualist convention in London, was not, like many others, spoiled by the relative extravagance of a small boat. Although her lifeboat sustained her, she had first fought off a man who clung, like an oversized ape, to her shoulders. A wave drew him off.

Another man passing close by was a ludicrous sight. Apparently he had wrapped two belts about his body and hips since he was floating high in the water.

154

"Do you see any rescue ships coming?" Miss Pope asked, thinking the fellow survivor was blessed with an Olympian perspective. He touched a hand to his forehead, looked solemnly around, then replied:

"No."

Someone else floated past on a piano, another on a huge tin can, several men clutched a raft trying to sing, "Tipperary," perhaps the same chance gathering heard by Donald.

Margaret Mackworth, the suffragist, was buoyed by varied wreckage, finally a wicker chair. Sailors of the fishing boat *Bluebell,* who rescued her, unconscious, had the impression she was rocking across the waves on it.

Oliver Bernard, in his lifeboat, and Elizabeth Duckworth, still mightily rowing hers, were the first to reach the nearest fishing boats. Bernard's was towing two collapsibles and a raft—a sea train carrying nearly 150 souls.

Elizabeth, however, refused to be helped onto the rescue smack by the fishermen. With several volunteers, she started back toward the scene of the sinking.

Still somewhere over the horizon was Admiral Hood with his Queenstown patrol and the three steamships that had answered the distress call.

About 3:45 P.M. and within thirteen miles of the *Lusitania's* last position, the *Narragansett* sighted a periscope, then a torpedo wake slicing through the sunny waters just astern. Captain Charles L. Harwood, concluding that the SOS had been merely a ruse, ordered course changed away from the Irish coast.

It did not much matter. The survivors were reaching tugs and the fishing fleet.

Sunset, and the harbor waters off Queenstown were a mirror as the rescue fleet began to arrive. The small vessels glided swiftly past the Royal Dock Yard and the Royal Yacht Club. There was a vague aroma of food and peat fires.

Survivors such as Archie Donald were busy tending to others in more desperate condition as the vessels neared the quays. The tug *Flying Fish* stood offshore for what seemed hours

155

to her passengers while blinking back and forth for permission to berth in a slip she did not generally use. It appeared to Bernard, for one, that the red tape they encountered, in harbor traffic and customs, displayed the "magnificent unconcern" of the shore officials.

As skiffs swarmed alongside, survivors obtained the impression that no one was particularly surprised that the *Lusitania* had been sunk.

An old man in a rowboat remarked, matter-of-factly, "She's been waitin' for ye for days."

Other remarks revealed that submarines had been sighted in bays such as Glandore, Dunmanus, and Dingle with a regularity that hinted at their always having been there.

When finally the tug *Julia* came alongside, a doctor stepped aboard. He examined Theodate Pope, who had been in the water almost four hours, in the captain's cabin, then called two sailors to assist her ashore. They made a chair out of their locked hands. Failing to hold onto their shoulders as they lifted her, she almost fell over backward.

The captain of the *Bluebell* asked Margaret Mackworth if she was ready to disembark. Seized with a sudden modesty, she protested she had only her "tiny" blanket for covering, but might manage a couple of safety pins. This brought "hoots of laughter" from the sailors. Someone produced a "British warm" soldier's greatcoat. Wearing this and the captain's carpet slippers, she started up the gangway.

"I must have been pretty weak," she recalled, "for I had to get down on my hands and knees and crawl onto it. At the other end of the gangway my father was waiting."

Captain Turner, wrapped in a blanket like some solemn Indian chieftain, was recognized as he padded off. A restrained chorus of cheers arose from the Irish townspeople.

A male survivor leaped onto the wooden barrier at the gangway of the pier. Shouting hysterically, he seemed to think he was back on the *Lusitania*. Two policemen finally pulled him down.

Wesley Frost, the American consul at Queenstown, waited at the strangely hushed wharves. Appalled by what he saw, Frost reported:

> We saw the ghastly procession of these rescue ships as they landed the living and the dead that night under the flaring gas torches along the Queenstown water front. The arrivals began soon after eight o'clock and continued at close intervals until about eleven o'clock.
>
> Ship after ship would come up out of the darkness and sometimes two or three could be just described awaiting their turns in the cloudy night to discharge bruised and shuddering women, crippled and half-clothed men and a few wide-eyed little children. . . .
>
> Women caught at our sleeves and begged desperately for word of their husbands, and men with choking efforts of matter-of-factness moved ceaselessly from group to group, seeking a lost daughter or sister or even bride.
>
> Piles of corpses like cordwood began to appear among the paint kegs and coils of rope on the shadowy old wharves. Every voice in that great mixed assemblage was pitched in unconscious undertones, broken now and then by painful coughing fits or suppressed hysteria. . . .

Of the 1,959 who had sailed on the *Lusitania,* 1,198 had perished, including 785 passengers.

Of the 159 Americans aboard, 124 had died. Of the 129 children, only thirty-five survived. All but 4 of the infants in arms of this number were lost.

The multi-millionaire Vanderbilt was not among the survivors, neither was Elbert Hubbard and his wife, Charles Frohman, the producer, and others whose names had the ring of easy familiarity in 1915.

The outrage in America, already giddy from "Preparedness Parades" was predictable. The New York *Sun* depicted Kaiser Wilhelm fastening a medal around the neck of a mad dog, as a small flag labeled *Lusitania* disappeared beneath the sea. The Philadelphia *North American* caricatured Hohenzollern as a roaring monster drowning a woman with his own hands.

An "appalling crime . . . contrary to international law and the conventions of all civilized nations . . . wholesale murder," thumped the coroner's jury at Kinsale.

Captain Turner himself was exonerated by Lord Mersey, sitting on his third major ship disaster commission in as many years.

"Will" Turner, however, would survive a transport sinking barely a year and a half later before Cunard decided their skipper had used up his luck and then some. He was put on shore duties.

Meanwhile, "Lucky" Tower, who had lived through the sinking of the *Titanic* and the *Empress of Ireland,* found that fortune still smiled in his direction. He had managed to swim away from the mortally crippled *Lusitania* and be picked up by one of the rescue boats.

Scarcely two months after the *Lusitania* went down within sight of the Irish coast, Americans were stunned anew—this time by another inland waterway disaster that almost rivaled in casualties the *General Slocum* accident. The steamer *Eastland,* on July 24, carrying twenty-four hundred persons bound for a Western Electric Company picnic, capsized even as a tug was drawing her away from her Chicago River pier, at LaSalle Street, in the heart of the great city.

A total of 835 persons, the majority of them woman and children, died in this seemingly inexcusable disaster of a top-heavy excursion vessel. As in the case of the *General Slocum,* whole families were wiped out. Police and undertakers, calling at more than one residence to inquire about the disposition of a body or bodies, knocked and knocked—and received no answer.

This was sheer waste of life. The sacrifice of those aboard the *Lusitania* added up to a great deal more.

There now ensued a succession of "Wilson notes" in which the President of the United States demanded with increasing force that Imperial Germany provide guarantees of neutral rights.

War clouds grew darker. On January 31, 1917, Germany announced her policy of unrestricted submarine warfare. Less than a month later another torpedoed Cunarder, the *Laconia,* went down in a snowstorm off the Old Head of Kinsale. Mrs. Mary Hoy and her daughter Elizabeth, of Chicago, froze to death in a lifeboat. They were among the 22 who perished out of a total of 289 aboard.

Incidents such as this hastened President Wilson's decision to arm American merchant vessels. On March 17, three medium-sized American freighters, the *City of Memphis, Vigilancia,* and *Illinois* were torpedoed in the war zone. A total of twenty-four Americans were lost.

Other ships followed the three to the bottom, while still more Americans perished.

Finally, on April 2, at 8:30 P.M., President Wilson went before a hushed Senate Chamber to ask that the existence of a state of war with Germany be declared. It was Monday, in Holy Week. By Good Friday the House of Representatives had completed the ratification. And at 1:13 P.M. that Friday Wilson signed the declaration, expressing his conviction that "America has found herself."

159

14.

The VESTRIS

. . . SOMEWHERE ON THE WESTERN FRONT A FORMER OILER, Frank Tower, settled down with the rest of "the forces" to trench warfare's muddy tedium.

The Liverpool newspapers had revealed that "Lucky" Tower had managed to survive his third major ship disaster. When he attempted to sign on another vessel, the crew—to a man—walked off. The same thing happened on his second try.

It was bad enough sitting with the rats and lice, wondering if the next "Jerry" shell had "your number." Fortunately, for the men in Tower's platoon none of them yet knew his terrible secret: He was a jinx.

And there the trail of "Lucky" Tower ended. None ever saw him again in the old waterfront haunts of Liverpool or Southampton. Yet, there was nothing to prove that he did not survive the war.

Meanwhile, Germany was having her troubles against the combined military might of Britain, France, and the United States.

Before very long, the Kaiser, Chancellor von Bethmann-Hollweg, Admiral von Tirpitz, and others of a tottering Fatherland's doomed leadership would concede that if the *Lusitania,* as a Royal Navy auxiliary, were a legitimate prize, her torpedoing had been one of history's supreme political blunders. It is more than likely that America would have gotten into the conflict sooner or later, but certainly the role of the sunken Cunarder in hastening our direct involvement could not be overlooked. Finally, after endless months of trench warfare, the vast carnage ended on November 11, 1918.

The years moved on, bringing a sense of disillusionment among many discerning people who sensed that it had been a war which probably, after all, was not going "to end war." Meanwhile, wherever one went, one heard the hedonistic cry of "back to normalcy." Then came the Roaring Twenties with jazz, the Charleston, prohibition, booze, bootleggers, big-time crime, flappers, raccoon coats, and the rising influence of the automobile in an economy that suddenly began to burgeon.

Yet anachronistically, like some hand-me-down in the corner, yesterday's "things" still predominated: stucco houses from the early 1900s, cumbersome trolley cars, heavy telephone sets, and men's double-breasted suits and straw hats. True, the style in automobiles and airplanes was changing, but not in ships. Most of the freighters and passenger liners that butted and smoked their way across the Seven Seas either had been witness to blackout and convoys of the war or had been constructed during it.

One example was the 10,494-ton Lamport and Holt liner *Vestris*, out of Liverpool, a coal burner that steamed into service in 1912. A trim-appearing, single-stacker with comfortable accommodations, the British cargo carrier had borne a charmed life. In January, 1915, she boiled into New York harbor under a forced head of steam, having outrun the German cruiser *Karlsruhe*.

In May, shortly before the *Lusitania* went down, the *Vestris* ducked a submarine's torpedo in those same fatal Irish waters. She carried beef to France from Argentina and troops in the Mediterranean for the remainder of the conflict.

Her luck almost ran out in September, 1919, when a serious cargo fire erupted. She safely made St. Lucia, in the West Indies, where the blaze was extinguished.

On a blustery "mean" Saturday afternoon, November 10,

161

1928, *Vestris* quit her usual pier in Hoboken for another run to Barbados, Rio, and, finally, Buenos Aires. It was her Christmas voyage. There was something unique, if not actually exotic about this route and, indeed, the ships that plied it, the Lamport and Holt Line told its customers. In fact that morning their advertisement in the New York papers started:

> For the traveler who wishes a change from the conventional. . . .

On board were 198 crewmen and 127 passengers, including a number of families with their children, heading home for the December holidays, at least one honeymooning couple, members of the diplomatic corps, businessmen, and a sprinkling of vacationers who merely sought such a "change" as was suggested by the steamship line.

Edward F. Johnson, thirty-five-year-old Standard Oil Company attorney, of Scarsdale, New York, en route to Trinidad, was among the representatives of industry. His wife, Katharyn, remaining at their Webster Avenue residence to care for a young son and daughter, nonetheless saw her husband off. Especially impressed by the near-shining quality of the holystoned decks, she concluded that "Ed" couldn't have picked a sturdier ship for his voyage.

A minority on the pier waving goodbye held rather vague contrary opinions, wondering if the *Vestris* showed a slight port list. It was true she had been overloaded by some two hundred tons; beneath her Plimsoll line was six thousand tons of cargo, including automobiles, and three thousand tons of bunker coal and half that weight in water.

William J. Carey, her stocky, jowly sixty-year-old master, expressed no doubts, however, but what his command was in trim. Making his final voyage before transfering to a sister vessel, the *Voltaire*, he considered the ship seaworthy in all respects.

He was joined in this confidence by a seasoned traveler, William W. Davies, American correspondent of *La Nacion*, of

Buenos Aires. All in all, Davies would comment, the voyage had commenced "very auspiciously."

By supper, the outlook was slightly less auspicious. A strong northeast wind called in strident voice from out of the Atlantic's blackness.

While the bridge did not log it as gale force, the sea kicked up was sufficient to send glasses and plates scurrying across tables. Children began to cry and mothers paled perceptibly as they started for their cabins along the passageways of this aging vessel.

Slowly, the port list assumed its counterpart to starboard. As the black evening wore on, Paul A. Dana, the tall South American representative of the Radio Corporation of America, perceived the intensity to be accelerating until "we were in the worst storm I ever saw on the sea."

"It was late that night," he added, "perhaps a little after midnight—that two big waves hit her almost simultaneously, bow and stern. The ship quivered from end to end. You could almost feel her wrenching."

Alfred Duncan, the second steward, steadied himself on deck against the spindrift and wind to peer out. He concluded that the *Vestris* was being "jolted with troughs fifty feet deep."

Sunday morning, the "moment" Dana walked from his cabin, he began to feel uneasy.

"The *Vestris* was listing," he later recalled. "I had been on steamers before that listed, but I had never seen quite such a list. It looked bad.

"In the dining saloon I ran into Captain Frederick Sorenson [of the Merchant Marine] and we started to talk things over. He did not like that list either. Inasmuch as he was a sailor, I decided he must know what he was talking about—that he was a good man to stay with."

Because of the rough seas and the severe rolling of the ship, only four other passengers besides Dana appeared in the dining saloon for breakfast.

Topsides, beside the chart table, behind the helm, the inclinometer registered a steady list of 5 degrees to starboard.

163

Because of the mounting winds, such a list was considered normal, even by passengers deprived of their appetites.

William Davies, the correspondent, was not among their number. He entertained the idea that the off-center attitude was "rather alarming." With questioning eyes, he watched his fellow travelers feeling their way about deck "at a queer angle to keep their feet, and laughing with each other as some of the minor officers assured them that the list would be corrected in an hour or so."

It was not. By Sunday afternoon, few people were seen out of their cabins. Most, according to Paul Dana, had become "violently seasick . . . in their bunks." Soon, he noted, "the list had become so pronounced that all the furniture that wasn't fastened down in the dining saloon and in the smoking room had slid over to the starboard side, where it was crashing around as the ship rolled."

The *Vestris,* as Davies seconded, "was clearly at the mercy of the waves." It seemed singularly disquieting to him since the liner was rolling more heavily than in tempo to the size of the turbulent seas.

The correspondent would report that about four o'clock

I was lying on my berth in my cabin while Sidney S. Koppe (a New York newspaper publisher's representative) was reading in an opposite berth. We were joking about the way the ship was rolling when suddenly a heavy sea broke in the windows carrying all the glass and sash clear across my bed, absolutely swamping the cabin. I called the steward and he gave us a cabin on the opposite side of the ship while they tried to clear up the one I formerly occupied. That was on the port side, while the list was to starboard.

When we shifted over to the starboard cabin we found the floor was sloping so badly that it was extremely difficult to walk about.

On Sunday night the list was too great to eat in the dining room. There were a few people gathered there. While we were eating, the boat gave a sudden, startling lurch and almost every table in the dining saloon was swept from its base and thrown across the room. Food and chairs were scattered in all directions.

Ed Johnson, of Scarsdale, at the table of Chief Engineer J. A. Adams, was not a little startled when a waiter was catapulted over his shoulder onto the table. Then, along with the wreckage of plates and glasses, assorted food and beverage, the crew member tumbled down hard to the floor.

The *Vestris* continued to "roll and roll" until Johnson wondered "if she was ever going to stop." Slowly, after what seemed endless moments of silent terror, the ship began to recover. But she did not return to even keel.

To the son of a Chesapeake Bay captain, as Ed was, and himself a onetime summer purser on the same old sidewheelers, this was scarcely reassuring.

There next issued a rumbling from somewhere forward. The diners could not know its origin. The crewmen berthed in the fo'c'sle did. Three of the crated automobiles had been hurled through a bulkhead into the living space.

Davies decided to continue the meal in his cabin. He obtained a plate of cold meat and left. En route, the correspondent encountered one of the crewmen, who insisted all would be "corrected." He obviously was not among those confronted by the vehicles.

Two of the ship's company, twenty-nine-year-old Chief Wireless Operator Michael O'Laughlin, and the second operator, James MacDonald, stuck it out, although the latter would admit he was "struggling with the fish" to keep it on the table. Topsides, the third Marconiman, Charles Verchere, on only his second trip to sea, had been hurled out of his chair at least once.

Dana was another who tried not to allow a plunging ship to upset his supper and his evening. With his Merchant Marine acquaintance, he wedged himself into a corner of the smoking lounge and put away a couple of whiskeys and sodas.

Feeling "a little better," the RCA representative retired

about 10 P.M. He became in likelihood the only soul aboard to be pampered with a good sleep.

It was foul sailing on much of the North Atlantic that night. To the east, Europe-bound, the *Mauretania,* sister of the lost *Lusitania,* reported she was bucking gales that gusted up to eighty miles an hour.

Ed Johnson, like the majority aboard, found it "very difficult to stay in bed. Sleep was almost impossible with the creaking of the ship and the howling of the winds."

Others were too uneasy to undress or lie down at all. William C. Quiros, of the Argentina consulate, New York, had been in bed feeling "the *Vestris* dance to the rhythm of the waves" and listening to "the tune of the throbbing engines."

He dozed only to be "abruptly awakened by shock. An empty bed, which faced my own had been torn loose from its fastenings. My watch and other articles which were on my night table had crashed to the floor.

"I put on my shoes and trousers and went out on deck. It may have been ten or eleven o'clock. I met an officer who when I pressed him for information told me that everything was okay. He advised me to go back to bed, so I did."

At midnight, Chief Engineer Adams had reason to believe matters were much less than "okay." He called the bridge to report that he was "holding the water," although the bunkers were "full of water and the bulkheads leaking."

At 4 A.M. a concerned Captain Carey personally visited the engine room, asking, "How are things down here?"

"Things look pretty bad," Adams answered.

The master ordered three ballast tanks pumped out. This was done. Instead of bringing the ship back to even keel, the operation only worsened her list.

All on the starboard side awoke Monday, if indeed they had slept at all, to the unnerving sight of water on a level with their portholes. Ed Johnson had been disturbed several times before daybreak by the unusual phenomenon of having sheets and blankets slide off the bed. When he finally aroused himself, he

166

looked at the curtains, still on their rods but hanging halfway across the cabin.

Perhaps more perplexing was the eerie, almost unreal quiet that pervaded the ship. There were no sounds of people, no throb from the engines. He mused if, somehow, he were the only human left aboard the *Vestris*.

Paul Dana, the sturdy sleeper, opened his eyes to watch water actually forcing through the port and "swishing around on the floor." He summoned the steward who arrived holding a badly wrenched shoulder from bailing with a bucket the night through. The steward volunteered that there "was apparently a leak." It seemed apparent.

With unaffected appetite, Dana ate a banana brought by the steward, dressed and made his way with considerable difficulty to the port bow deck.

Davies, glancing out of his porthole, found "it was like looking at the bottom of a well. The list was so great that I could not see the horizon at all. It was very difficult to stand upright."

Through his opened door, he noticed one passenger who seemingly was not unduly perturbed: a child, laughing and cooing, in a perambulator that was tied against a wall handle.

When Johnson came on deck he observed "knots of people talking in whispers." Still, he remained to be convinced of how serious conditions really were until he saw that the canvassed hatches had been opened and the crew was struggling to hurl odd items of cargo overboard.

There was no steam on the winches, necessitating the use of muscle power.

Dana later observed:

> It looked like bales of cloth and such stuff. They couldn't get rid of the heavier things like automobiles. A little crowd of men stood up there, leaning over the railing and watching the crew.
>
> Some of them had come with their life preservers on. They looked badly scared. Although I had dressed myself that morning with the idea that I'd probably have to leave the ship before

167

the day was over, I tried not to take such a dark view of the thing. Some of us did what we could to cheer the more timid ones—told them this was just a precaution, and so on.

The sky had cleared during the night and now the sun was shining brightly. The wind was still blowing, however—and those towering, black waves looked forty feet high.

"Well, anyway, we've got a nice day to be wrecked on," one of the men remarked with a grin.

Officers were going about, cheery but noncommittal. I went into the smoking room for a little while that morning, and tried to read and divert my mind. I thought I heard the radio sort of sputtering.

Once I went back to my cabin to try to rescue my money that I had left in a trunk; no use, the trunk was under water and wedged under my bunk. I got my passport, stuck a pack of cigarettes in my pocket, and left—for good.

The ship kept on tipping. It looked to me as though she had a list of 45 degrees. You could hardly walk on the deck. The women and children were brought up, and were told to put on life preservers. Still, we got no definite information from the officers or crew.

William Quiros, the Argentine consul, one of the distinguished passengers, contemplated the spectacle of seamen bailing water from the lower decks with buckets. Although this struck him as a rather futile undertaking, he made his way to the bridge to ask the master if there actually were any danger.

"No danger at all," the latter replied. "We shall have this trouble over soon, then everything will be all right."

Quiros, disregarding the ostensible optimism, returned for his life preserver, assuring himself the while that he was not really "afraid, but cautious."

While Quiros was on the bridge, Second Mate J. O. Bolger had asked O'Laughlin to flash a "CQ," simply meaning that other ships should "stand by" their wireless receivers. This was 8:37 A.M.

Davies, who had gone to the wireless shack to transmit a story of the *Vestris'* troubles, had to wait because of the stand-by.

He sat down on the steel decking and clamped his legs firmly around a table.

Then, a few minutes before 10 A.M., Bolger strode into the wireless cabin again and told O'Laughlin to go ahead and send for help:

"Vestris in distress. . . !" This was followed by her approximate position, about 240 miles east of Norfolk.

An unusually large number of ships within a 150-mile radius picked up the message. These included the Hamburg-American liner, *Berlin,* the *Santa Barbara,* of the Grace Line, the *American Shipper,* of the United States Lines, and the battleship *Wyoming,* accompanied by five destroyers.

A small freighter, the *Montoso,* steamed some thirty miles distant. She carried no radio. Not being a passenger vessel she was not required to be so equipped.

The Navy had in effect been waiting for such a call since Sunday. The Naval Radio Compass Station at Bethany Beach, Delaware, had plotted all night, with radio fixes, the Lamport and Holt liner's positions. Since she was making such little headway, it became obvious that the ship was in trouble.

Within a few minutes, at least half a dozen vessels had altered course to push themselves through heavy seas toward the *Vestris.* None, however, who heard the SOS could arrive much sooner than twelve hours' time.

Even the dirigible *Los Angeles,* at Lakehurst, was ordered to make a try, in spite of the exceptionally "dirty" flying weather. The Coast Guard dispatched the cutter *Davis.*

Along the coast, commercial radio stations as far north as New York went off the air so as not to risk interference, even though their frequencies differed from the "short wave" adopted by ships. Housewives, storekeepers, the sick and aged, all began to wonder what had happened to their noon programs: baritones and orchestrals, news and stock market reports, cooking recipes and gardening hints.

Captain Carey, deliberate as ever, was not quite ready to

169

abandon. On the bridge with him, Duncan, the second steward, marveled how the master "gave his orders unexcitedly. He instructed that the lifeboats be stocked with proper food and water and that assurance be given there was no need for excitement."

"Are they well provisioned?" Carey asked. "Is everything well for the women and children?"

Duncan, aware that the boats were *not,* scurried to the pantries of the three classes, snatching up cans of Fig Newtons, bananas, and all the cracker tins he could find. He moved between clusters of women, some holding or carrying children, being assisted by other stewards into their lifebelts.

"The ladies were wonderful," Dana recalled as he remained on deck. "Some were crying quietly, but there was no hysteria. One of them held in her arms a baby not more than eight months old.

"All the children had been bundled up. They knew now that they probably would have to leave the ship.

" 'Isn't this fun?' I said to one little fellow with bright blue eyes trying to cheer him up. He looked at his mother who was crying and nodded—solemnly."

Meanwhile, within the past quarter of an hour, ships from Cape Farewell, the southern tip of Greenland, to the Cape of Good Hope knew that "HWNK," the identifying letters of the *Vestris,* was in trouble. The big RCA towers at Tuckerton, New Jersey, had picked up the distress call and repeated it in a many-times magnified Morse code voice.

At ten-twenty, the *Santa Barbara* advised that she could be abeam of the Lamport and Holt liner in nine hours. A few minutes later the Japanese freighter *Ohio Maru* called to say she was coming at full speed and should arrive at 5 P.M.

This seemed, at the very least, optimistic. The small vessel was 135 miles distant and at best couldn't coax more than twelve knots out of her old steam pistons.

O'Laughlin, barely able to sit at his transmitting table against the list and thrashing motion, tapped back, "rush at all speed to our side immediately!"

170

At 10:52 A.M., nearly an hour after the first SOS had spoken out over the Atlantic, Captain Carey informed Lamport and Holt's offices in New York:

Hove to since noon yesterday. Last night developed 32-degree list. Starboard decks under water. Ship lying on beam ends. Impossible to proceed anywhere. Sea moderately rough.

This message had the effect of peaking the curiosity of the Brooklyn Navy Yard who asked:

Please advise more details.

O'Laughlin spontaneously snapped back:

Oh, please come at once! We need immediate assistance!

At eleven-fifteen, the *Santa Barbara* broke in optimistically:

We have you on direction finder, dead ahead, 135 miles away . . . expect to reach you about 7 P.M. speed seventeen knots.

The *Montoso,* without a radio, even now was passing abeam of the *Vestris,* slightly over the westerly horizon.

At eleven-thirty a stranger joined the radio conversation— the White Star liner *Cedric,* well out in the Europe-bound lanes:

Do you need assistance?

O'Laughlin did not answer. Hardly able to hold the key, the perfectionist radioman transmitted an apology into the air for his possible blurred sending:

"It's the devil's work with this list. . . " He paused as Mac-Donald struggled to his side, with a note, then added, "getting lifeboats out now."

It was noon. The final rupture of the bunker bulkhead,

171

showering the "black gang" with coal, water, and steam, precipitated the master's order to abandon.

William Quiros, the Argentinian, could see the captain, "white-faced, without cap, on the hurricane deck . . . a broken man." To Johnson, he appeared "haggard, unshaven."

"Women and children to the right!" Carey shouted.

Quiros then watched, "a rush, and all women and children on board were soon lined up and placed in two boats . . . utterly lacking in ability to handle the boats, the crew were befuddled and were unable to disentangle the ropes which made the craft fast to the sides of the steamer."

Duncan, the second steward, saw the tableau against the backdrop of a ship at an almost impossible angle:

"It was an awful scene what with the weepings, pleadings and shoutings and dashing of waves over the now almost three-quarters-covered deck."

But, not all witnesses saw the drama in quite the same perspective.

"I watched the boats being lowered from the port side," Johnson, the lawyer, would report, "as other boats went over from the starboard side. The ship at the time was almost entirely on her starboard so that the port lifeboats went right against her hull.

"There was no disturbance. Everyone was calm and seemed particularly anxious to be of some assistance to someone else. Wives and husbands said goodbye and parted to their separate boats without display of emotion.

"Our lifeboat, Number 10 aft, had more than fifty in it when lowered. We were without officer or a sailor. It was with the greatest difficulty that we swung clear of the ship. One man had his hand crushed as the boat smashed against the steel side-plates. The ax provided was so dull it would not cut the davit rope which held the lifeboat to the larger vessel."

Fortunately, Captain Sorenson, the Merchant Marine officer, produced a jacknife. He managed to hack the tough hemp through.

172

With another group, Davies "walked aft. As the starboard rail was awash, it seemed almost impossible to board a boat there. Moreover, I got a fleeting glimpse through the sloping shaft that had been the midship deck of a boat being smashed up, so the prospects of getting aboard on that side did not seem very encouraging. We then went back to the captain and said there seemed to us to be room in the boat that was still hanging on the port side. He said, all right, that he would arrange for us to get aboard that."

Dana went off in No. 8 boat, which had to be patched with a piece of tin as it hung to its davits. The banging against the side of the liner had knocked a hole in the keel. With him were ten women and two children, about six and eight years old, and Clara Ball, a burly stewardess of many years at sea. She was wearing a heavy coat over her dress and sweater.

On the bridge Duncan was coaxing the captain to don his lifebelt and be prepared to join the rest in abandoning:

> I said, "Well Captain, here's a belt for you!" He merely stuck his hands in his overcoat pockets and rejoined, "Never mind about me, Duncan. Take the belt yourself and go!"

Davies and Quiros shared some of the master's innate reluctance to relinquish what was still habitable. Quiros had "heard that ships sometimes remain afloat several days." He thought that "by staying aboard we had a better chance to save our lives."

Cline F. Slaughter, a traveling auditor for International Harvester Company, refused to be separated from his wife. He had been standing on the now towering port side, holding her hand for an hour, watching the crew with legs canted against the immense list, trying to get the boats loose and over.

The terror in the seamen's eyes, as they waited, was something neither Slaughter nor anyone on board had ever before witnessed. Presently, the Slaughters were assisted into No. 4 boat, along with twenty-six women, ten children, six other men, and a few of the ship's personnel.

173

It bumped down the side, everyone clutching one another so they wouldn't be dumped out. Before it reached the water a heavy spar crashed through the middle, cracking the little craft in two. The water was filled with the dead and the living. The Slaughters were separated.

The clock was racing. At 1:17 P.M., the *Vestris* transmitted: "Can't wait any longer. Going to abandon."

O'Laughlin, who had turned over the key momentarily to MacDonald, asked Verchere for lifebelts. The latter soon returned with three, one of which he threw over his own shoulders.

MacDonald, turning to his chief operator, said he supposed he'd put his on "just to please Verchere." O'Laughlin wasn't that interested in obliging. He arranged it on his chair as a cushion against the slant.

Verchere, a drawn look on his face, was insistent.

"If you are going to take to the boats, you have to go now," he pleaded.

Duncan, too, remonstrated once more with Captain Carey. He still "wouldn't take the belt" even though the bridge was beginning to "sink into the water."

The second steward leaped off, holding the belt but without taking time to fasten the laces.

Five minutes after the last message, the first operator flashed:

Now taking to lifeboats.

Meticulous as always, O'Laughlin added,

Goodbye to WSC.

This was the RCA station at Tuckerton. After that he gave the signing off signal—"SK."

HWNK, the *Vestris,* had left the air.

"Time to go!" Quiros called to Davies, glimpsing the captain out of a corner of his eye, "standing to his post."

First Officer Johnson, about to dive off, heard the captain exclaim:

174

"My God! My God! I am not to blame for this!"

The *Vestris* "suddenly tilted," according to Davies. He found himself clinging to the rail which instead of being in its usual horizontal position was now absolutely perpendicular. His feet were dangling and it was hard to maintain his grasp of the rail.

"Below I saw a seething mass of water rushing up through the midship deck to meet me, carrying with it deck chairs and debris of all kinds."

The correspondent also obtained "a glimpse of the captain, who had been directing operations from the boat deck above the main promenade deck. He shouted, 'Goodbye, boys,' to such officers, crew, and passengers who were around him, clinging to the rails on the deck below.

"He was a tragic figure, without collar, unshaved, and showing every sign of having been on duty day and night. There was an awful hopelessness in his face as he shouted these words."

When the water was almost at his feet, Davies shook hands with Quiros and the two men jumped.

Striking out toward a boat—one of eight that had gotten away—Duncan looked back and saw that the greedy waves had already engulfed the bridge, while the captain had vanished.

For a moment, the liner—as it looked to Dana—was "lying entirely on her starboard side. Several members of the crew were walking on her port side, which was out of the water, and seemed to be making their way toward a lifeboat that was adrift."

The men, about forty in all, began to run, "racing madly down her side and diving off from her keel." In the madness of the moment, the pitiful spectacle seemed to be one of the "funniest things" Dana had ever witnessed.

His boat fell into the trough of a wave and when it rode up again, the crewmen and the lifeboat had all vanished from sight. The "funniest" scene had disappeared—a projection upon a screen that has been flicked off, as though there had never been a picture at all.

Davies, who had taken so long to surface he feared suffoca-

175

tion, heard "explosions, and it seemed one queer gulping sound as if some gigantic animal had swallowed too much water. A moment later the *Vestris* was out of sight but the surface of the sea was boiling with eddies. Passengers and crew were trying to cling to chairs, hatch covers, pieces of wood, and other wreckage."

Then, a "very quick drifting current" carried most of the survivors away before "the tremendous suction of the great liner could pull them down with it."

To Dana, the actual sinking was almost anticlimactic. According to his later account, the ship went "silently, with just a little puff of steam."

Slaughter thought the Lamport and Holt vessel had broken in the middle as she "glided under with dipping, horizontal motion forward." He tried swimming toward his wife, but "could make no headway. I was in one current and she in another. People were all separated that way . . . a great grinding of wreckage floating up and churning together."

A chicken coop floated past, and the auditor for International Harvester grabbed hold of it.

Dana's boat, already full of water, was turned topsy turvy by "a great black wave that looked one hundred feet high." All occupants were hurled into the water.

The RCA representative and the other men managed to right the boat, which still was buoyed by air tanks. Most of the women and children clambered back in.

However, the waves pounded it until the boat broke up and the air compartments floated off. The women and children disappeared.

Dana and Mrs. Ball, the stewardess, "with never a whimper" clung to a large piece of wreckage. The water he discovered to be "warm, warmer than you find in an indoor swimming pool." Then, he was surprised to notice an extra pair of shoes stuck in his companion's life preserver. She explained her feet were so narrow in relation to length that she was compelled to have her shoes especially made. Thus she did not want to lose them.

Davies, the newspaperman, once he recovered his breath from being underwater, found he could swim fairly well with the boost of his lifebelt.

He later asserted:

> I supported myself, by clinging first to a chair, then to part of a hatch, on which I scrambled, next to a piece of heavy timber which offered good support. In this boiling and seething mass of water and wood, I caught sight of my friend, Mr. Koppe, who was clinging to what looked like a small raft, but this may have been the top of a hatch. A heavy wave came along and I was hurled off the board to which I was clinging when it collided with a tightly wedged mass of heavy wreckage.
>
> I last saw Mr. Koppe floating on his heavy covering or raft as the current swirled us apart. I was able to look around me and I saw numbers of people swimming in the water, but most of the boats were standing off, apparently feeling that they had their full complement. I saw two boats which were cruising around in the wreckage, but they did not come very near. I found that I had time to shift from one piece of timber to another, until finally I reached a broken overturned boat. It was lying completely upside down in the water, and I managed to scramble on top of it, and from this position to look around. . . .
>
> How long I remained there I do not know, but it was possibly half or three-quarters of an hour. I hailed one boat which had picked up a man nearby, but they made no response. Then I saw another one making in my direction and I called to them and waved my arm. They came in within about twenty feet and said that they could not approach any nearer because of the danger of smashing the boat on the heavy timber floating about. They told me to swim. I managed to throw off my overcoat quickly and jumped into the water. As I got near the boat they handed me the end of a boat hook and lifted me aboard. I was suffering somewhat from cramp.
>
> Meanwhile I noticed two other boats cruising among the wreckage and picking up some of the men who were floating about. The boat that picked me up was smaller than most of the others. I understand it was known as the captain's boat.

Quiros, who had jumped with Davies, was invited into another boat by a fellow South American, "a young lady with

177

golden hair." When he saw it was too full already he declined, and struck off for another.

The golden-haired woman was, as a matter of fact, the Argentine-born bride of Orrion S. Stevens, the thirty-five-year-old assistant manager of a Buenos Aires branch of the First National Bank of Boston.

Quiros later wrote:

> The Negroes pulled me in. For a while we drifted. Other passengers came to our boat and were lifted in.
>
> When night came, the Negroes began to get uneasy. They rowed madly in all directions and sent rockets up in the sky. I thought it would have been better to remain still. Rowing made the boat cut the waves too sharply and we shipped a lot of water.
>
> There followed a procession of dreary hours. Cold, hungry and thirsty, I lay down. An Italian, a thin fellow, was shivering next to me. I went to sleep, but not for long. A kick in my shins brought me back to life. A giant Negro, sitting near me, was the donor of the kick. Why he did it I do not know. I know, however, that I got angry and let slip a number of words not fit for publication. The Negro began to tremble. "Now, man," he said, "don't swear just now. Please, man, don't swear."
>
> As time went by and not a ship appeared I began to have serious fears for our safety. We had more than a foot of water in the boat and I doubted that we could keep afloat very much longer. Just as I was putting my soul in the care of my Maker two steamers approached.

Dusk, then night came "awfully fast." All in Johnson's No. 10 boat began to think, reflexively, of rockets. Almost each one they could find under the seats was waterlogged and wouldn't light. It was about 10 P.M. when the first flare sizzled redly into the gloom.

The occupants bailed and bailed some more, all but one man who had sailed on the *Vestris* with his broken wrist in a cast. Attention focused on him every hour and at the half hour by the ringing of a pocket alarm or chime clock.

He was William P. Adams, a wealthy Iowa cattle raiser. He confided to Ed Johnson that he was a man of exact habits.

He liked to know what time it was and *where* he was, or *should* be, at a given moment.

Davies, in his boat, bespoke the reactions of many when he would observe, "There is no sign of anything—nothing but waves and skyline. If the night had been clear it would not have been so bad. But storms and rain, occasionally snow, made conditions almost unbearable."

When someone suggested it must be 2 A.M., another rejoined "No, it is about midnight." A third read the luminous dial of his watch and discovered it was only 9 P.M. The other occupants sighed and went on with their bailing.

Dana was not that well off. Every once in a while a fish brushed past him and he "squirmed." Then he and Mrs. Ball would salve their emotions by "cussing out Captain Carey for not getting those radio messages out earlier."

By midnight, perhaps sooner, many of the survivors noticed searchlights bouncing off the low clouds. This "seemed to cheer" the complement in Johnson's boat for it was obvious that help was near. One of the most persistent of the beams kept moving in such a way as to suggest the ship was following a square or "box" type search, compressing in the sides at each circuit.

Near 4 A.M. the Scarsdale attorney discerned the silhouette of a ship. But there were no more flares with which to signal.

In his boat, Quiros organized the castaways into a chorus. He counted "one, two, three," for them to hold their breaths, then in unison they would shout:

"Help!"

At exactly 4 A.M., Captain Schuyler Cummings, of the *American Shipper,* a veteran of at least two earlier rescues at sea, completed his "box" and hove to near a boat bearing twenty-one persons. Two men, one with leg fractures, together with a woman who had collapsed from exhaustion, were pulled on deck in a cargo net.

Now rain squalls punctuated by the illumination of intermittent lightning swept over the cold, predawn Atlantic coast.

Within the next three hours, Captain Cummings rescued

179

crewmen and passengers from five lifeboats. Some contained pitifully few persons, hinting that others had gained their safety after the sinking only to slip overboard again.

Johnson, on the *American Shipper,* was dressing in make-do clothes in the cabin assigned him when he saw through the porthole a woman floating, face down, "with her beautiful golden hair streaming on the water in front of her." The sight was at once compelling and shocking, even as she drifted almost like a wraith out of a dream, past the ship. Perhaps no one else had noticed her.

The lawyer knew who she was, though—the Argentinian bride of Orrion S. Stevens, the same young lady who had invited Quiros into her boat.

Indeed, Stevens had mentioned to Johnson when he also came aboard the *American Shipper* that he was not worried. She would "certainly be aboard another ship."

Cline Slaughter, the auditor for International Harvester, expressed the same faith about the fate of his wife.

Daybreak, according to Dana, had been the "worst moment for us. As dawn broke not a ship was in sight. And our piece of wreckage was beginning to break up. We had to hold it together while using it for support."

About ten o'clock, the pair sighted the battleship *Wyoming* at least twelve miles distant.

"How about it?" Dana asked Mrs. Ball. "Shall we swim for it?"

Without a word, the stewardess swam away toward an all but impossible horizon. Fortunately, the *American Shipper,* already with more than one hundred saved, had spotted the two from afar and sent a boat after them. Their heroic fight for survival was at last over after twenty hours in the Atlantic Ocean. And neither had caught so much as a head cold.

Their ordeal was at least equaled by that of Carl Schmidt, a Chicago passenger from third class, who was rescued by the *Berlin.* Others were picked up by the battleship *Wyoming* and the *Myriam.* Among those on the French tanker was Mrs. Cline

180

Slaughter. She happened to be observing her twenty-first birthday.

Ernest Smith, a refrigerating engineer, had dried out from his third sinking. The Liverpool crewman had been torpedoed twice in the war.

Coast Guard cutters and Navy destroyers retrieved a number of the bodies. These did not include the captain nor Wirelessman O'Laughlin who were missing.

It was all over. The stock-taking and fault-finding alone remained. Approximately one-third of those who had sailed—110 —had been lost. Not a child was saved, and only ten women, including Mrs. Ball, other stewardesses, and a laundress.

Whereas more than one out of every two passengers who had embarked died, only one out of four crewman perished.

This crew-passenger ratio was not so adversely pronounced as in the *Arctic,* of a few generations earlier, where a paying traveler's chances of survival had proven but one in twelve, contrasted with ship's company who won a better than one in three odds for survival.

On the *Titanic,* by contrast, 62 per cent of the passengers lived, nearly three times more favorable than the crew's adverse percentage.

The chivalry of the sea was proven once more to be a mercurial unknown when the natural and familiar order of things was challenged, then fragmented.

The press itself, which apparently had come, finally, to believe the shipping companies' boasts about their wares, was exceptionally dismayed. The New York *World* editorialized:

> When in a great modern harbor people go aboard of a good-sized steel ship of an old and well-known line, they have every good right to assume that it will not founder under stress of not unusual weather at sea.

The Boston *Post* added, with a weary sigh:

> We have learned nothing from a long succession of disasters. We shall probably learn nothing from this new tragedy of the sea.

181

Still, the New York *Telegram,* citing the twenty thousand already killed in automobile accidents the same year, held out the belief that "modern science . . . *can* conquer the sea."

The maritime writer, Karl Baarslag, castigated the "scandalously inadequate American radio laws," referring to the *Montoso.*

The British Board of Trade met for three months the following spring and early summer to hear testimony, consuming several working days' more time than the *Titanic* inquiry. Its members were dumbfounded, as they prefaced their final report:

> Speaking generally, the evidence is unsatisfactory, contradictory, inconsistent, and piecemeal. Much of it is unreliable, some of it untruthful.

However, they did find a stevedoring firm in New York "guilty of wrongful acts and default," including "overloading" and fined its officers $2,500, which represented court costs. The latter conceded with some relief that it was not too severe a decision at all.

The late master was not charged, although he was criticized for not sending out an SOS "six hours earlier." He also was found to be at fault for not loading passengers on "the lee side." Chief Engineer Adams was, as well, blamed—for not "sooner anticipating the vessel's fatal condition."

The London inquiry tended to agree with the Steamboat Inspection Service of the United States Department of Commerce that the *Vestris,* like the *Waratah,* was a "tender" or "negative" ship when overloaded. That is, her fulcrum, or vertical metacentric balance point, became off-center. This would be like a seesaw by rough comparison, which has slipped slightly in one direction making it likely that someone will be thrown off.

In this shaky state, a series of coincidences caused by the storm resulted in her destruction. These, it was theorized, started with water breaking scupper or drain pipes below the waterline, allowing the sea to surge into the coal bunkers in ever-increasing

182

quantity. Once they were broken, it was held possible that steel plating then tore away, increasing the diameter of the hole and the amount of water flow.

When a bulkhead or bulkheads broke under the crushing weight of water and coal at noon, the ship was doomed.

Dickerson N. Hoover, inspector-general of the service, who signed the report, then spoke in more philosophical vein:

> The thing that stands out most prominently in this disaster and the lesson first to be learned is that we must hereafter stress MEN more than THINGS.
>
> In this modern age we are prone to direct our efforts as far as possible toward the invention of mechanical devices that will make things safer, and this is true not only on ships but also on shore. As a result of it, I fear that we have come to unconsciously become the slaves of these things that we have invented to help us, forgetting that no matter how excellent a device there may be, there must be competent men to handle it, and this competency in men must be stressed at sea more than in any other place.

It rather intoned the epitaph for the *Vestris* and those who manned her.

15.

The Combustible Thirties:
GEORGES PHILIPPAR
and MORRO CASTLE

ONE WET, WINTRY MORNING IN PARIS, FEBRUARY 26, 1932, THE offices of the Compagnie des Messageries Maritime, 9 Rue de Sevres, received a phone call.

The Sûréte General—the French FBI—was advising this shipping line to the Far East that the $4 million, 21,000-ton *Georges Philippar,* sailing that day from Marseilles on her maiden voyage, might be blown up in Suez. An informer in the demi-monde of the Mediterranean waterfront had whispered of an overheard plot that related to the Sino–Japanese–Manchurian strife on the other side of the world.

The Sûréte was thanked. The Messageries Maritime was not, however, concerned because the cargo did not include items that would be of any interest to a provocateur. There was a small "quick-firing" gun and some cases of bullets consigned to Shanghai. Otherwise, the manifest read along customary, peaceful lines: caviar, perfumes, shoes, dresses, a few automobiles, and disassembled bicycles.

The all-white, funnel-less *Philippar* was not designed as a freighter. Her *raison d'être* for entering the Far East trade was to

184

carry people and in luxury. Every extravagance had been built into this 542-foot-long diesel ship. Named after the company's president, she replaced the *Paul Lecat* which had burned in her Marseilles drydock on New Year's Eve, 1929.

The deluxe cabins, complete with verandas, varied in French Renaissance decor. Possibly the Louis XV suite was the largest and most lavish with its carvings, polished walls, tapestries, and even chandeliers. It commanded a passage running into tens of thousands of francs.

The first-class smoking lounge featured a walled veranda recalling the Château de St. Germain de Livet, Calvados. The château motif dominated first class, making the *Philippar* a sort of floating Sans Souci.

The swimming pool "arena" was in harmony, offering a fresco inspired by Quellin's "Cupid Astride a Dolphin." The pool was of cassis stone and dark blue marble.

The nursery walls were adorned with paintings representing the life of Gargantua the Great, who looked like a great rubber balloon ape.

All in all, this posh eyrie of the carriage trade's sea set did not resemble a ship as known to most voyagers. The *Philippar's* first-class gaudiness outdid even the *Titanic's*, created as the former had been without a hint of British restraint.

Second and third classes were something else again.

Despite hints of sabotage, the *Philippar* sailed on schedule. Captain M. Vicq indicated that he placed little credence in the auguries. It was true that his mates had discovered some fire extinguishers mysteriously empty, but they had been refilled.

Several days out of Suez, the electric alarm rang in the gold bullion strong rooms, "for no accountable reason," as the fifty-four-old captain would log. Perhaps there was a short-circuit in the system. At the same time, a number of the storage batteries, used to power emergency lanterns, were found to be dry.

Nonetheless, the liner completed her outbound passage, arriving at Hong Kong on March 29 and Shanghai, April 1, where she remained eight days. She finished her calls to the Far East on May 2 when she sailed westward from Saigon, with approximately 600 passengers and a crew of 250. In her holds rested ten thousand sacks of mail.

Early Monday, May 16, the *Philippar* was nearing Djibouti, French Somaliland, from Colombo, Ceylon. Her position was ten miles off Cape Guardafui at the entrance to the Gulf of Aden, and thence the Red Sea.

Just before 2 A.M., Mrs. Leon Valentin, wife of a mining engineer working in Tientsin, returned to her deluxe "D" deck cabin after watching the Cape Guardafui light winking brighter and brighter. With all of the *Philippar*'s splendor, she depended only on air ports for ventilation, and it was stifling hot below decks in this western extremity of the sultry Arabian Sea.

"Typhoon breeder," the old salts might have observed in the China Sea. Here, in this northern part of the Indian Ocean, the weather was usually moist, everlastingly brooding.

As Mrs. Valentin lay down atop her bed and before she had reached for the mother-of-pearl wall switch, the central light group in the ceiling suddenly dimmed.

"I sensed that something was wrong," she would recall. "I went to ring for the steward but the bell switch dropped off the wall into my hand and the ends of the wires were hot."

The wife of the French mining engineer then ran from her cabin calling for a steward. She encountered one pumping a small hand extinguisher toward tongues of fire licking through a panel of the companionway. He explained to her that he had not rung the fire alarm—of which there were thirteen call buttons on "D" deck—for fear of disturbing the sleepers.

Scarcely reassured, Mrs. Valentin returned once more to her cabin to find it already filling with smoke and to hear "the wires crackling inside the wall." In the next moment, the partition to the adjacent suite started to burn through.

The French lady watched in disbelief the partition melting as though it were pastry, while the beige tint varnish blistered, sizzled, then popped.

186

Someone had finally told Captain Vicq that all was not as it should be on "D" deck. He ran down from the bridge to find "the blaze spreading rapidly in spite of prompt measures to check it." At once he ordered the *Philippar* stopped from her normal seventeen-and-a-half-knot cruising speed and turned stern-to in the direction of the light breeze which had sprung up over the flat sea.

Fearing the lifeboats might become "inaccessible" if the flames continued their present acceleration, Vicq rang the general alarm and took position at the evacuation station to supervise abandoning. All ventilators were plugged in an effort to smother the flames.

The "SOS" was transmitted, with a position that should have made the *Philippar* easy to locate: now little more than five miles east of Guardafui Light.

A Dutch passenger, A. G. Boot, was awakened by the abandon bells. Nonetheless, "some time elapsed before I realized the significance." When he did, he "saw flames and smoke on all sides and the blaze was spreading with amazing speed. It could not be isolated."

Boot hurried up on deck to attempt to secure places for himself and his family in a lifeboat.

Other travelers would never hear the alarm, or awoke too late to save themselves. These were on the fatal "D" deck, apparently the origin of the conflagration, and were overcome by the thick smoke from burning paint and electrical insulation.

One nimble passenger, Lucien Basset, a French stockbroker living in Shanghai, leaned out of his porthole and shouted at a group of sailors to throw him a line. Grasping it, he crawled outside and hand-over-hand along the rope until he was assisted onto deck in the unscorched fore part.

Almost as soon as the first distress signal was tapped out, three ships responded—the Russian tanker *Sovietskaia Neft,* and two British cargo vessels, the *Liverpool Contractor,* and the *Mahsud.*

There was not time to repeat the "SOS."

187

"The wireless cabin," according to the captain, "the emergency electrical generator on the upper bridge, and the passage below burst into flames almost at the same time, although removed from the point of origin of the blaze on "D" deck."

While A. G. Boot was impressed by the lack of panic, others, terrified by the lightninglike rapidity with which the flames were engulfing the ship, jumped overboard. The clothing of some was ablaze. Almost all of the saloons, cabins, and other compartments were burning fiercely, and emitting clouds of oily, noxious smoke.

One woman, in flames, was seen plunging down a fiery elevator well. A number of boats were blazing at their davits, reminiscent of the luckless *Cospatrick*.

A twelve-year-old girl, "suffering agonies from her burns," was placed in Boot's lifeboat. It had hardly cast off before the child "died before our eyes."

Six boats in all got away. These were not sufficient to accommodate even half of the passengers and crew. However, the water was pleasantly warm for those in their lifebelts. Captain Vicq, impressed by the "composure" of the passengers and the "admirable devotion" of officers and crew, was the last to leave the ship, by then "a solid mass of fire." He placed the time at 8 A.M., although it was doubtful that anyone could have remained alive on the burning hull for six hours.

The rescue vessels were already on the scene, some having arrived before dawn, guided by the liner's own funeral torch, crackling hundreds of feet into the sky. The *Liverpool Contractor*, the first, simply lowered all of her gangways. People stepped upon them from the lifeboats. Swimmers were assisted directly onto the steps.

When the last survivors had been disembarked during the next two days at Aden, some three hundred miles west, it was found that ninety were missing—approximately 10 per cent of those aboard. It was far from a high toll among sea disasters, but the loss seemed especially unnecessary, a maiden voyage *Titanic* of another time, place, and circumstance.

188

In an unexpected, tragic postlude, two French passengers who had survived the sinking perished on the twenty-seventh of May when their plane crashed in mountains sixty miles north of Rome. They had boarded the Paris-bound aircraft in Brindisi, with a gay wave to reporters who had just interviewed them.

While marine underwriters and secret police launched their separate investigations, the blackened hulk floated, unattended, back into the Arabian Sea. For five days the derelict pursued her listing, ghostly course, drifting 160 miles. Then, with a few native fishing boats—dhows—as the sole mourners, the most beautiful ship the Massageries Maritime had ever created settled lower and vanished. Fast dissipating vapor clouds attested that her hull plates were still hot.

"A number of strange events occurred aboard the ship," asserted *Le Matin,* of Paris. "The whole disaster cannot be regarded as solely due to fate."

Or was it?

Before the inquiries could be completed, another French liner, the 41,000-ton *L'Atlantique,* burned in the English Channel, January 4, 1933, with the loss of seventeen of her crew.

The two disasters, coming so close one upon another, were shattering to the prestige of the French Merchant Marine, whose minister, Leon Meyer, charged that criminal neglect was each time involved. For some reason, neither the line nor the ministry ever released its findings. The paper *Paris Midi* printed what it purported to be a comment, *in camera,* by Meyer:

He reportedly had alleged "negligence" in not heeding the "warnings" of short circuits, such as the ringing of the alarm bells. Contrary to the master's own praise, the probers were quoted as claiming that "certain of the men lost their heads, among the crew and the high command."

Further, it was charged, "the fire was not fought vigorously from the beginning. The captain waited too late."

New fire laws were prescribed late in 1933 by the same ministry: fireproof paint, no glazed surfaces, fire-retardant draperies and upholstery, no wooden partitions or panelings unless protected by a layer of asbestos, a back-up fuse system and other rules.

They all sounded reasonable enough. It seemed that each precaution should have been anticipated decades earlier.

Unfortunately, American shipping executives appeared unable to read French. The very next year, the smoldering, hissing hulk of what had been a ship almost as ornate as the *Georges Philippar* floundered, pilotless, against the Convention Pier in Asbury Park, New Jersey.

The date was September 8, 1934, the gutted victim: the 11,520-ton twin-funneled *Morro Castle*, of the Ward Line. She was completing not her first but her 174th, and last voyage.

The *Morro Castle*, less than four years old, was beyond dispute the most attractive of the east coast and Caribbean cruise ships. Propelled by quiet turbine-electric drive, she rode well and was tastefully but not garishly decorated in harmony with her advertised purpose—"the finest and fastest," to Havana.

She sailed from New York every Saturday, offering complete packages for the seven days starting at a mere $65. As travel agents, to whom she was a natural enough darling, used to suggest in fun to their customers, "You can't live at home any *cheaper* than that."

Mindful, however, of the several major liner disasters in the century, the Ward Line studiously avoided any hint of a previously fatal boast that she might, as well, be "the safest." The company hoped that passengers would soon enough assume that on their own.

Then *what* might have brought this liner ashore at Asbury Park, still aflame, and attracting the morbidly curious from miles around?

What had happened?

Once again, it fell to Dickerson N. Hoover to report to the Secretary of Commerce on this latest disaster. Since the Ward Line, also known as the New York and Cuba Mail Steamship

190

Company, flew the United States flag, a formal inquiry rather than a statement as to the liner's seaworthiness was in order.

When the last witness had been called, the final inspection of the twisted carcass of the *Morro Castle* completed, certain facts were established:

When she put Morro Castle, her namesake at the entrance to Havana harbor, astern on September 5, she carried 318 passengers and a crew of 230, including officers, and comprising at least half a dozen nationalities.

Absent from the farewell dinner on Friday, September 7, the master, Robert F. Wilmott, suddenly slumped in his chair while eating supper in his cabin, as he was about to bite a melon. Wilmott was pronounced dead about an hour later by the ship's surgeon, Dr. DeWitt Van Zile.

The cause was attributed to "acute indigestion." Dr. Van Zile reminded Chief Officer William F. Warms that the fifty-five-year-old captain's health had been "indifferent" for some time.

Warms, who was forty-seven, assumed command of the ship, advising the Ward Line at 9:08 P.M. of these wholly unexpected developments.

It was a squally, wet night, with a twenty-two-knot north-easter whipping up the coastal waters. Warms, however, kept the powerful cruise liner butting into the storm at nearly her twenty-knot "service speed." The grueling one-day turn-around on Saturday had to be maintained. With a large ship manned by a substantial number of crew, this ferry-boatlike schedule imposed its hardships on the lives of personnel and created difficulties in fueling, reprovisioning, and cleaning.

By midnight, lights of the Jersey shore resorts were sighted to port. The New York channel should be raised before dawn. The pride of the Ward Line ploughed on.

About 2:45 A.M. the *Morro Castle* was twenty-five miles south of Scotland Light Vessel, at the approaches to New York's Lower Bay. At this time, smoke and possibly flames were observed by several crewmen and at least two passengers in the

191

small writing room on the port side of the promenade or "B" deck, immediately beneath the forward funnel. The room, like other lounges, was in the French period motif, with polished mahogany, satinwood, ebony, and rosewood veneer panels.

A deck watchman observed smoke issuing from a ventilator immediately above the room. Inside, Daniel Campbell, assistant beverage steward, among the first of the crew to be made aware of the trouble, would later testify, as noted in the official U.S. Coast Guard report:

> About five minutes to three or three o'clock a passenger came into the smoking room and asked me if I smelled smoke and I said "no." He said, "Well, I think there is a fire somewhere, because I can smell smoke very strongly."
>
> Being a member of the crew my business is to go and find out just where that smoke is, so I dropped what I was doing—I was just cleaning the smoking room—and I went into the lounge. In the lounge there was a little party there drinking straight brandy, or just having a good time—they didn't seem to be causing any trouble or anything or any undue disturbance, just a regular party, that is all, having a lot of fun, and from there I went into the writing room.
>
> In the writing room there is a concealed locker and I looked and I just saw the smoke coming from that concealed locker. There is a little knob on that, and also a Yale lock but the Yale lock is never closed, because for some reason or other it is not necessary. There is nothing valuable kept in there. I opened the door and what I knew once as a locker was just one mass of flames, flames from top to bottom and from one side to the other side.

The interrogation continued:

Q. Was this fire burning heavy?
A. Very heavy. It is my opinion at that very moment that fire was out of control. It could not be taken care of.
Q. Were there any flames above it?
A. The locker itself was one blaze. The whole locker was one blaze. There was no such thing as seeing anything in it. There was just a blaze. Completely gutted.

Arthur J. Pender, the night watchman, was on deck when he observed:

What I first thought was steam, but which I later found out was smoke, was coming from a ventilator on the hurricane deck on the port side just alongside of what we call the auxiliary lighting system. I thought this was unusual. I went right to this ventilator, which is a cargo ventilator. It was trimmed aft due to the weather, which gave me a very good view, and upon coming close to this cargo ventilator, which I have later been told leads to No. 3 hold, but which at that time I thought led to No. 2 hold—

Q. You could not tell the difference between No. 2 and No. 3 by the position of the ventilator?

A. At that time I was not familiar with the ventilating system of the ship, that is, referring to the cargo ventilating system. I did not know just directly to which hold that went, of course, not having been a cargo officer, and my duties were just a little different. I did not know just exactly where this cargo ventilator went to.

Q. What did you do after you saw that smoke coming out there?

A. I did the only thing, only reasonable thing to do. I went to find the source of that smoke.

Q. Did you report it to the bridge before you went down?

A. No sir, I did not.

Q. What about the smoke from the cargo ventilator?

A. I immediately forgot about that when I finally saw the fire. I realized now that there must be two separate fires, as the cargo ventilator led into the cargo hold, and I did not get to the source of that, but I had only got two decks below and this was the writing room.

I proceeded in this lobby and there were two fires. From my vision or point of view there was no connection between the two fires. The overhead from the writing room to these two suites was not in flames. There was no sign of a fire overhead of the lobby through which I passed, although I passed through two fires, the two forward suites, and it seems ridiculous to think that there was a connection between the two fires when both suites simultaneously burst into what I term an inferno. The heat was so intense in both the writing room and these suites that it does not seem reasonable, although it is possible, that

193

there would be a connection between these two fires. If there was a connection, it must have been between the partitions or between the over head, and that doesn't seem very reasonable.

One of the few passengers still up at this hour, Doris Wacker, of Roselle Park, New Jersey, watched Campbell and Pender, soon joined by a third crew member throwing buckets of water on the blaze.

"There were no flames outside the room," she later reported. "The room itself seemed to us all afire on the inside, though I couldn't see much except smoke."

When she volunteered to run for assistance, one of the trio held up his hands and urged her not to say "anything to anybody" since "the fire was not bad."

Miss Una Cullen, of Brooklyn, also up and about at this early hour, was certain she saw the smoke in the passageway leading to the writing room, "coming from the cracks in the ceiling," but not from the room itself.

The bridge was advised of the blaze already proving more dangerous than "not bad." No warning of a fire had yet been registered in the automatic detecting systems. This was not especially surprising to Acting Master Warms since neither the electric device nor the smoke-sampling tubes connected to the writing room. Furthermore, there had been a "pretty lively" blaze in No. 5 cargo hold on August 27 without an indication on the bridge. Charred cardboard and "funnels" of newspapers apparently had been set as tinder.

At two fifty-five, shortly after receipt of the information, the bridge phoned the engine room to inquire about the presence of smoke below. The answer was negative. Second Officer Clarence C. Hackney was ordered to the writing room. He observed the futile efforts to extinguish the conflagration.

Quickly, the condition down below changed. Chief Engineer Eben S. Abbott asked his first assistant, Antonio R. Bujia, for a report.

"Good," replied Bujia, "but we can't stay much longer."

194

"Don't leave until you are driven out."

The seeming contradiction in Bujia's reply to Abbott's query was the result of a curious situation that existed in the engine room. The fire was raging in the superstructure, not below. But the ventilating system was drawing smoke into the machinery space, creating the illusion of fires that were not present there and causing oilers and firemen to quit their stations prematurely.

Abbott [he would claim] left his office and walked down a steel ladder into the machinery space.

"As soon as I stepped in the engine room," he later testified, "the lights went out."

Third Assistant Engineer Arthur Stamper put steam on the second pump. The other was already running to maintain pressure on the sanitary lines. In a moment, Aubrey H. Russell, the second assistant, turned on the main pump, thus putting three into operation.

As rapidly as it had on the *Philippar,* the fire spread beyond the writing room and into adjoining, equally polished and inflammable public saloons. It soon tumbled, almost capriciously, down the forward staircase to the next deck below. Some passengers were awakened not by any alarm bells but by the smell of smoke or sounds of mounting confusion.

"When the fire was discovered," the official inquiry was to observe, "there does not seem to have been any uniform or concerted effort on the part of the stewards to wake up and assist the passengers and lead them to safety. While that unfortunate condition generally existed, it is only fair also to say that there were instances of persons employed in the stewards' department who undoubtedly did their duty in this respect."

Mrs. Lena Schwartz, a stewardess, who ran coughing down corridors to bang on doors, was cited as one of the laudatory exceptions.

Many of those who opened their doors slammed them shut again as smoke billowed inward. Then they tried to move the heavy, glass, bolted-down portholes.

Herman Cluthe, a cruise director, happened to be one of the fortunate persons who were experiencing insomnia. In the inquiry he testified as follows:

Q. Now, would you kindly state, therefore, what you were doing when the fire started?

A. When the fire started, sir?

Q. Yes. The purpose of that question is [to ascertain] if you were asleep. I just want your statement as to what your condition was at that time.

A. To the best of my knowledge I retired to my room about two o'clock or shortly after. I went down to my room and I made things ready for the morning, got my uniform ready so that I would have a clean uniform to put on. Then I went to bed and I was unable to sleep. So I turned the small light on over the head of my bunk and took a Spanish textbook that had been given to me by some friends in Havana, and tried to study it. Very shortly after, I cannot say the exact time——

Q. This was about two when you started?

A. Two or shortly after two. I smelled smoke, and naturally I was surprised at this and sat there for a moment trying to realize what was wrong. Then I turned to the left, turned my head to the left, and looked out the porthole and I could see the glare of the fire.

Q. Where was your room?

A. My room is Room 318 on the forward foyer of "D" deck.

It was not until 3 A.M., by officers' testimony, that the fire bells were rung. There were passengers who could not remember ever having heard such an alarm.

At 3:18 A.M. when, as the inquiry would assert, "the fire had been out of control for some time," a "CQ" standby was flashed by thirty-seven-year-old George W. Rogers, the chief radio operator. He would aver that this was transmitted, not by order, but on his own initiative after hearing the nearby freighter *Andrea Luckenbach* asking the shore if there were any reports of a ship afire.

Rogers, overweight and perspiring, repeated the "CQ" three

196

times. It brought silence on the ship-to-shore frequencies as captains prepared to divert their vessels for a rescue. Smoke rolled into the *Morro Castle*'s radio shack, then the lights flickered off. Emergency illumination failed to flash on.

Six minutes later, at three twenty-four, word came from the bridge to speedout the "SOS" "KGOV," the *Morro Castle*'s letters, declared she was afire twenty miles south of Scotland Light.

Before Rogers had completed the first distress call, the corner of his transmitter table smoked, then flamed. There was an explosion, as if a tube had burst. Solder connections within the set began to melt. The chief operator twisted one wire coupling back together.

Nearby ships commenced to answer, first the *Monarch of Bermuda* followed by the *President Cleveland,* homeward bound from Manila, the *Luckenbach*, the *City of Savannah*, and the Coast Guard cutter *Tampa*.

Nothing on board the *Morro Castle* was going according to plan, if there ever had been any on this "finest and fastest" cruise liner.

The report made by the board of inquiry revealed a considerable amount of confusion on board and a lack of discipline and planning in instituting emergency procedures among crew and officers:

> When the passengers were awakened by the fire alarm and endeavored to make their way to the boat deck they were not able to use the two main stairways and the only recourse left them was to find their way to the after decks. This they did, large numbers of them, gathering on "B," "C," and "D" decks aft. It is apparent that no successful effort was made on the part of any of the officers or crew to lead these people up to the boat deck by way of the crew's service stairways or to lead them up outside. No successful effort was made by any of the lifeboats that left the burning vessel to go under her stern and render assistance to the large number of passengers gathered there.
>
> Mr. Hackney let go the painters on these lifeboats and no effort was made on the part of the officers to keep these boats in close proximity to the burning vessel to render assistance to

197

those persons who could not reach the boat deck, and some of whom were jumping overboard at the time. Thus these passengers were cut off from the lifeboats by the flames and their only means of escape was to lower themselves into the water by means of ropes or by jumping overboard from the stern of the vessel.

In the engine room, meanwhile, Chief Abbott shouted, "Let's get out of here!"

There was no more communication with the bridge, either by telephone or speaking tube. Steam pressure, for which the gauges were located next to those of the fuel oil lines, was shut off. The turbines were dead, the electric drive motors whined into silence. The propellers had stopped, although the ship's momentum continued to carry her forward, even as had the *Lusitania*.

The *Morro Castle* could have steamed on indefinitely had there been some way to block off the fires above the "black gang."

"Hurry, can't hold out much longer!" Rogers transmitted within the near-cauldron of his radio shack. Then the emergency generator exploded. There would be no more messages from the *Morro Castle*.

It was time for everyone to save him- or herself. Captain Warms, however, had a number of responsibilities yet to be performed. As the inquiry brought out:

Q. What happened to Captain Wilmott's body?
A. I went down to the captain's cabin to try to get his body out. The flames were coming right out of his cabin. [Here, Warms paused until he could control his sobs.] I couldn't reach him. Then I went down the ladder forward to the forecastle head.
Q. Did the fire ever reach you?
A. No.

Smoke hung lower and lower, all but suffocating the passengers clustered on deck, milling, like sheep without a leader, jamming closer and closer together. There was increasing lack of confidence in the lifeboats. Families and other groups put on their lifebelts and warily eyed the dark, stormy sea.

198

"Black smoke poured down stairways and there was a rush of running feet," Leroy C. Kelsey, a crewman from East Chatham, New York, would later report in an interview. "Flames crackled and roared and the black windows were shot with red and yellow gleams . . . flames swept down upon us from forward and closed in from aft. She was no longer a ship. She was a flaming hell from which the consuming fire shot upward in angry, lurid iniquity."

John Kempf, a New York city fireman, had taken this vacation for the express purpose of getting away for at least a week from the smoke and flame which was almost his daily fare. However, there was probably no one aboard in a better position to survive a holocaust.

As he began to entertain serious notions of abandoning ship, Kempf heard a girl beside him remark, "Why worry? We're all in the same boat!"

At about that point, it seemed to him, any reluctance on the part of the passengers to leave commenced to dissipate.

"One or two began to jump in the water," he would recall, "and then like a barrel of apples they began to go over the side until one hundred jumped."

Kelsey, the crew member, soon was inside a loaded boat halted at the edge of the deck by its falls. He grabbed a fire ax and hacked away. As it lowered, plate glass in the ballroom windows buckled from the fierce heat inside, then burst. The boat's occupants were showered with molten glass.

Still on deck, Father Raymond Egan, of St. Mary's Church in the Bronx, was offering absolution to all who asked, regardless of their particular faith or religious persuasion.

A prominent New York physician, Dr. Gouverneur Morris Phelps, Mrs. Phelps, and their twenty-five-year-old son, Morris, Jr., jumped from the stern. Somewhere amidships a naked woman was seen to squeeze through a porthole and plunge into the surging waters.

Kelsey's boat pushed off, its occupants burned, cut, and bleeding from the glass splinters and shards.

Two sisters from Shrewsbury, Massachusetts—Ethel and Gladys Knight—were not as fortunate as some family members who managed to keep close together. They were separated as soon as they surfaced from their dive over the side of the *Morro Castle*.

Ethel, who was twenty, three years older than Gladys, soon collided with a child. He turned out to be Benito Rueda, seven, of Brooklyn. When he shrieked through a mouth filled with water that he could not swim, Ethel held him with one arm and dog-paddled with her other to keep them both afloat.

By 4 A.M. the last of the eight boats to clear the burning liner was gone. Many passengers bobbed in the choppy night waters, supported only by their lifebelts. Others, with no faith in rescue, were stroking out for the shore lights, evanescent through the scud and rain showers. In fact, the storm was so heavy at times that passengers and crew alike wondered why it had not quenched the flames.

About half an hour later a twenty-six-foot surfboat from the Coast Guard Station at Sea Girt, seven miles south of Asbury Park, attracted by the fire on the horizon, together with the *Luckenbach* arrived at the *Morro Castle*'s side. The *Luckenbach* immediately put over boats whose crews, together with the Coast Guardsmen, began to haul people out of the water. Others, who had been fearful of jumping off the liner, did so with the rescue craft so near.

Only fifteen crewmen remained aboard, including Warms and the radio officer, Rogers. Even in the midst of the smoke and flames some hope was entertained of salvaging the *Morro Castle*. By 6 A.M., the little group took shelter in the bow, the only space left that was not swept by fire.

Although there was no power of any sort on board, the windlass locks still could be opened by hand. Warms pulled a lever, and the starboard anchor chain clattered out. It touched bottom and held. The flaming carcass of the Ward Line's $65-and-up weekly cruise ship was hove to, less than three miles off Sea Girt.

200

For the next five hours a converging fleet ranging from the *Monarch of Bermuda* and *President Cleveland* down to fishing craft such as the fifty-four-foot-long *Paramount* were pulling survivors out of the Atlantic. The Abraham Cohens, of Hartford, had swum all the way in, collapsing, exhausted, on the beach at Sea Girt. Mrs. Cohen would confide to nurses who checked her over, "My vacation is over."

Dr. Gouverneur Morris Phelps and Mrs. Phelps were rescued under the guidance of no less a personage than the governor of New Jersey, A. Harry Moore, circling in a plane above the choppy seas. A smoke flare from the National Guard aircraft brought a launch to their side.

Their son, however, had clung through the long hours to a stern line from the *Morro Castle* and from it he was finally saved.

Gladys and Ethel Knight were almost on the beach when small boats hauled them, chilled and exhausted, aboard. The seventeen-year-old sister, Gladys, was holding the Rueda boy at the time.

(Ethel was awarded a medal by the Massachusetts Humane Society for her part in saving the child's life. Also, wedding bells rang for her soon after her experience. The society, however, had waited too long for the actual presentation. Within four weeks of her marriage, Ethel was dead of a heart attack. The silver medal was fastened to her grave stone.)

The Coast Guard cutter *Tampa*, which had attempted to tow the fiery liner to an anchorage in New York Lower Bay, abandoned the effort Saturday afternoon when the twelve-inch hemp hawser burned through. By this time, Warms, Rogers, and all remaining personnel had been removed.

That evening before tens of thousands of awed spectators, the smoking skeleton, reeking with charred death, wallowed aground at Asbury. She was so near Convention Pier that a gangway could have been placed between the two—just as though some publicity man ghoulishly had arranged it.

Soft drink and all the other midway stands, stores, and attractions which had largely been boarded up reopened. All during

201

the following week business along the boardwalk in Asbury boomed. Only the most earnest representations by clergy and others of conservative mind canceled a float depicting the burning liner in that same week's event for local residents—a "baby parade." It did seem somewhat less than in good taste.

The Department of Commerce investigation of the disaster which claimed 134 lives commenced in New York almost immediately. It proved at once a sounding board for impassioned assertions, recriminations, and broad vilifications.

George Alagna, the first assistant radio operator, arrested as a material witness, appeared bent on convicting Warms. He testified, among other damaging allegations, that he had found the acting master in a daze, muttering, "Am I dreaming or is *it* true?"

Alagna also stated he saw Chief Engineer Abbott wringing his hands and shouting in supposedly a crying voice, *"What* am I going to do?"

Sweepingly, Alagna alluded to all "the madmen on the bridge."

It was true enough that Abbott, in his dress whites, had abandoned ship in No. 1 boat with twenty-eight other crewmen and only three passengers. His was among the first to come ashore at Spring Lake, five miles south of Asbury Park.

Some of the crew were charged by other members with being Communists. All—and they represented several nationalities—agreed that they had been improperly briefed on their fire stations. The International Seaman's Association succinctly branded the holocaust as "inexcusable."

The New York County Lawyers Association denounced a radio broadcast of the investigation. The hastily formed *Morro Castle* Survivors Association condemned the federal proceedings, which proved to be more concerned with what had *not* started the blaze.

Interestingly, there was some agreement, if not full conviction, that arson was the cause. Second Officer Hackney would so testify:

Q. What makes you believe that the fire had been set?
A. The way it burned so fiercely all of a sudden. If it was like a cigarette fire, it would start on the outside and burn a rug or chair.
Q. You say it burned so suddenly and spread so rapidly; how would you explain it?
A. The fire must have been inside there and burned away before it broke through.
Q. Would you explain it that the fire had been in there for some time?
A. It must have been.
Q. In that locker?
A. Around the place.

In his assumption he was seconded by Acting Chief Officer Ivan Freeman who was yet more specific:

The only conclusion I can come to is that it was deliberately set by someone who saturated oil all around to feed it.
Q. What motive do you think anyone would have had for setting the fire deliberately?
A. God knows what the motive was.
Q. Had you had any labor troubles?
A. Not directly. There was some trouble in Havana, but there always is labor trouble there.
Q. How do you think it was started?
A. Someone watched his opportunity when the watchman had gone by.

Warms himself was in agreement.

Q. What started the fire?
A. I have two theories. One, it was incendiary.
Q. Why?
A. I think somebody put something in that writing room locker.

His second was that someone "tossed a cigarette butt" into

203

the same locker. The acting master did not elaborate on how that act, necessitating the opening and closing of the storage locker door, could have been an "accident."

When asked, "How did it happen there was a delay in sending the radio message?" Warms snapped back: "There was no delay. It was ordered at three-fifteen and sent about three-twenty."

While only hinting at "spontaneous combustion" as a possible source, Dickerson Hoover, in summing up his report of the hearings noted:

> What does stand out clearly is that the ship's officers failed to control the situation with the strong hand that was necessary in such an emergency. When the fire alarm sounded, the crew did not take their regular fire stations nor was any effort made on the part of the officers to organize them and make a concentrated effort to meet the emergency existing. The testimony shows that No. ten lifeboat, the first boat to leave the vessel, was lowered by a seaman without orders from the master or any officer. This boat contained only three passengers, all women. The rest were crew.
>
> Lifeboats Nos. one, three, five, nine, and eleven were lowered and contained a large percentage of crew. These six lifeboats, which had a total carrying capacity of 408 persons, only had a total of 85 persons, mostly crew. If the testimony of Acting Captain Warms be carefully examined it will be found that he seemed to satisfy himself with sending officers to do certain things, but it does not appear that there was any follow-up by the officers reporting back that they had done those things or even that they were unable to do them.
>
> The engine and fireroom watch stayed at their posts until driven out through the emergency exits. It is apparent that the same cannot be said of the chief engineer, who never appeared in the engine room (contrary to Abbott's own testimony) during the fire to inform himself as to the condition of his department, and the first assistant engineer paid but a short visit to the engine room, and he was apparently the first member of the stand-by crew of the engine department to make his exit.
>
> In the first testimony given by Captain Warms he says little or nothing about the turning of the ship. When he was re-

204

called for further examination he said considerable about the turning of the ship. Yet if the testimony be carefully studied, it will be found that Captain Warms, after being notified that the ship was on fire, continued on his course at 18.8 knots for 3.1 miles before sounding the fire alarm, and the testimony indicates he continued for some distance thereafter before undertaking to turn the ship.

Had he taken prompter action in this respect it is possible that he may have been able to have controlled the fire or at least to have controlled it to such an extent as to have been able to have saved a larger number of passengers.

According to the testimony of Captain Warms and Mr. Hackney, the vessel passed three miles east (true) of Barnegat Light Vessel at 1:55 A.M. September 8 and the course was set 1 degree (true) for Ambrose Light Vessel. Testimony of the chief engineer shows that the vessel's engines were turning 130 revolutions a minute, which would give the vessel a speed of 18.8 knots. Weather was rainy, wind east twenty miles, also seas choppy. The testimony of Captain Warms and Mr. Hackney shows that the course of 1 degree (true) was continued to at least 3 A.M.

At 2:40 A.M., when the first indication of fire was observed by the watchman, the vessel was twenty-seven miles from Scotland Light Vessel, and at 2:45 A.M., when open fire was seen in the writing room, the vessel was twenty-five-and-a-half miles from Scotland Light Vessel. At 2:55 A.M., when the telephone call came from the bridge to the engine room asking if there was a fire below, the vessel was twenty-two-and-a-half miles from Scotland Light Vessel, and at 3 A.M., when the fire alarm was turned in, she was twenty-one miles from Scotland Light Vessel.

It is evident that the vessel was navigated on various courses until shortly before she was brought to anchor two miles east (true) of Sea Girt Light, and the fact that the lifeboats drifted ashore between Spring Lake Coast Guard Station and Sea Grit Light is further indication that she was navigated northward of the anchored position.

Much as he had concluded in the case of the *Vestris,* the pensive Hoover suggested that "the human equation failed." Later, a federal court accused Warms and Abbott of "negli-

205

gence and inattention to duties." Convicted, they were sentenced to prison terms. An appellate court, rightfully, reversed the cruel verdict. Henry E. Cabaud, executive vice president of the Ward Line, was fined $5,000.

The only "hero" to emerge from the catastrophe was Rogers, the chief radio operator, awarded a medal by the mayor of Bayonne, New Jersey, and another by the Veterans Wireless Operators Association. However, it turned out that the bestowals were somewhat premature.

Joining the Bayonne, New Jersey, police force, Rogers was convicted in 1938 of willfully planting a bomb which exploded and nearly killed a superior officer. Released from prison, the former radio operator was convicted in 1954 of the murder of an eighty-three-year-old retired printer and his fifty-eight-year-old spinster daughter, involving $7,500 he owed them.

The story of Rogers ended on January 10, 1958, in New Jersey State Prison in Trenton, with his death from coronary occlusion. It was one of the most natural, positive, and definitive acts of his life.

With his passing, the full secret of the *Morro Castle* went with him. There were, however, those, including police and insurance inspectors, who still were not satisfied. Thomas Gallagher, who published *Fire at Sea* in 1959, effected the most searching study of Rogers and his shady past, culminating with an interview in the penitentiary two years prior to the radio operator's death.

Gallagher discovered that Rogers was a pathological liar with a record since he was a twelve-year-old of thievery, arson, and child-molesting. Yet, Gallagher does not say Rogers actually set the blaze that destroyed the *Morro Castle* and also reports the prison interview as not clinching that crucial point.

The same author also hints that Captain Wilmott may well have been poisoned. There was, he develops, a mysterious absence one day of the first captain's remains in his charred cabin, then the appearance of a skull and other bones.

Since Dr. Van Zile, the ship's surgeon, perished in the blaze, one source of vital testimony had been forever lost.

Considering the disorganization in firefighting, it is perhaps no wonder that the cruise liner burned so briskly and devastatingly. What started the fire can never be proven, other than circumstantially. It is a fact, however, that the forward funnel flue, carrying away the heat, smoke, and gases from three furnaces went directly behind the fatal writing room closet. At least, this was a very poor place to locate a locker where polishing rags and other combustibles were normally stored.

In retrospect, nonetheless, it would appear that the chances of arson as a cause for the loss of the handsome Ward liner proved greater than in the case of the *Georges Philippar*.

On January 24, 1935, not quite five months after the *Morro Castle* disaster, the Ward passenger-cargo ship *Mohawk* was rammed in tragically familiar waters, four and a half miles off Sea Girt, by the Norwegian motorship *Talisman*. Grounded, she rolled over and partially sank an hour later. Of her 53 passengers and crew of 110, 45 were lost, including Captain Joseph E. Wood, who returned to the derelict after being saved.

Bitter weather following an east coast blizzard which already had sheathed in ice the Havana and Vera Cruz-bound vessel caused most of the deaths from exposure. A faulty steering mechanism on the *Mohawk* was blamed by the Department of Commerce for the accident itself. The steering motors shorted out, swinging the *Mohawk's* rudder and projecting her into the path of the *Talisman*.

Still, the luckless Ward Line sailed on, minus two ships. Assaulted further by the outbreak of World War II in Europe in September, 1939, and, two years later, the United States' entry into the conflict, the New York and Cuba Mail Steamship Company "suspended" service the last of March, 1942.

The loss of a ship, or ships to a private corporation was one thing. When a government like that of France maintained an appreciable interest in the destinies of an ocean transportation company, catastrophes assumed a national mien. Ill fortune in the thirties, as well as in the succeeding decade, continued to plague vessels flying the French tricolor.

On May 4, 1938, the 25,000-ton *Lafayette,* nine years in the transatlantic service, was razed at her pier in Le Havre. Fast and beautiful as this large, single-funnel liner was, she had been a jinx, having survived two previous small fires and two collisions. One of the latter had occurred in 1936 in the St. Lawrence River within a few miles of the *Empress of Ireland*'s submerged wreck. Some three weeks after the *Lafayette* had burned herself out, a charred, unidentifiable body was found at one of the forward fire stations. All the members of the anchor-watch or port crew had been accounted for.

Who was he?

On April 19, 1939, the 34,569-ton *Paris* was swept by flames, also in Le Havre, after which she capsized. Threatening messages had been received prior to the outbreak of the blaze. Considering Chancellor Adolf Hitler's "softening up" prior to the invasion of Poland, his accelerating war of attrition against the West, one had reason to speculate as to whether international arson rather than "accident" was the villain in this destruction of the French Merchant Marine. And it would reel under yet another major blow.

The *Normandie,* at eighty-three thousand tons one of the three largest liners in the world (along with the *Queen Mary* and *Queen Elizabeth* of comparable tonnage) and surely the most graceful and exquisitely conceived, had been moored to her Hudson River dock ever since the war started.

Commandeered, in effect, first by the Coast Guard, next by the Maritime Commission, and successively by the United States Navy, the Army Transportation Service, the Army, then again by the Navy, she proved no less than a nightmare each time conversion to war service was contemplated. For one major consideration—like the far smaller *Vestris* or *Waratah,* among other twentieth-century liners whose lofty superstructures had been an *idée fixe* among marine architects—she possessed "a low metacentric height, whereby the shift of small weight could cause dangerous listing . . . a very tender ship."

That is to say, less euphemistically, the exquisite *Normandie* was top-heavy. Nevertheless the U.S. government went ahead with plans to convert her into a troopship.

On February 9, 1942, during the conversion of the grand saloon, a workman's torch set ablaze stored bales of lifejackets. New York City firemen poured in tens of thousands of tons of water all that afternoon and evening. They won their battle against the fire, but the *Normandie* rolled over onto her side in the ice floes and muck of the river and lay there like some wounded, beached monster out of the deep.

She was truly "a very tender ship."

In the decade since the *Georges Philippar* floated unmanned and incandescently in the Arabian Sea, Norman ship designers seemed already to have forgotten warnings against unfireproofed wooden partitions, highly glazed and varnished surfaces, flimsy curtains.

The *Normandie,* queen of the Compagnie Generale Transatlantique—the French Line—was as inflammable as any ship of earlier vintage, and a dramatic, fiery symbol of the destructive years ahead of World War II.

16.

War and Postwar Casualties: ATHENIA, LANCASTRIA, WILHELM GUSTLOFF, CHAMPOLLION, DARA, and LAKONIA

ON SUNDAY, SEPTEMBER 3, 1939, PRIME MINISTER NEVILLE Chamberlain announced that a state of war existed between Great Britain and Nazi Germany. Far too late, the slight gray man with the umbrella had concluded that Hitler "can be stopped only by force." Appeasement had proven disastrous. But now—it was over.

That very evening, just after dinner, the 13,581-ton Donaldson Atlantic liner *Athenia,* carrying 1,102 passengers, mostly tourists and neutrals hoping to take refuge in Montreal, was torpedoed and sunk 250 miles west of Ireland by the German submarine, U-30. There were one hundred and twelve lives lost, sixty-nine of whom were women and sixteen children, in this first passenger ship "atrocity" of World War II.

A few of the number drowned were Americans. Even so, this sinking did not prove another *Lusitania.* For one consideration, no one in the United States was especially surprised. Persecution of the Jews and other minorities, the brutal invasion of Poland, following upon the recent annexations of Austria and Czechoslovakia, broken promises tumbling one atop another, blood baths within his own National Socialist party—all of those events combined to convince the Western World that only the worst could now be expected of Adolf Hitler.

For another, World War I had underscored the fact that civilians, whether neutrals or nationals of a belligerent nation, traveled in a war zone at their own risk—no matter if the war were only days or even hours old.

A second steamship tragedy followed on June 17, 1940, as German armies consolidated their *blitzkrieg* against France. Jammed with troops, diplomatic personnel and their families, other civilians, the ex-cruise Cunarder *Lancastria,* of 16,243-tons, was dive-bombed and set ablaze in the harbor of St. Nazaire.

At least twenty-five hundred died.

This figure closely approached the total of the victims of the *Titanic* and *Lusitania* combined. And yet, almost at war's end there would be the worst single marine disaster in history. As victorious Russian armies surged westward in the winter of 1945, like Ghengis Khan's eastern hordes of earlier centuries, Germans in conquered Poland, Silesia, and East Prussia fled before them.

On a snowy day, January 30, families mingled with submarine personnel of the Third Reich's dwindling *Kriegsmarine* to swarm aboard the former Nazi "strength through joy" cruise liner, *Wilhelm Gustloff,* at Danzig (Gydnia), Poland.

The Führer himself had spoken at the 25,484-ton vessel's launching, shortly before the war's outbreak, as if to burn deeper the curse already attached to the big vessel's name. Wilhelm Gustloff, a forty-one-year-old bully-boy of the Swiss Nazi party, had been assassinated in February, 1936, by a Jewish medical student.

No accurate count was kept of those embarking. The only thing that mattered now was to escape the foe who had returned with all the menace of a wounded grizzly bear. The *Gustloff* was a large ship, by any measure. If overcrowding were permitted, and it was, she could carry ten thousand persons. An estimate put her final complement at about that number.

She headed out of Danzig Bay through blinding snow and mounting winds in the thick dark of a bitter northern evening. The *Gustloff* was just away from the headlands and turning westward for Rostock in East Prussia, when a Russian submarine, waiting for anything to move out of the port of Danzig, sighted her.

One and probably not more than two torpedoes sank the shallow-draft "strength through joy" ship in a few minutes. The results were pure horror, with entire families drowning in their cramped cabins.

No more than one thousand survived, meaning that between nine and ten thousand perished.

The war at sea had left in its turbulent wake new depths of savagery.

The loss was approximately twice that of the Nazi prisoner of war ship *Riegel,* sunk by a British bombing plane in November, 1944, off the Norwegian coast. Only four hundred of the five thousand Yugoslav and Russian prisoners aboard, crowded below, survived. The RAF had no way of knowing the nature of the vessel, since it was not flying the International Red Cross flag. (As this went to press, twenty-six years after the horror, divers had located the wreck and were commencing the ghostly task of searching for bodies, or skeletons.)

It required some years for the international merchant marine to rebuild. When it did, nations whose shipping had been virtually wiped from the oceans—Japan, Norway, and Holland, for example—would return with greater strength than ever. The dawn of the supertanker, for one innovation, was at hand.

Still, certain old-timers survived torpedo and aerial bomb to wallow in postwar senility. One was the thirty-year-old *Champollion,* of the Messageries Maritime, which smashed into a reef, December 22, 1952, off Beirut.

Known as the "pilgrim ship," the 12,546-ton liner was carry-

212

ing, among other passengers, fifty-seven nuns of the order of Notre Dame de Salut, as well as members of the French Fathers of the Assumption to visit Bethlehem on Christmas. Fifteen lives were lost during the difficult rescue operations by buoy and surfboat.

In nearby waters, on April 8, 1961, the 5,000-ton *Dara,* of the British India Steam Navigation Company, caught fire in the Persian Gulf, en route to Bombay, and was destroyed along with 212 of the 697 persons aboard.

Another Christmas sailing, in 1963, ended in disaster 180 miles north of Madeira, in the Atlantic. The 20,314-ton, thirty-three-year-old *Lakonia,* operated by the Greek Line, was swept by flames believed to have originated in the barber shop. She had escaped major damage in two previous fires, one of which was thought to have been the result of arson.

Lost were 132 persons, out of 1,036. Aboard had been many retired men and women, who had spent a great portion of their life's savings to make the expensive cruise.

The casualty figure would have been higher had not British and United States aircraft dropped life rafts and rings to those in the water.

17.

The YARMOUTH CASTLE

THE *Yarmouth Castle,* OF ONLY FIVE THOUSAND GROSS TONS, was much the same vintage as the *Lakonia.* A steel vessel, she was constructed in 1927 in Philadelphia for the Eastern Steamship Company to be used in the overnight Boston to Yarmouth, Nova Scotia, service as the *Evangeline.* In spite of her small size, she proved durable as a troopship in the Pacific. She survived World War II to be reconverted in 1947.

Moving south for cruises, the belle of Nova Scotian waters aged not so gracefully into a crochety old lady past due for a snug harbor. She broke her moorings, failed to sail on schedule several times, a whale was caught in her rudder, and her water system broke down, evoking the comment from one cruise passenger, "I had to brush my teeth with soda."

By 1965, after several changes of ownership and national flags, *Evangeline,* like some multiple-divorcée, had become the *Yarmouth Castle.* Her operators were listed as the little-known Chadade Steamship Company, of Panama.

She sailed at 5 P.M., Friday, November 12, 1965, under hot, clear skies, on a routine bi-weekly voyage to Nassau. Aboard were 376 passengers (50 less than her certified capacity) and 176 crew members, approximately a normal complement. Most of the travelers were Floridians, with a few exceptions. The largest single group aboard was the contingent—sixty-one men and women—from the North Broward, Florida, Senior Citizens Club.

Scarcely a senior citizen, however, was Carole Pendleton, of Cleveland, a recent graduate of the Andrews School for Girls, in nearby Willoughby. Married, Carole, of medium height with dark brown hair, was traveling with her mother, Mrs. John Kekelis.

Carole would later admit she became "a little concerned the minute I saw the ship." The *Yarmouth Castle* was sufficiently sparkling in her white paint. But no matter how many coats were applied, like makeup to a dowager's complexion, the liner's sunset years could not be hidden.

Carole's concern, however, was occasioned mostly by the fact that she had become aeronautically adapted. In fact, she went to her stateroom and recommenced studying for her forthcoming commercial pilot's license. She hoped to pilot the plane for the tool company owned by her husband, Lee Pendleton.

All along, Carole had wanted to fly to Nassau, and made no secret of this desire to her somewhat distressed mother.

Almost as soon as the ship cleared the narrow channel leading abruptly into the Atlantic, it was dinner time. The passengers, who for the most part had spent the pre-sailing hours at goodbye parties and then had gone directly into the *Castle*'s several bars and drinking terraces, were by now as ravenous as wolves. They crowded into the dining saloon which, following its several conversions and expansions, was still lacking in amplitude.

Since the captain, thirty-five-year-old Byron Voutsinas, had ordered full speed—fourteen knots—the vessel began to roll from side to side from her own forward motion. Her beam was wasp-waisted.

This was too much for a number of the diners. They left for deck or cabin. The sturdier continued to dance, imbibe, and play the seagoing version of horse races.

Carole Pendleton, among others of the vacationists, switched off her cabin lights at 10 P.M. "It was easy to fall asleep because of the beautiful moonlit night and the calm ocean."

The last floor show, however, did not come on until eleven-thirty. It attracted some, including Charles Matias, of Berwyn,

215

Illinois, and his wife, Edna. When the party started getting "a little wild," Charles, who was fifty-eight, suggested that they call it a night.

Edna wanted to stay, but he persuaded her, after a final drink, to return with him to their cabin, No. 719 on the promenade deck, "a death trap if I ever saw one." Even though their fare had been $200, the room was so small that he could barely squeeze up the ladder to his top bunk.

Midnight came and passed. It was now Saturday, November 13. The *Yarmouth Castle* was in Northwest Providence Channel, abeam of Great Stirrup Cay. The security watch started his rounds at twelve-thirty and completed them at ten minutes before 1 A.M., at which time he relieved the man at the helm. Inadvertently, perhaps, he had missed several of the watch clock stations, including Room 610, on the main deck, used for storage. Its contents included mattresses, damaged chairs, pieces of scrap paneling, a vacuum cleaner, and miscellaneous items.

There was nothing unusual about this storeroom except for two factors: There was no sprinkler outlet and a "jury-rig" lampcord type electric line with a "naked" light bulb served as illumination.

While the watchman was making his imperfect rounds the engine room crew was routinely blowing the boiler tubes—that is, clearing away the exhaust-pipe carbon. When this operation was completed, about 1 A.M., a smell of smoke was detected in the engine compartments through the ventilator system.

The engine watch thought that the smoke must be coming from the "pantry-galley-bakeshop area," where loaves of bread or cakes were often done to somewhat more than a turn. A search in this culinary space proved inconclusive.

However, by this time—just a few minutes after one o'clock —others, including the radio operator, members of the night cleaning staff, and several passengers had smelled smoke and were searching independently for its source. Most of them soon converged on the men's toilet on the promenade deck from which smoke was issuing. None had any way of immediately knowing,

216

however, that the source actually was on the next deck below, in the storeroom, at approximately the same location.

The hunting party had grown almost to comic-tragedy proportions, now led by Captain Voutsinas himself, with such lesser functionaries as the cruise director and the telephone operator trailing close in his wake. Rumors and counterorders only augmented the confusion.

When, finally, the mixed assemblage of amateurs and professionals arrived at the true origin, Room 610, on the main deck, fire extinguishers were brought into play. They did not retard the flames. Fire hoses were next tried after the engine room was ordered to operate fire pumps.

When these streams of water proved equally ineffective, the master returned to the bridge. The firefighters one by one retreated from the mounting heat of the conflagration, now spilling into the corridors and toward the stairwells. Although no alarm was rung, the passengers were being awakened by the rising babble of chaos.

Carole Pendleton, who had been sleeping heavily, came alive with the jolting realization that "all hell had broken loose." She later wrote:

. . . . a shout of fire, a tap on the door and the sound of running feet. Mother grabbed her handbag and opened the door to be faced with flames to the right of the door and billowing thick black smoke. I glanced at my watch. It was 1:05 A.M. Saturday, November 13.

Mother ran out toward the main lobby. I ran out the door after her. I turned to go back into my stateroom, took too many gulps of smoke, then grabbed my train case (all it had in it were curlers, etc.). I found my way to the main lobby where my mother was, but I had to sit down and vomit as I had already inhaled too much smoke. By this time, even though only a few minutes had elapsed, our stateroom was completely destroyed by fire.

The main lobby was almost empty except for two women (one badly burned). I thought at first it was a small fire that could be put out. I also was mistaken to think that the crew had awakened all the other passengers and would take care of them and me. It was at this time I noticed that the sprinkler system was not working and the water hose was flat with no pressure. We heard no fire alarm.

After discovering our hair was singed from our close call with fire, we regained our composure and headed for the outer deck as it was hard to breathe where we were. We had no lifejackets, only our night clothes which were already blackened by the smoke. Everyone alive was gathered in the aft sections of the ship. A crewman rushed out with two lifejackets and handed them to my mother and me. We put them on, then I noticed an elderly lady with no lifejacket. As I am a good swimmer and have no fear of the water, I took off the jacket and put it on her.

Charles Matias was awakened by what he believed to be "a bunch of drunks screaming and yelling." Then his wife, Edna, who had wanted to stay on for the floor show and dancing, spoke out, "Charlie, there's something wrong."

He opened the door and was immediately enveloped by a rush of smoke. Without saying anything, Edna jumped from her bed and pushed past him.

"Edna! Edna! Come back!" he shouted.

Unable to breathe and not struck by the premonition that he would never see his wife again, Matias shut the door long enough to grab his wallet and pants, then in his bare feet exited through the cabin window onto the safety of the promenade deck.

Mrs. Morris Herman, of Cleveland, in a nearby cabin, opened the door to hear and see "a naked woman running down the passageway screaming: 'My baby! My baby!'"

It was Mrs. Herman's first venture on a ship.

Among the last to be made aware of the trouble were the staunch breed of "night people," loath to forsake the ballroom bar on the boat deck aft. Suddenly, a young woman, her hair streaming, burst in, yelling "fire!"

She was quickly followed by another lady, badly burned. Since there was no smoke in this small saloon and the lights were on, their appearance was all the more unbelievable.

218

The late drinkers emerged on deck to be hit in the face by thick smoke and to see fellow passengers pushing toward the stern like a disorderly march of ants. Crewmen mingled with them. Some assisted the passengers in locating lifejackets, others helped with the fire hoses, since pressure was being maintained below.

At least one of the officers was smashing in windows of deluxe cabins along the promenade deck to be sure none was still trapped within.

At 1:20 A.M., the bridge ordered the engines and ventilation blowers stopped. All but one of the burners on each boiler were cut off. Watertight doors in the fire and engine rooms were closed.

The master ordered a distress message but it was too late. The radio shack was already burning. Voutsinas then called for the same SOS by blinker since he had observed the lights of two vessels, both within eight miles of the *Yarmouth Castle.*

Five minutes later, at 1:25 A.M., the abandon ship alarm was ordered. This could not be accomplished since the wheelhouse, afire, had itself been abandoned. The bells were controlled from within. The best that could be coaxed was a forlorn toot or two on the whistle.

Five girls from Lima, Peru, now approached Carole Pendleton and asked for assistance.

"I assured them that everything was going to be all right and not to worry. The poor girls could speak very little English and my Spanish is limited. I fastened their lifejackets so if they had to jump into the water they would not drown. The lifeboats were not being lowered so I assumed that the fire was under control and the captain did not want passengers to board the lifeboats, as lifeboats are very risky and can tip easily. It was still very difficult to breathe so mother and I headed for the stern to put ourselves behind the steel reinforced swimming pool in case the ship blew up."

Curiously, perhaps from a broken valve, the swimming pool which had been empty, began to fill. Although the *Yarmouth Castle* had developed a list of some 4 degrees, it was not sufficient to allow water to pour over the sides.

219

The fire was burning fiercely amidships, with flames "eight stories high," it seemed to Charles Matias. At that time he heard the captain urging passengers not to jump without life preservers. Then Voutsinas himself left the ship in one of the first boats to drop clear. He would later explain that his intention was to seek help.

Gerald McDonnell, a resident of Silver Spring, Maryland, was heard to comment with a certain air of detachment to a man next to him that this was certainly "a very poorly run ship." With that, he tightened his lifebelt and jumped.

At about five minutes before two o'clock—a few minutes after Captain Voutsinas had quit his command—the Finnish ship *Finnpulp,* about six miles astern, radioed the Coast Guard that she had sighted a vessel afire. Rescue aircraft in Miami were at once ordered to prepare for takeoff.

The *Finnpulp* altered course toward the burning stranger, followed shortly by another vessel, the Panamanian cruise liner *Bahama Star.*

Passengers soon saw the lights of the pair rushing at full speed toward them.

"In the meantime," Carole continued, "I wanted to get my mother into a lifeboat, as she is deathly afraid of water, so we headed for a crewman who told us that all the lifeboats that could be lowered were being lowered. Ours was stuck and would not budge. Out of our fourteen lifeboats only four could be lowered. The first one had the children in it and the second had all crew members except for four passengers. Some of the passengers had started jumping into the water. I decided we had better take a chance and wait."

The *Bahama Star,* meanwhile, hove to and speedily put fourteen boats in the water. Carole observed:

"The lifeboats that were lowered started sending flares, but unfortunately our rescue boats were still quite a distance. I turned to see a holocaust of flames coming at us very rapidly. Another crewman noticed that I had no lifejacket and gave me one. Mother and I went back to the swimming pool and waited."

220

Soon she suggested a song since "we were in a dark section of the stern and I did not think we would be noticed. That went over like a lead balloon and everyone decided to yell 'help!' instead. The brave captain of the *Bahama Star* told us to jump and we would be picked up by lifeboats.

"So Mother and I headed for a lower deck. When we arrived there, about twelve crewmen were taking charge of the rescue and told us not to jump as the water might be filled with sharks. They said they would get us on a lifeboat."

About 2:15 A.M., the boat containing Captain Voutsinas came alongside the *Finnpulp*. The master, or "someone" in it explained that there were "six hundred persons on board" and help was required at once. The Finnish motor vessel put over her two boats. Since she was not a passenger ship, she carried no additional boats.

Officers on the *Finnpulp's* bridge observed "towering flames on the *Yarmouth Castle* forward of the stack and engulfing the bridge area."

Voutsinas then returned to his ship. By 3 A.M., he was among the few remaining aboard. Carole Pendleton handed over her lifejacket before leaving in a lifeboat of the *Bahama Star*.

As the rowers pulled away, she heard "the strange noises of a dying ship. By this time the fire was three-quarters of the way to the stern. I noticed large blisters all along the hull.

"We got to the *Bahama Star* at three-thirty, by my watch. When I seated my mother in the lounge, I ran to the doctor's quarters to help administer first aid. There I saw around eight people badly burned and cut. I grabbed a bottle of peroxide and a box of cotton and went back to the lounge.

"I gave first aid but no one felt faint or in shock. I have never seen a braver bunch of people in my life. I was on the sinking ship two-and-a-half hours after leaving my cabin and on two different decks, never seeing any signs of panic.

"At around 6:03 I witnessed the sinking of the *Yarmouth Castle*. It was a very strange sight. The water and smoke separated just as the sun came up."

221

Eighty-five passengers and two crewmen were lost, one of whom was the ship's surgeon, Dr. Lisardo Diaz-Torrens, a Cuban. The North Broward Senior Citizens Club sustained the heaviest casualties of any group on board, losing twenty-two out of the sixty-one who had embarked.

After its inquiry, the Coast Guard concluded that the fire had originated in Room 610 from any one of a number of potential causes including a short-circuit or a smoldering cigarette.

"The proximate cause of the debacle was failure of early detection," the Coast Guard charged, adding, "that the magnitude of loss of life stemmed from failure of early use of the general alarm or the public address system."

The *Yarmouth Castle* was not of United States registry. No disciplinary action could be taken, nor was any suggested. In leaving his ship, however, Captain Voutsinas was criticized for "abandonment of command responsibility and an over-all failure to approach and cope with the difficulties attending the accomplishment of a task of this order of magnitude."

EPILOGUE

EARLY IN 1970, A MEETING OF SHIPBUILDERS, OPERATORS, underwriters, and many world leaders in the water transport of petroleum met by invitation in the formal, ultramodern board rooms of Shell Centre, London. There were depressing tidings to ponder.

On December 12, 1969, 110 miles northwest of Dakar, the 206,000-deadweight-ton supertanker *Marpessa,* owned by Royal Dutch Shell, was rocked by fire and explosion, claiming two lives. An SOS brought another Shell tanker to her side, along with several ships steaming nearby.

For the better part of two days the blaze was fought. Then, by the company's own account the following events occurred:

At 11:30 P.M. (the 13th), alarm came from the engine room of rapidly rising water in the pump room. The water was entering the engine room through a horizontal gash in the bulk-head. A large leak must have sprung somewhere down in the pump room, possibly a seal or flooding valve was gone, and the pumps could not cope with the water.

At 3:30 A.M. on the 14th the master gave the order to leave the ship, only he himself remaining on board with the wireless officer. At 6 A.M. the master also decided to abandon the ship together with the wireless officer as he was afraid that the ship would break with the risk of sparks and further explosions.

Marpessa was sinking very slowly. About noon the funnel

223

emblem was just above the water and the bow out of the water. She stayed in this position for about twelve hours.

At 11:37 P.M. on the 14th she suddenly sank. After an explosion and a leaping flame the ship with her bow standing up on end was seen foundering within a minute.*

The mighty *Marpessa,* like greater and lesser ships before her—the tiny *Essex,* the larger *Portland,* the great *Titanic,* the *Andrea Doria,* all of the doomed lot—was gone. The sunken, ghostly chasms of her broken hull in their "sea change" were the habitat of fish, barnacles, and other creatures of the deep.

The *Marpessa* had all at once become as extinct as the dinosaurs, the civilization of the Aztecs, the builders of Stonehenge, the Hanging Gardens of Babylon. She had proven as mortal as man himself.

She had not been the largest tanker afloat. One, 372,000 tons, has been launched in Japan, where the *Marpessa* also had left the ways. But she was the most massive ship ever to be sunk, including losses, in wartime. In fact, her tonnage approximated that of *all* the eight battleships sunk or damaged in the Pearl Harbor attack, December 7, 1941.

After a century of concerted effort to construct the unsinkable ship, *Marpessa*'s loss underscored several truths, including the immutable paradox: The bigger they built them, the more readily they sank. It could not, however, be assumed flippantly that man had been mocked by fate at every turning. He had come far in the science of marine progress since the time of the Phoenicians, at least twelve centuries before Christ. He had accomplished much. He was betrayed only by his boasts, for the sweeping, immeasurably powerful, and unpredictable sea would remain master with a mien that was varyingly beneficent and vengeful.

If the Lord, as the Bible would assert, had but to speak to calm the angry oceans, such prerogatives were reserved exclusively for the Almighty.

*From *Shell Magazine,* London, February, 1970.

Man has not succeeded in taming the waters or fully guaranteeing his dominance in navigating across them. On the other hand, the era of shocking passenger liner disasters is ending. Transoceanic travel has shifted to the skyways, leaving the sea route for assorted cargo carriers.

Cunard operates only one name in transatlantic service, the *Queen Elizabeth II*, and that irregularly. The fastest liner in the world, the *United States,* has been mothballed. The once glittering American Export Line, which could carry to the Mediterranean in any one of several fine liners more people than fleets of ancient triremes, now exports freight.

The docks along the Hudson River are empty, many of them rotting away. Some have been converted into truck terminals. The lengthy ship departure and arrival columns in the newspapers have shrunk to the relative depth of a help wanted advertisement.

A way of life, with all of its inherent excitement and promise of adventure, has gone.

The long lines of personal baggage being trundled aboard a towering liner at a pier reeking of tar and a hundred indefinable smells, the confetti and streamers, then the daily distance "pool," horse races in the lounge, refreshments at bedtime and, in fact, at odd hours all day long, the ever-compelling sidewash and the boiling wake with the gulls flapping and crying overhead—all of these nuances are fading into memory, keepsakes for granny's attic trunk of days that occasionally were perilous, disturbing, or merely upsetting, sometimes tragic, but, for the most part, rich, wonderful, and exhilarating.

One may "go down to the seas again," but soon the beautiful liner, with its throaty bass call, will be waiting there only in dreams.

Acknowledgments and Bibliographical Notes

CHAPTER ONE

The author is indebted to many persons who assisted him in researching the *Andrea Doria-Stockholm* collision: Mrs. Barbara (Boggs) Benziger; Captain Piero Calamai, of Genoa, Italy; Stewart P. Coleman, retired vice president and director of the Standard Oil Company of New Jersey; Richardson Dilworth, then mayor of Philadelphia; Mrs. Henrietta Freeman, of San Francisco; A. Newell Garden, of the Raytheon Company, Lexington, Massachusetts; Carl W. Hallengren, Swedish-American Line; Dr. Leonard E. Laufe, of the Western Pennsylvania Hospital, Pittsburgh; Alvin Moscow, Stamford, Connecticut; J. F. Waller, Decca Radar, Ltd., London.

All of the comments and navigational directions in the last hour preceding the crash are taken directly from testimony in the United States District Court for the Southern District of New York and as reported in *The New York Times.*

According to Edward P. Morgan, still a radio commentator in Washington, his daughter Linda went on to complete recovery. She attended Sarah Lawrence College, joined the Peace Corps, and later worked on the New York *Herald Tribune.* The "miracle girl" is now Mrs. Philip Hardberger and lives in Odessa, Texas. Her husband is a lawyer.

Concerning the opening paragraphs of this chapter, mention should be made, as well, of Mrs. Edith M. Rowe, of Vancouver, who as a six-year-old—the captain's daughter—was aboard the *Cromartyshire* when the sailing vessel collided with the *La Bourgogne.* Mrs. Rowe (née Henderson) communicated recently with the author. She had read an account of the disaster in his earlier work, *They Sailed Into Oblivion* (Thomas Yoseloff, New York, 1959).

These books were consulted:

Benziger, Barbara, *The Prison of My Mind,* New York, Walker and Company, 1969.

227

Monasterio, Aurelio, *Tragedy on The Andrea Doria,* Havana, Editorial Neptuno, 1958.

Moscow, Alvin, *Collision Course,* New York, G. P. Putnam's Sons, 1959.

Publications not referred to in the text include *Collier's,* September 28, 1956, and *Shipping World,* January 14, 1953.

The daily newspapers of New York, Boston, and Pittsburgh proved particularly helpful.

Primary libraries used in the preparation of this chapter as well as most of the succeeding chapters were the Army Library, the District of Columbia Public Library, the Library of Congress, the Navy Library, and the New York Public Library.

CHAPTER TWO

The saga of the whaleship *Essex* has long been a part of America's seafaring lore, as unpleasant as it is true. The primary source is, of course, Owen Chase's own account published by W. B. Gilley, New York, in 1821, and running to 128 pages. The title, if not quite a model of the terse description, at least was all-inclusive. It was:

> *Narrative of the Most Extraordinary and Distressing Shipwreck of the whaleship Essex, of Nantucket; which was Attacked and Finally Destroyed by a Large Spermaceti Whale, in the Pacific Ocean, with an Account of the Unparalleled Sufferings of the Captain and Crew.*

In 1832, the Reverend David Tyerman alluded to the account in his *Journal of Voyages and Adventures.* It was published in New York by Crocker and Brewster for the Missionary Society of London.

Although Melville's *Moby Dick* appeared in 1851, nothing further, in book form, on the *Essex* was printed until 1884 when R. B. Forbes wrote *Loss of the Essex, Destroyed by a Whale,* published by John Wilson and Son, Cambridge.

Other works consulted:

Brady, Cyrus Townsend, *South American Fights and Fighters,* New York, Doubleday Page, 1910.

Haverstick, Iola, and Shepard, Betty, *The Wreck of the Whaleship Essex,* New York, Harcourt, Brace & World, 1965.

Stackpole, Edouard A., *The Loss of The Essex,* Nantucket, Inquirer and Mirror Press, 1958.

Copies of Chase's original volume can be found in the Harvard College Library, with Melville's marginal notes, in the Library of Congress, and the New York Public Library, among others.

CHAPTER THREE

Source material for the forty-niners, our hardy ancestors who joined in the gold rush some 120 years ago is virtually infinite. There is almost no major library, historical or marine society, or museum on the east or west coasts or in the Midwest that does not contain at least a few pertinent items, whether a letter, a diary, the facsimile of an old newspaper or a book. The New York and Boston newspapers were especially replete with sailing notices or chronicles of completed voyages.

Important testament for this chapter was autobiographical *Incidents on Land and Water* by Mrs. D. B. Bates, published by James French, Boston, in 1857. It was a matter of some frustration that the author could not trace down any living descendants. Inquiries to Kingston, Massachusetts, given as her home town, have elicited only a blank. However, the fact that the sailing of the *Nonantum*, "an A-1 ship," was announced in the Baltimore *Sun* the last week of July, 1850, tends to substantiate the author.

Recent books on the gold rush include:

Cook, Elliott, *Land Ho!*, Baltimore, Remington-Putnam Book Company, 1935.

Hale, Richard L., *The Log of a Forty-Niner*, Boston, B. J. Brimmer Company, 1923.

Lewis, Oscar, *Sea Routes to The Gold Fields*, New York, Alfred A. Knopf, 1949.

Low, Garrett, *Gold Rush by Sea*, Philadelphia, University of Pennsylvania Press, 1941.

Riesenberg, Felix, *Cape Horn*, New York, Dodd, Mead, 1939.

Rydell, Raymond A., *Cape Horn to the Pacific*, University of California Press, 1952.

CHAPTER FOUR

The definitive book on the loss of the *Arctic*—*Women and Children Last*—was published in 1962 by G. P. Putnam's Sons, New York. The author, Alexander Crosby Brown, is a great grandson of James Brown, the president of the ill-starred Collins Line.

A naval officer in World War II, Mr. Brown is book editor of the Newport News (Va.) *Press* and Newport News *Times-Herald*.

Other sources are found in Devens, R.M., *Our First Century*, Springfield, Massachusetts, C. A. Nichols & Company, 1876, The *Evening Star*, of Washington, D.C., October 16, 1854, and *The Naval Institute Proceedings*, January, 1968.

While historians have not forgotten disasters such as that of the *Arctic*, the *Austria* has all but faded from documented memory.

Primary sources for the Austria, however, are *The Times*, of London, *The New York Times*, and *Leslie's Illustrated Newspaper*.

229

America's worst river disaster, involving so many lives in mid-America, was bound to capture national attention, and, subsequently, its imagination, for many decades to come.

Chester Berry, the survivor, waited until his own middle years until he could reflect objectively, then wrote, in 1892, *Loss of the Sultana*, published by D. Thorp Co., of Lansing, Michigan.

The accounts of Joseph Taylor Elliott and others were published by the *Indiana Historical Magazine*, Vol. 5, in 1913.

A grandson, James Elliott, wrote *Transport to Disaster* in 1962, New York, Holt, Rinehart and Winston.

The *Wisconsin Magazine of History* covered the topic in its April, 1927, issue: "The Burning of The Sultana."

It was, of course, alluded to in that massive recapitulation, *Official Records, War of the Rebellion*, U.S. Government Printing Office, Washington, D.C., 1880–1901.

Acknowledgment, too, should be given John Means, now a U.S. congressional staffer, formerly of the Memphis *Commercial Appeal*, who did a comprehensive look-back in the newspaper's *Midsouth Magazine*, April 25, 1965.

Margaret McKee wrote a similar piece in the Memphis *Press Scimitar Magazine*, May 28, 1969.

News articles are to be found in the May, 1865, issues of the Memphis *Appeal*, Memphis *Avalanche*, and Memphis *Bulletin*, all on file at the Memphis Public Library.

CHAPTER SIX

The author expresses appreciation to the Shaw Savill Line, of Leadenhall Street, London, for their assistance in researching the story of the *Cospatrick*, and for supplying historical information and a photograph. Other sources include:

Bowen, Frank C., *The Flag of the Southern Cross*, 1939–45, London, Shaw Savill and Albion Co., Ltd., 1948.

Mitchell, Alan Q., *Splendid Sisters, A Story of the Planning, Construction and Operation of the Shaw Savill Liners*, London, George C. Harrap & Co. Ltd., 1964.

Shaw, Frank H., *Full Fathom Five*, New York, The Macmillan Co., 1930.

Waters, Sydney D., *Shaw Savill Line*, London, Whitcombe & Tombs Ltd., 1961.

Weiss, Nathaniel, *Personal Recollections of the Wreck of The Ville-du-Havre*, New York, Anson Randolph Co., 1875.

The Times of London, *The Illustrated London News*.

CHAPTER SEVEN

As a reporter for the Portland (Maine) *Telegram* during 1957–59, the author had access to the files of many repositories, including the Maine Historical Society, the Peabody Museum, and Essex Institute. Several kin of those lost on the *Portland,* including Mrs. Nora Metcalfe, then eighty-five years old, Henry T. Hooper, another son of the frugal Oren Hooper, and Mrs. John Liscomb, whose husband was a grandson of the old steamship line's manager, were among those who searched memories and family albums, Bibles, and such shrines of storage to provide information. Clyde Doyle recalled to the writer how he arrived too late at the wharf to put a half-sister, Miss Florence Pierce, aboard the doomed vessel.

General research was acccomplished through the files of the Portland *Press,* Portland *Herald,* and Portland *Evening Express,* the Boston *Herald,* *The New York Times, Leslie's Illustrated Weekly,* and the *Literary Digest.*

Through the good fortune of being able to consult living memory, the author wrote shortly thereafter what he believed to be the first contemporary definitive account of the *Portland*'s loss. It appeared in his book *They Sailed Into Oblivion,* previously acknowledged.

The present chapter on the sidewheeler is adapted from the earlier book through the kind permission of Thomas Yoseloff, president of A. S. Barnes Co., Inc.

Relics from the *Portland,* washed ashore, fitfully, for many years, can be found in several New England societies or museums including that in Orleans, on Cape Cod, where the name *"Portland"* is kept alive through succeeding generations.

Edward Rowe Snow has written of the *Portland* in *Great Storms and Famous Shipwrecks of the New England Coast,* Boston, Yankee Publishing Company, and in other books. He has dived for the fabulous wreck and believes he has located it in the wilderness of the Cape Cod–Nantucket shoals seafarers graveyard.

CHAPTER EIGHT

The basic source of research on the *General Slocum* is the "Report of The United States Commission of Investigation Upon the Disaster to the Steamer *General Slocum,*" Government Printing Office, Washington, D.C., 1904.

Those New York newspapers of the time with the most comprehensive stories and personal interviews were the *Times, Herald,* and the *Tribune.*

Two books were at once published, condensing what the press had already printed:

Northrop, N. D., *New York's Awful Steamboat Horror,* Philadelphia, National Publishing Company, 1904.

Ogilvie, J. S., *History of the General Slocum Disaster,* New York, J. S. Ogilvie Publishing Company, 1904.

231

Recent books bearing on the subject are:
Buchanan, Lamont, *Ships of Steam*, New York, McGraw-Hill Book
Company, Inc., 1956.
Werstein, Irving, *The General Slocum Incident*, New York, John Day
Company, 1965.
Mr. Werstein's almost nostalgic effective little treatise concludes with the belief that no survivors are alive today. One might wonder, considering the fact that there were a number of children survivors. Clara Hartmann, for example, would be seventy-seven, if she is alive.
There could be others, under eighty years of age.

CHAPTER NINE

The disappearance of the *Waratah* remains one of the great sea mysteries of all time. Thus, all that is truly factual ends with her last sailing from Durban and sightings within the subsequent few hours by two and possibly three other ships.
The findings of the formal inquiry were necessarily conjecture and were based on very scanty circumstantial evidence.
Thus, source material is itself scanty. *The Times* of London, which covered the inquiry, also printed periodic stories first dealing with her "overdue" state, then details of the search, finally the inevitable items of probate: wills of the various passengers.
Otherwise, research grist on the Lund's liner is slim. More rumor than fact is available. Chapters or paragraphs, however, may be found in these books:
Bennett, William E., *Last Voyage*, New York, John Day, 1956.
Breed, Bryan, *Famous Mysteries of The Sea*, London, Arthur Barker, 1965.
Villiers, Alan, *Posted Missing*, New York, Charles Scribner's Sons, 1956.

CHAPTER TEN

The author drew on his previous correspondence and other file material concerning the *Titanic*. Among those who assisted were Leslie Reade, of London, author of a forthcoming book on the *Californian's* role in the tragedy, Walter Lord, and Washington Dodge, a New York stock broker who survived the sinking at the age of five.
Among the spate of literature on the subject are these more or less primary books:
Baarslag, Karl, *S.O.S. to the Rescue*, New York, Oxford University, Press, 1935.
Baldwin, Hanson, *Sea Fights and Shipwrecks*, New York, Hastings House, 1955.
Beesley, Lawrence, *The Loss of The Titanic*, Boston, Houghton Mifflin, 1912.

232

Gracie, Archibald, *The Truth About the Titanic,* New York, M. Kennerley Company, 1913.
Lightoller, Charles H., *Titanic and Other Ships,* London, Ivor, Nicholson and Watson, 1935.
Lord, Walter, *A Night to Remember,* New York, Henry Holt and Company, 1955.
Padfield, Peter, *The Titanic and the Californian,* New York, John Day, 1965.
Rostron, Sir Arthur H., *Home From the Sea,* New York, The Macmillan Company, 1931.
The two formal inquiries are:
Great Britain, *Court to Investigate Loss of the Steamship Titanic,* The Board of Trade, His Majesty's Stationery Office, London, 1912.
Titanic Disaster Hearings Before a Subcommittee of the Committee on Commerce, United States Senate, 62d Congress, U.S. Government Printing Office, Washington, D.C., 1912.
Almost every daily newspaper in the world carried comprehensive stories on the ship that struck an iceberg, and for a considerable period thereafter. The London, Manchester, Liverpool, and Southampton papers, in England, carried the most details for British readers, as did *The Graphic Illustrated London News, Sphere,* and *Tatler.*
The New York and Boston papers were especially concerned in this country. Articles of interest appeared in the *Literary Digest* and *Harper's,* among other periodicals.

CHAPTER ELEVEN

The *Volturno's* burning was documented in the issues of that period of *The New York Times, Literary Digest, Illustrated London News,* London *Times,* and many other sources.
The account can also be found in *S.O.S. to the Rescue,* previously acknowledged.
The Great Lakes Storm of 1913, not surprisingly, is well covered in the Chicago, Cleveland, and Detroit newspapers of that date. The Cleveland *Plain Dealer* printed the most comprehensive coverage.
Otherwise, history has largely forgotten the disastrous blizzard except for one book, *Freshwater Fury,* by Frank Barcus, Wayne State University Press, Detroit, first published in 1960.
For a lively chronology of individual, earlier Great Lakes sinkings, read Dana Bowen's *Shipwrecks of the Lakes,* Freshwater Press, Inc., Cleveland, Ohio, 1969.

CHAPTER TWELVE

Captain Kendall went on to command the merchant cruiser *Calgarian* in the First World War. She was sunk in 1918 with the loss of forty-nine

233

lives. That seemed to be pushing his luck too far. He went "on the beach" as the Canadian Pacific's marine superintendent for the next twenty years, retiring in 1938. He died in 1965.

The wreck was paradoxically near the surface. The masts and some of the superstructure were dynamited to lessen this menace to navigation. And still her hulk rested offshore, perilously close to the channel. And there the *Empress* is today. Every day, the ferry to Baie Comeau makes a wary "S" turn as she heads out from Father Point into deep water, and safety.

The same year of Captain Kendall's death a daring group of skin divers repeatedly visited the wreck to retrieve an anchor, the helm, the brass annunciator on the bridge connecting to the engine room, wine bottles (still corked), and other relics including even a leg bone.

All are on display at the Maritime Museum, L'Islet-sur-Mer, fifty miles downriver from Quebec.

At Father Point, the little cemetery of forty-seven unknown victims of the sinking still is faithfully tended by the Canadian Pacific.

The author especially wishes to thank Maurice Gingerysty, press representative of the Canadian Pacific, in Montreal; John Hanna, librarian, Toronto *Globe.*

So far as can be established, two survivors of the *Empress* still reside in Canada. They are Mrs. M. E. Martyn, the former Grace Hanagan, and Colonel Alfred T. Keith, both of Ontario.

Lord Mersey's proceedings were published in Ottawa in 1914 under the title, *Report and Evidence of the Commission of Inquiry into the Loss of the British Steamship Empress of Ireland of Liverpool.*

Books on the subject include:

Dayall, Valentine, *Famous Sea Tragedies,* London, Hutchinson, 1955.

Marshall, Logan, *The Tragic Story of the Empress of Ireland,* Philadelphia, John C. Winston Company, 1914.

An excellent article was carried in *Maclean's Magazine* of March 28, 1959, under the title, "The Night the Empress of Ireland Went Down."

The *Montreal Star Weekly,* July 10, 1965, tells how divers reached the wreck.

Principal newspapers consulted were the Toronto *Globe* and London *Times,* and periodicals: *Literary Digest* and *Illustrated London News.*

CHAPTER THIRTEEN

The account of the *Lusitania's* torpedoing is based entirely on *The Last Voyage of the Lusitania,* by the author and his wife Mary Hoehling, published in 1956 by Henry Holt & Company, New York. This was the first of various editions, serials, excerpts, and condensations in several languages.

Their research was based on direct interviews and correspondence with some sixty survivors of the sinking, in the United States and overseas, as far distant, in fact, as Australia, where the captain's son, N. H. Turner (a bee keeper), was then living.

It is known that quite a number of those sixty, perhaps the majority, are since deceased.

CHAPTER FOURTEEN

A few years after the *Vestris* sank, Edward Johnson was attending a stockholders meeting of the Standard Oil Company. He kept staring at one of those present, and as he did so he could almost hear the chiming of a "fancy" pocket watch.

The man turned out to be none other than William P. Adams, of Chicago and Iowa, his companion in the lifeboat.

Mr. and Mrs. Johnson still reside in Scarsdale. Keen and active "Ed" Johnson retired the second time on January 1, 1970, as company attorney. It seemed a bit too much to ask a man of seventy-seven to ride the commuter trains from Westchester every morning. He has served during and since World War II on various high level Department of Defense advisory panels.

The best published eyewitness accounts are contained in contemporary issues of the Baltimore *Sun* and New York *Daily News*. Karl Baarslag has an excellent chapter on the subject, focused on the radio operators, in *S.O.S. to the Rescue,* previously listed.

Principal official reports are those of the Board of Trade London, *Loss of the Steamship Vestris,* published in 1929; and that of the Steamboat Inspection Service, Department of Commerce, "Investigation of Accident to the Steamer Vestris," mimeographed and distributed in December, 1928. *The New York Times* carried a full day-by-day account of the British inquiry.

CHAPTER FIFTEEN

The author wishes to thank Mrs. Valentine Pottle, of Annapolis, Maryland, for her help in researching the loss of the *Georges Philippar.* Lucien Basset, one of the survivors, since deceased, was her stepfather.

This maiden voyage tragedy evoked surprisingly little attention in the world's news media. The most conspicuous notice was to be found in the *Illustrated London News* which published many photographs of the doomed vessel and her gaudy interiors. Articles of varying length can be read in *The Times* of London, the Paris *Herald, Le Monde* and other Parisian dailies, as well as the North China *Daily News.*

The only book treatment of any consequence consists of a chapter in Otto Mielke's *Disaster at Sea,* New York, Fleet Publishing Company, 1958. He also treats at length the *Champollion* disaster.

235

The author of this present work, while on duty in the Navy, met Warms, called to duty as a reserve lieutenant commander commanding a small "section base" of small craft in the Gulf of Mexico. Junior officers quipped, unkindly enough, that this was the St. Helena of the gaunt, stooped acting captain of the *Morro Castle* for a few fateful hours. The author also corresponded with his widow, Mrs. Grace Warms, and daughter-in-law, Mrs. William Warms, Jr., shortly after Warm's death in 1953. Both felt keenly that the master was a victim of cruel circumstances and that his memory continued to be accorded grave injustice.

Thomas Gallagher's *Fire at Sea* was published in 1959 by Rinehart and Company, Inc., New York.

The Department of Commerce published the results of its investigation and hearings on October 26, 1934.

The Senate Committee on Commerce published the results of an investigation on the *Morro Castle* and *Mohawk* losses in 1937 (U.S. Government Printing Office, Washington, D.C.).

Three years later, on May 6, 1937, the dirigible *Hindenburg* exploded as she was coming in for a landing at Lakehurst, New Jersey. Many lives were saved because of lessons learned in treating *Morro Castle* burn cases at Asbury Park, Lakewood, and adjacent hospitals.

This story is told in *Who Destroyed the Hindenburg?* by A. A. Hoehling, Little Brown, Boston, 1962.

The account of the burning of the *Normandie* is the subject of a chapter in another book by this author, *Home Front, USA,* Thomas Y. Crowell, New York, 1966.

CHAPTER SIXTEEN

The research for the *Wilhelm Gustloff* sinking is taken from an earlier magazine article by the author and is based on an interview with one of the survivors of the tragedy. The brief narratives covering the other ships in this chapter are based on research conducted in the Navy Library, the Library of Congress, and the District of Columbia Public Library.

CHAPTER SEVENTEEN

The author wishes to acknowledge the splendid assistance of Mrs. Carole Pendleton, of Ashtabula, Ohio. She took time out from flying and doing extracurricular work for the Junior Chamber of Commerce to pass along her vivid memories of that night off the Florida coast.

The other principal source was the report of the United States Coast Guard, published February 23, 1966. Good eyewitness account are also in the Miami *News* and the Miami *Herald*.

The author, as a boy, sailed on the *Yarmouth Castle* when she was the *Evangeline,* plying between Boston and Yarmouth, Nova Scotia. Impressed even then with the diminutive qualities of the cabins, he tends to marvel that so many managed to escape under the circumstances.

EPILOGUE

The author is indebted to Hugh Harvey, of Shell International, London, for his assistance in information on the loss of *Marpessa*.

For general assistance in supplying photographs and research matter, he also wishes to thank John Lochhead, of the Mariners Museum, Warwick, Virginia. The staff and facilities of the Library of Congress and the Navy Library, Washington, also helped to make this book possible.

Finally, but far from least, the author is most grateful to Charles N. Heckelmann, senior editor of Cowles Book Company, who conceived the original idea for the manuscript and who, by the same token, must bear at least a portion of the responsibility therefor.

237

Almanac of
Ship Disasters

This is a partial list of additional ship tragedies, involving civilians. It does not include war vessels or wartime accidents, with the exception of several cadet training ships, mostly sailing craft.

Charles Hocking, in his *Dictionary of Disasters at Sea, 1824–1962,* lists some fifteen thousand losses, great and small, sail and steam, many of which went down with few or even no casualties. His massive work, in two volumes, was published in 1969 by Lloyds of London, but is available in this country in only the large libraries.

Mr. Hocking, surprisingly, missed a number of disasters. Other source material for this highly selective list includes many of the reference books, periodicals, and newspapers already mentioned in the acknowledgments section and other papers on either side of the Atlantic Ocean in the "old" category. Students who may be pursuing this subject further should be warned to crosscheck quick reference sources such as some almanacs, which contain a certain number of ambiguous or incorrect insertions.

May 11, 1833——*Lady of The Lake.* Struck iceberg en route from England to Quebec; 215 perished.

August 24, 1848——*Ocean Monarch,* 1,301-ton sailing ship. Caught fire in Irish Sea en route to America with immigrants. There were 178 lost.

February 26, 1852——HMS *Birkenhead,* 1,400-ton iron paddle steamer carrying troops and some family members during the Kaffir War. Struck rock off Cape Agulhas, South Africa, with 420 lost out of 630 aboard. The stoic formation "as if on parade" maintained by the troops waiting their turn to abandon inspired the term *"Birkenhead* Drill." Not one of the seven women and thirteen children was drowned.

September 29, 1853——*Annie Jane,* emigrant ship of American registry. Sank off coast of Scotland; 348 drowned.

April 27, 1859——*Pomona,* 1,181 tons. Emigrant ship en route from Liverpool to New York, ran aground on east Irish coast. There were 388 drowned, including the captain.

April 27, 1863——*Anglo-Saxon,* steamship. Hit rocks off Cape Race, Newfoundland, en route Liverpool-Quebec. At least 250 lost.

July 31, 1865——*Brother Jonathan.* Went on rocks off Oregon coast en route San Francisco-Vancouver; 146 lost.

October 3, 1866——*Evening Star,* 2,147-ton steamer. Foundered in hurricane off Georgia coast en route New York-New Orleans. Approximately 300 were lost. This number included the unusual group of seventy-five known prostitutes making their annual fall and winter business transfer to Louisiana.

October 29, 1867——*Rhone,* 2,738-tons, of the Royal Mail Steam Packet Company, foundered during a hurricane near St. Thomas, Virgin Islands, with a loss of 124. Another vessel of the same line also sank, with forty-one casualties, and three more ships of the Royal Mail Line were damaged. Of some sixty ships in harbor and adjacent waters during the tremendous storm only two escaped any damage. The combined loss of life exceeded one thousand.

October 27, 1869——*Stonewall,* paddle steamer. Caught fire below Cairo, Illinois, and 222 died.

July 30, 1871——*Westfield,* Staten Island ferry. Exploded at her Manhattan slip, killing one hundred.

January 31, 1878——*Metropolis,* eight hundred tons, Collins Line. Beached near Norfolk after storm damage which hampered navigability. Approximately one hundred were lost, largely on account of ineffective and clumsy abandoning.

March 24,1878——*Eurydice,* Royal Navy training ship. Capsized near Isle of Wight, England, in storm, drowning approximately three hundred cadets and crew.

September 3, 1878——*Princess Alice,* 251 tons, excursion steamer on Thames, London, sank after collision. Nearly seven hundred drowned. an indication that the relatively small craft was hopelessly overcrowded.

April (?), 1880——*Atalanta,* Royal Navy training ship, disappeared off Azores, with 290 aboard. She had replaced the ill-fated *Eurydice.*

November 24, 1880——*Oncle Joseph,* 823-ton emigrant steamer bound for South Africa. Sank after collision off Spezzia, Italy. More than two hundred drowned.

May 24, 1881——*Victoria,* excursion steamer. Collapsed, presumably from overcrowding, in Thames River, London, Ontario, Canada, with 202 lost.

August 30, 1881——*Teuton,* 2,317 tons, Union Line. Struck rock off Cape Agulhas, South Africa. Although none was hurt in the grounding and abandoning was proceeding in orderly manner, a bulkhead was stove in, the stern upended, and 236 (most of those aboard) were drowned.

240

April 18, 1884——*State of Florida,* 3,138-ton steamship. En route from her port of registry, London, collided twelve hundred miles west of the Irish coast with barque *Ponema,* out of New Brunswick, Canada, with 123 lost from *Florida,* twelve out of the *Ponema*'s crew of fifteen which also sank.

January 20, 1887——*Kapunda,* 1,095-ton emigrant iron barque. En route London to Australia hit another British barque, *Ada Melmore,* off Brazilian coast, with 360 casualties.

February, 1893——*Naronic,* 6,594-ton White Star Line freighter. En route Liverpool to New York, vanished with crew of fifty-five. From notes in two bottles it was concluded she hit an iceberg.

January 29, 1895——*Elbe,* 5,100-ton North German Lloyd liner. In collision off Dutch coast; 335 drowned.

March 24,1899——*Stella,* 1,059 tons, English channel steamer. Hit rocks off Alderney Island; 112 drowned.

August 4, 1906——*Sirio,* 2,401 tons, Italian steamship. Struck rocks off Cartagena, Spain; 442 drowned.

February 12, 1907——*Larchmont,* 1,605 tons, of the Joy Line. En route from Providence to New York, collided with schooner off Watch Hill, Rhode Island. Approximately 130 died, including ten members of the Salvation Army. (See Chapter 12, *Empress of Ireland.*) A peculiarly unlucky ship, *Larchmont* had been sunk in Boston harbor and raised, burned once, and grounded twice.

February 21, 1907——*Berlin,* 1,775-ton British North Sea ferry. Driven onto breakwater off hook of Holland. One hundred lost.

August 4, 1909——*Maori,* British, 5,317 tons. Stranded on rocks off Table Bay, South Africa. Thirty-four lost.

March 5, 1916——*Principe de Asturias,* 8,371 tons, newest and finest steamer of the Spanish mercantile marine. Hit rocks off Brazil going from Barcelona to Buenos Aires; 338 passengers and 107 crew drowned.

April 20, 1923——*Mossamedes,* 4,615 tons, Portuguese. En route Cape Town to Lisbon, ran ashore at Angola, West Africa. Although the survivors were a week in lifeboats moving farther up the coast for a more populated spot, only thirty-one out of the nearly three hundred aboard were lost.

March 5, 1921——*Madimba,* 2,013 tons, Belgian. Lost by collision outside of Antwerp. All forty-three aboard were drowned.

December, 1928, Missing at Sea——*København,* 4,000-ton five-masted barque, used as a Danish school ship. Vanished en route Uruguay-Australia with sixty aboard, mostly cadets.

June 14, 1931——*St. Philibert,* 189 tons, excursion boat. Sank in squall in Loire River, off St. Nazaire, France. There were 368 drowned.

Spring, 1938——*Admiral Karpfanger,* 2,853-ton, four-masted steel barque of Hamburg-American line used for training ship. Vanished

241

in Pacific west of Cape Horn, where some wreckage was later found. Perhaps hit iceberg.

March 20, 1945——*Mapocho*, 2,652 tons, Chilean. Caught fire off Chilean coast. Seventy-eight were lost.

January 19, 1947——*Himera*, 1,500 tons, Greek. Sank after hitting mine in the Aegean Sea, twenty miles south of Athens. More than three hundred perished.

April 16, 1947——*Grandcamp*, French freighter. Exploded in Texas City harbor, Texas, loading cargo of ammonium nitrate, setting off a chain reaction of fires and blasts in neighboring oil and chemical plants over a two-day period. More than 550 lives were lost.

July 17, 1947——*Ramdas*, ferry, four hundred tons. Capsized in Bombay harbor, India, drowning all aboard (about 626).

November 25, 1947——*Clarksdale Victory*, Army transport. Foundered off Hippa Island, British Columbia.

January, 1948——*Samkey*, American Liberty ship operated by New Zealand Shipping Company. Disappeared off Azores. Forty-three aboard.

September 1, 1948——*Euzkera*, Honduran. Capsized in storm off Colombia. Forty-seven lost (mostly circus performers), plus fifty-nine animals.

December 3, 1948——*Kiangya*, 2,100 tons. Chinese ship containing refugees from advancing Communists sank after explosion in China Sea, eleven-hundred believed lost.

January 27, 1949——*Taiping*, Chinese freighter, 4,000 tons. Loaded with refugees for Formosa, collided with collier *Kienyuan*, 2,700 tons, 140 miles southeast of Shanghai. More than six hundred drowned.

September 17, 1949——*Noronic*, 6,905 tons. Burned at her pier in Toronto during her last cruise of the season. A total of 136 died in their cabins on this, the largest passenger vessel plying the Great Lakes.

June 19, 1950——*Indian Enterprise*, British freighter. Exploded in Red Sea. Seventy-two lost.

August 25, 1950——*Benevolence*, 11,000-ton Navy hospital ship. Sank after colliding with freighter, *Mary Luckenbach*, off Golden Gate, San Francisco. Eighteen drowned.

September 1, 1951——*Pelican*, party fishing boat. Capsized in rough seas off Montauk Point, Long Island, taking forty-five, including the captain, to their deaths.

January 9, 1952——*Pennsylvania*, 7,608 tons, owned by States Steamship Company. En route Seattle to Yokohama abandoned by crew in storm. No trace found of men or ship after last radio message.

December, 1952——*Melanie Schulte*, new 6,367-ton German motor cargo vessel. Vanished northwest of the Hebrides en route to Mobile, Alabama, with crew of thirty-five.

January 10, 1953——*Chang Tyong-Ho*, South Korean ferry. Foundered off Pusan. Nearly 250 drowned.

242

January 31, 1953——*Princess Victoria,* British ferry. Sank in Irish Sea; 133 lost.

Early August, 1953——*Monique,* 240 tons, French motorship. With seventy-five aboard, disappeared without trace en route from the Loyalty Islands to Australia.

September 26, 1954——*Toya Maru,* 4,337 tons, Japanese train ferry. Sank in typhoon in Tsugaru Strait off Hakodate. There were 794 lost, 196 lost.

October 27, 1954——*Mormackite,* American freighter. Capsized off Cape Henry. Thirty-seven lost.

May 11, 1955——*Shiru Maru,* Japanese ferry. Sank in collision in Inland Sea; 173 lost.

January 18, 1956——*Salem Maritime,* tanker. Sank in Lake Charles, Louisiana, after explosion. Fifty-two died.

September 21, 1957——*Pamir,* 3,103-ton West German merchant marine training ship, four-masted barque. Foundered in hurricane six hundred miles west of Azores. A total of eighty-six (mostly cadets and crew) lost; six survived.

November 10, 1957——*Ave Del Mar,* Spanish fishing boat. Capsized on reefs off Vigo Bay. Twenty-eight drowned.

January 28, 1958——*Nankai Maru,* Japanese ferry. Vanished in Inland Sea with 170 aboard.

March 21, 1958——*Uskudar,* 148 tons, Turkish ferry. Capsized in Sea of Marmora; 361 drowned.

January 30, 1959——*Hans Hedtoft,* 2,875-ton diesel Danish ship. During maiden voyage, struck iceberg off Greenland. Last SOS— "slowly sinking. . . ." No trace ever found of vessel or the ninety-five aboard.

December 14, 1960——*Peter Zoranic,* Yugoslav tanker, 17,830 tons. Collided in Bosporus and exploded, with fifty-two lost.

July 9, 1961——*Save,* Portuguese motorship, 2,037 tons. Caught fire after grounding in storm off Mozambique, with 243 passengers and sixteen crew lost.

September 3, 1961——*Vencedor,* tourist ship. Capsized off Colombia coast, South America, with loss of seventy-four.

November 6, 1961——*Clan Keith,* 7,129-ton British freighter. Foundered in the Mediterranean off Tunis, Tunisia. Sixty-one drowned.

November 18, 1962——*Tharald Brovig,* Norwegian cargo ship. Sank after collision off Japan. Thirty-nine perished.

February 3, 1963——*Marine Sulphur Queen,* about 10,000 tons, World War II T-2 medium tanker. Apparently broke up in storm two hundred miles east of Jacksonville, Florida, with all thirty-nine aboard. Traces of her cargo—hot sulphur—were seen on water but no signs of wreckage or bodies.

May 16, 1966——*Pioneer Cebu,* Philippine inter-island passenger ship. Went down in typhoon with loss of 132 lives.

243

October 22, 1966——*Golden State,* American freighter, 7,598-ton. Sank in Manila Bay after collision, with seventy-one drowned.

December 8, 1966——*Heraklion,* Greek ferry. Foundered in Aegean Sea; 264 drowned.

August 1, 1970——*Christena,* an inter-island ferry in the British West Indies. Sank off St. Kitts, with approximately 125 lost. Overcrowding tentatively blamed.

246

250